Silas Wright

THE LIFE

OF

SILAS WRIGHT,

LATE GOVERNOR OF THE STATE OF NEW YORK.

WITH AN APPENDIX,

CONTAINING A SELECTION FROM HIS SPEECHES IN THE SENATE OF THE UNITED STATES, AND HIS ADDRESS READ BEFORE THE NEW YORK STATE AGRICULTURAL SOCIETY.

BY JOHN S. JENKINS,

AUTHOR OF THE "HISTORY OF POLITICAL PARTIES IN THE STATE OF NEW YORK." "LIFE OF ANDREW JACKSON," ETC., ETC.

"The Cato of the American Senate."
THOMAS H. BENTON.

AUBURN:
ALDEN, BEARDSLEY & CO.
ROCHESTER: WANZER, BEARDSLEY & CO.

1852.

THOMAS B. SMITH, STEREOTYPER,
216 WILLIAM STREET, N. Y

PREFACE

The biography of Silas Wright can be but little more than the political history of the State and Nation for the last twenty-five years. His life was spent in the service of his country;—not in a sphere requiring the exhibition of military capacity, or physical daring and fortitude, but in one demanding, at least, as high an order of talent, and far more of those nobler qualities, which so exalt and dignify the human character—moral courage and integrity. He had but just established himself in the practice of his profession, when he was elected to the New York Senate; and from that time until within a few months previous to his death, he remained in public life.

In preparing this volume, the author has not been free from diffidence, and distrust of his ability, to execute the task without favor or prejudice. If, however, anything has been omitted which should have been said, or anything inserted that would have been more wisely left unsaid, no one can regret it more deeply than himself. It is an error of judgment on his part, and not of intention. Of one thing he is quite confident, that not a single word has been written, with even the most distant hope of furthering the views or interests of any class, or faction, or party; but the work has been prepared simply and solely to present a complete and impartial life of one of the ablest—by many regarded as the ablest—statesmen that New York has ever produced.

To commend this book to those who are familiar with the character and extent of Mr. Wright's services to the State and to the Union, would not only be unwise and indelicate in the author, but it would be justly considered as labor lost. To his political friends and—not his foes, for he had no personal enemies—to those who disagree with him in regard to questions of public policy, it cannot be unpleasant to speak well of the memory of so great and good a man. The sources of information to which the author has had access have been various, and he has freely made use of them. In this connection he takes pleasure in acknowledging his indebtedness to those friends of the deceased who have cheerfully responded to his numerous inquiries. He has spared no pains in his attempt to render the work as full and complete as possible; the utmost care and accuracy have been preserved; and he is conscious of omitting nothing that it was in his power to supply. Errors and imperfections there may be; yet he trusts that he can rely upon a generous public to overlook them.

The Appendix contains several of the speeches of Mr. Wright in the Senate of the United States: those relative to the pressure and the removal of the deposits—to Mr. Clay's resolutions of Censure—and to the revision and modification of the Tariff law of 1842. Extracts from others of special importance are given in the body of the work, or his views upon the important questions agitated in the State and National Legislatures are stated as briefly and as distinctly as the size of the volume, and the ability of the author, would admit. The Address read before the New York State Agricultural Society has also been inserted, as well because of the importance of the subjects discussed, as for the reason, that it contains the last words of its lamented author to that large class of which he was an honored member—the Farmers of New York.

CONTENTS.

CHAPTER I.

CHAPTER II.

CHAPTER III.

CHAPTER IV.

CHAPTER V.

CHAPTER VI.

1*

CHAPTER VII.

CHAPTER VIII

CHAPTER IX.

APPENDIX.

LIFE OF SILAS WRIGHT.

CHAPTER I.

1795.—Introductory Remarks—The Ingratitude of Republics—The Objects of a True Ambition—The Statesman's Reward—The Ancestors of Silas Wright—His Parents—His Birth and Early Life—Enters Middlebury College—His Political Sentiments manifested—Graduates—Politics of his Father—Battle of Plattsburg—Commences the Study of Law at Sandy Hill—Removes to Albany and enters the office of Roger Skinner—Is Licensed as an Attorney—Travels for his Health—Anecdote—Locates at Canton—Traits of Character—His Popularity—Appointed Postmaster and Surrogate—Kindness as a Friend and Neighbor—His Public Spirit—Nomination as State Senator—Political Parties in the State of New York—The Electoral Law—Canvass for the Presidential Nomination—Movements of the Friends of Adams, Crawford, Jackson, Calhoun, and Clay—Dewitt Clinton—Martin Van Buren—Election of Mr. Wright—1823.

The ingratitude of republics has furnished, from time immemorial, a fruitful theme of invective to the enemies of democratic institutions. But there was never uttered a more ungenerous sentiment—one having so little of fact upon which to rest for support. Because the demagogue who had cajoled and flattered, but to deceive and betray; who had made his way to power but to further his own schemes of personal aggrandizement, may have been thrust, in a moment, and perhaps without one note of warning, from the position he had dishonored; the example, which, viewed aright, shoula only be regarded as an admonition to be heeded ana observed, is held up to view as an act of political martyrdom, demanding sympathy for the victim, and the severest condemnation of the perpetrators. Temporary causes, indeed, may produce temporary forgetfulness of those worthy of reward, and temporary alienation and distrust towards the public servant who has labored faithfully and zealously in the discharge of his duty. In a republic, all start equal; and so long as selfishness exists in the hearts of men, the contest for superiority will often beget feelings which may, for the time, lead to unfortunate consequences, or produce unfavorable impressions. But he who, girt about by the panoply of honor and truth, "possesses himself in patience," and presses steadily forward, keeping his eyes fixed on the goal before him; disdaining the vile arts that must debase and contaminate, and never forgetting that

> "Lowliness is young Ambition's ladder,"

will be sure, sooner or later, to win confidence and respect, and achieve a name and a reputation which the coarse denunciations of partisan violence can never tarnish.

It is a blessed thing in the history of our country, that the merits of the truly great man never fail to be acknowledged; that even those who entertain different views, in regard to the policy which should control the administration of the government, cherish a feeling of pride when they behold the independent spirit which does not bend to circumstances, and the uncompromising integrity that will not yield to expediency. When the career of such a man is ended, the event is mourned as a public calamity. All feel the shock—all hasten to bestow the tribute of their sorrow. And then it is, that men can see and appreciate these truths: that, although it may afford a transitory gratification, to be lauded as the head of a political party, it is a far higher triumph for the statesman to secure a place forever in the affections of his countrymen; that wealth and official honors are not the only evidences of the gratitude of a republic—that they are mere baubles, frail and unsubstantial, in comparison with the fame which has no grave!

We have a forcible, though melancholy illustration of these sentiments, in the death of the distinguished citizen, the incidents of whose life are detailed in the present volume. Cut down in the prime and vigor of manhood, when just entering, as it were, upon the brilliant destiny which the fond anticipations of his friends had confidently predicted, his loss has been universally lamented. It argues well for our institutions—well for the hearts of our countrymen—that all classes and parties were so prompt in the expression of their regret, and are so willing to perpetuate whatever of good example he has left behind him. His biography, therefore, cannot be devoid of interest, notwithstanding it is, to a greater or less extent, that of a politician. Those who thought with him may be cheered and encouraged, and those who disagreed in opinion, can, at least, admire the greatness of soul, the qualities of mind and heart, which did him so much credit while in life, and, now that he is no more, have added to that glorious legacy bequeathed by the honored and the great who have gone before him.

Silas Wright was a lineal descendant of some of the earliest emigrants from the mother country. One of his ancestors, Samuel Wright, was among the first settlers of Springfield and Northampton, in the state of Massachusetts, and died at the latter place, in 1665. His son, Samuel, junior, was killed by the Indians, at Northfield, near the New Hampshire line, on the 2nd of September, 1675. Joseph, the son of the latter, died at Northampton, in 1697, leaving a son, Samuel, who died sometime after the year 1740. He left a son, bearing the same name with himself, who removed to the north part of Hadley township, now Amherst, and whose son, Silas, was the father of the subject of these memoirs.

The elder Silas was a tanner, currier, and shoemaker by trade. He was apprenticed at an early age, and never went to school a day in his life. When he had "served out his time," he could neither read nor write; but, with the assistance of his fellow-journeymen, he soon qualified himself to keep accounts, and to transact all ordinary business. His wife was also a native of Hampshire county; and, after their marriage, she instructed him in many things which he found of great service in his subsequent life. She had received a good education, and, it may well be presumed, was not more willing to teach, than her pupil was apt to learn. They had nine children—five sons and four daughters—two of whom died in infancy; the rest, with the exception of a younger sister, now reside in Vermont. Silas Wright, junior, was born in the town of Amherst, Massachusetts, on the 24th of May, 1795. In March, 1796, his father, having given up the occupation which he had previously pursued, removed with his family to the town of Weybridge, Addison county, Vermont, where he purchased a farm, and devoted his whole time to agricultural pursuits. The brothers of Silas likewise became farmers, and the sisters were married to those engaged in the same honorable employment. Thus, the family may be regarded as literally composed of tillers of the soil, since the younger Mr. Wright himself spent the latter years of his life, during his relaxation from public duties, in cultivating his farm; and hence, too, it is easy to account for the deep interest he manifested, on all suitable occasions, in everything appertaining to agriculture.

Like most of his young playmates and associates, Silas attended the common schools in winter, and worked on the farm in summer, until he had passed his fourteenth year. His rare natural endowments were remarked in the family, and the tradition is, that his father looked upon him with peculiar pride. In order to foster the germs of intellect which had begun to develop themselves, it was determined to send him to an academy, where he could fit himself for a collegiate course. Having completed his preparatory studies, he entered Middlebury College, in August, 1811, and remained a member of that institution until he graduated, in the summer of 1815. During the time he was in college, as is well known, party spirit ran high throughout the country. In the New England states, particularly, much ill feeling was exhibited on account of the war measures of the administration; and it required no little firmness to bear up against the torrent of public sentiment adverse to their prosecution, which it was necessary to encounter in that section of the Union. His fellow-students were all politicians, and ranged themselves with one or the other of the two great parties. The class to which he belonged averaged about thirty, for the whole course of four years, and of this number there were but four democrats, including young Wright. But he was never daunted at this disparity of strength, and in later years, he often referred to the political discussions which took place in the halls of his Alma Mater, as having first enkindled in his bosom that ardent attachment to the political party with whose fortunes he became identified.

The elder Mr. Wright was also a democrat. During the first contest for the presidency between Adams and Jefferson, in 1796, he took an active part in support of the latter. Between 1800 and 1810, he was repeatedly elected a member of the Legislature, and, in his limited sphere, labored faithfully to promulgate the political sentiments he had adopted. Up to the time of his death, which occurred but a few years since, he was regarded as a firm, consistent, and determined republican. Both he and his oldest son were in the battle of Plattsburgh, under Macomb, in September, 1814, and two of his sons-in-law were volunteers from the "Green Mountains," although the Governor of Vermont, like the Governors of Massachusetts, Rhode Island, and Connecticut, refused to call out a single man to assist in the defence of the New York frontier, on the ground that the militia could not be compelled to pass beyond the boundary lines of the respective states to which they belonged.

In the month of October, 1815, young Mr. Wright entered the law office of Henry C. Martindale, a gentleman widely known in the politics of the State of New York, who resided at Sandy Hill, Washington county. Here he remained about eighteen months, when he removed to the city of Albany, where he continued his studies with Roger Skinner, at that time the Attorney of the United States for the northern district of New York. His period of clerkship expired early in the year 1819, and he was licensed to practise as an Attorney at the January term of the Supreme Court. His health having become impaired in consequence of his intense application to study, and his labors at the desk, in copying law papers, he spent the greater portion of the following summer in travelling on horseback, with a view to its restoration, and for the purpose of selecting a permanent location. He soon regained his strength, as his constitution was naturally hearty and vigorous, and his frame stout and muscular.

In his younger days Mr. Wright was fond of athletic exercises, and there is an anecdote related of the manner in which his skill and prowess were put to the test, while on his journey, in company with a friend, through western New York. On one occasion, they halted for the night at a small country inn, in a newly settled part of the country. Towards the close of evening a number of the young men from the neighborhood collected together at the tavern, as was their usual custom, to indulge in the sports and merriment which are frequently resorted to, in order to relieve the tediousness of a backwoods life. Mr. Wright and his friend were then, as in after life, both simple in their habits, and plain in their appearance; but, as they had just been emancipated from a long and tedious course of study, they quite naturally gave freer vent to their mirthfulness and gayety. In some way or other, the honest, well-meaning countrymen, thought they had been insulted by the "young sprigs of the law," as they termed Mr. Wright and his comrade. High words passed, and then a challenge ensued. After a long and severe contest, in which the odds were greatly in favor of their opponents, the two travellers not only escaped the whipping with which they had been threatened, but came off the victors of the ring. This result, as a matter of course, settled the quarrel; and when they departed on their journey the following morning, none bade them a more hearty good-speed on their way, than their late antagonists.

Mr. Wright located himself at Canton, in the county of St. Lawrence, in the month of October, 1819. The village was then new; it was surrounded by a rural population, and the business of the courts was limited and unprofitable. The professional emoluments of the young lawyer, therefore, were very moderate; but his superior talents, the amenity of his manners, and the undeviating kindliness of his disposition, soon made him highly popular. There was no seeming effort on his part to secure the esteem and respect of his neighbors and friends; but they were insensibly drawn towards him, and it was not long before they learned to repose entire confidence in his capacity and integrity. The traits in his character which won him so much favor and regard, were finely illustrated by the remark of the shrewd and observing farmer, who stated, in conversation with an acquaintance of Mr. Wright, "that he was the first lawyer he ever saw whose law was all common sense; and that he always gave plain, sensible reasons, for his opinions on any subject." His duty to his clients was discharged with rigid fidelity and punctuality, and none ever complained of his inattention or neglect. In the trial of causes, he was uniformly kind and courteous; there was no affected dignity in his manner: the counsel arrayed against him endeavored to imitate his urbanity—the witnesses felt "at home" when he questioned them, and cheerfully responded to his inquiries—while the jurors looked on and listened with delight. The opposite party, too, even though unsuccessful, would feel that the bitterness of defeat was almost removed, if he could hear the pleasant tones of the fortunate advocate addressed to him in courtesy and kindness.

After a short residence in his new home, Mr. Wright was selected as the village Postmaster, Captain of the local militia company, and Justice of the Peace; and subsequently, on the 24th of February, 1821, he was appointed Surrogate of the county of St. Lawrence, under the administration of Governor Clinton. When he became a magistrate, instead of promoting and encouraging litigation, he always discountenanced it; and it was remarked, that he spent more time in reconciling differences and restoring harmony, than in performing his official duties, and attending to the actual practice of his profession. His advice was never asked in vain, by the poorest, or the humblest citizen; it was given unhesitatingly, though without fee or reward; and many still remember, with feelings of gratitude, the wise counsels which saved them from penury and want. Others who refused to follow the course he pointed out, were soon taught, by sad experience, to place a higher estimate on the prudence and sagacity which they had undervalued. In all the relations he sustained, whether of neighbor or friend, of counsellor or magistrate, he was ever the same—kind, frank, and generous—prompt to relieve distress—ready to sympathize with the afflicted—never censuring in anger, but admonishing with the tender solicitude of a parent.

One who knew him, long and intimately,* has said, that "whatever tended to promote the substantial interests of his town, was certain to receive his atten-

* Hon. R. H. Gillett.

tion. The construction of roads and bridges—the erection of churches and public edifices, were objects that attracted his early attention, and were essentially promoted by the labor of his own hands. Until public duty called him away, he often acted as pathmaster in his district, and personally performed as much labor as any citizen. The competition between his and other districts, led to results still visible in his town. * * * In case of sickness, he was always the first to offer his services. I have known him to walk miles in stormy weather, over muddy roads, to watch with the sick. No one performed this task more frequently or cheerfully. No one is more devoid of all selfishness. During my long acquaintance, I never knew him to be laying plans for pecuniary gain or personal advancement. No man has ever accused him of doing a personal wrong, or any injustice. He always fulfils his engagements, of every description, with scrupulous fidelity. The example of Mr. Wright on this, as on many other subjects, has exerted a most salutary influence upon the citizens of his town, often noticed, and frequently mentioned, by the people from other towns. There are but few among his neighbors, of either party, who do not feel heartily proud of him, and manifest an anxiety to act, so as to meet his approval. His frankness and sincerity have made impressions upon his friends and associates, which a stranger will readily notice."

But the narrow limits of a town or county, were scarcely calculated to display the eminent abilities of Mr. Wright, and his friends desired to see them tested on a wider and broader field. For this purpose, but without the slightest expectation of such an event on his part, his name was presented, in the fall of 1823, to the republican convention of the fourth senate district, (at that time consisting of the counties of Saratoga, Montgomery and Hamilton, Washington, Warren, Clinton, Essex, Franklin, and St. Lawrence,) and he was nominated as their candidate for State Senator. The opposition of Dewitt Clinton, and his friends, to the convention of 1821, and other minor causes, had produced an entirely new organization of parties. The supporters of Mr. Clinton were styled Clintonians, while his opponents were known as Bucktails, anti-Clintonians, or republicans. When Mr. Wright settled in St. Lawrence county, a large majority of the electors were friendly to Mr. Clinton. This was also the case in that entire section of country. But the first election under the new constitution, which took place in November, 1822, was suffered to go by default. Although Mr. Southwick took the stump, and received a few votes for the office of governor, no candidate was nominated in opposition to Judge Yates. Of the thirty-two senators chosen at this election, not one was friendly to Mr. Clinton. The fourth district, nevertheless, was regarded as debateable ground; and as Mr. Wright had at all times, and on all occasions, frankly avowed his political sentiments, and was well known to be a firm and decided member of the anti-Clintonian party, his election was a matter of very great doubt.

Another cause which, it was feared, might have a tendency to insure his defeat, was the question of the passage of an electoral law, which had recently become mixed up with the politics of the state. The presidential canvass for the successor of Mr. Monroe, commenced in the city of Washington early in 1822. A great number of candidates were brought forward, and the excitement continued gradually to increase, until the ensuing year, when it formed the principal topic of discussion and conversation among politicians. The federalists proper remained aloof from the contest, at least during its earlier stages. A majority of the democrats, in the northern and middle states, were in favor of the nomination of John Quincy Adams; but William H. Crawford, of Georgia, was probably the strongest candidate in the Union at large. General Jackson, John C. Calhoun, and Henry Clay, were also urged by their respective friends in different parts of the country. At first, the various factions were exceedingly jealous of each other; but, finally, those opposed to Mr. Crawford entered into a sort of conventional league, to force him from the field, leaving the question between themselves as an open one, to be determined after they had removed the common enemy. Martin Van Buren, Erastus Root, and other leading republicans in the state of New York, were in favor of Mr. Crawford, but those who acted with them were divided in regard to the several candidates. The same was true with respect to the Clintonians. While Mr. Clinton himself was anxious to see General Jackson elevated to the presidency, a great diversity of opinion prevailed among his friends upon the subject. At the session of Congress in 1822–'23 the views of the members were pretty well ascertained. It was evident that Mr. Crawford would be much the strongest candidate in a caucus; and the supporters of Adams, Calhoun, Clay, and Jackson, forthwith determined that one should not be called, although it had been customary to make nominations in that way, ever since the organization of the democratic party. This movement alarmed the Crawfordites, and they endeavored to bring the influence of the New York Legislature to bear in the premises. For this purpose, a meeting of the republican members of that body was held at Albany, on the 22nd of April, 1823, and a resolution adopted "in favor of calling a congressional caucus, to select candidates for President and Vice President." The proceedings of this meeting were immediately forwarded to Washington, but they failed to produce any impression, except that of increasing the zeal and activity of the opponents of Mr. Crawford.

In the summer of 1823, the New York American came out decidedly in favor of Mr. Adams for the next President, while the National Advocate, then edited by Mr. Noah, as warmly espoused the cause of Mr. Crawford, and claimed to be the only truly republican journal in the city. With a view of counteracting the influence of the Advocate, as far as possible, Henry Wheaton, who was then understood to be in the confidence of Mr. Calhoun, procured the establishment of a new paper, called "The New York Patriot," which was placed in the editorial charge of Mr. Gardner. This paper opposed the election of Mr. Crawford, but did not support any particular candidate. It was also feared, that a majority of the members to be elected to the next Legislature, upon whom would devolve the choice of electors, might be too much under the control of Mr. Van Buren; and to prevent this result, a plan was matured by a citizen of Albany, and advocated in the Patriot, for giving such choice to the people themselves. This measure, though nothing but a political stratagem in its inception, proved to be highly popular, and a party denominated "The People's Party," was formed for carrying it into effect. The friends of Mr. Crawford, in the state of New York, were called "The Regency Party," by their opponents; and the canvass previous to the fall election was conducted with much spirit and animation. The proposed alteration of the electoral law was certainly democratic in its character, and setting aside the circumstances under which it was presented, it would probably have commanded a very general support. As it was, a large proportion of the candidates put in nomination, were compelled to pledge themselves in its favor. Among others, Mr. Wright avowed himself in general terms, to be friendly to such a law ; and this declaration, added to his wide-spread popularity in the county of St. Lawrence, secured his election in a district which might otherwise have been carried against him. The Clintonian candidate, General Moers, of Jefferson county, received a majority in the district, out of St. Lawrence, but the friends and neighbors of Mr. Wright gave an almost united vote in his favor.

CHAPTER II.

1824.—State of Parties in the Legislature of 1824—Message of Governor Yates—The Electoral Question brought forward in the Assembly—Mr. Flagg—Reference of the Bill to a Committee in the Senate—The Presidential Canvass at Washington—Congressional Caucus—Report in the New York Senate on the Electoral Bill—Discussion thereon—Various Propositions to Amend—Mr. Wright's Plan—His Speech—Postponement of the Bill—The Seventeen Senators—Nomination of Colonel Young—Removal of Dewitt Clinton from the office of Canal Commissioner—Course of Governor Yates in regard to the Electoral Question—Extra Session of the Legislature—Adjournment—The Clintonian and People's Convention—Election of Mr. Clinton as Governor—Choice of Presidential Electors—The Subject of an Electoral Law referred to the People.—Objects of those who originated the Proposition—Mr. Wright's Course in relation thereto—Legislative Session of 1825—Unsuccessful attempt to Nominate a United States Senator—Defeat of Judge Spencer and the Causes thereof—Legislature of 1826—November Election—Mr. Wright chosen a Member of Congress—1826.

The people's party did not succeed in electing a majority of the members of Assembly at the November election in 1823, although it was understood that upwards of seventy were committed in favor of the electoral law. The republicans, or bucktails, had secured a greater share of the members, but the friends of Mr. Crawford were in the minority. Mr. Wheaton was elected in the city of New York, on the people's ticket, and General Tallmadge in the county of Dutchess. Among the Clintonian members chosen at this election, were Samuel J. Wilkin, of Orange county, and Gamaliel H. Barstow, of Tioga. The most prominent republicans were Messrs. Flagg, Edwards, and Ruger, who were friendly to Mr. Crawford; and Messrs. Hosmer, Whiting, and Mullet, who supported Mr. Clay.

The Legislature commenced its annual session on the 6th of January, 1824; at which time Mr. Wright took his seat as a member of the Senate. Mr. Wheaton, General Tallmadge, and others, who had been elected by the people's party, and were known as anti-Clintonians, met with the republican members at the caucus held on the evening preceding the first day of the session, and an attempt was made to nominate General Tallmadge as the candidate for speaker; but Mr. Goodell, of Jefferson county, received a large majority of the votes, and was afterwards elected in the House. Governor Yates called the attention of the Legislature, in his annual message, to the proposed change in the mode of choosing presidential electors; but expressed no definite opinion on the subject, though he left it to be inferred that he desired the Legislature to retain the power in their own hands. Soon after the preliminary organization had been completed in the Assembly, Mr. Wheaton gave notice that he would bring in a bill authorizing the people to choose the electors of President and Vice President. Mr. Flagg thereupon offered a resolution, referring the whole subject to a select committee of nine members.

For several years there had been but two parties in the state, and in the Legislature of 1824, the members were divided into Bucktails and Clintonians, on all matters affecting their internal politics. But the moment the question of the presidency was brought up, there were "six Richmonds in the field." Although the friends of the other candidates united in their opposition to Mr. Crawford, they were very cautious that nothing should be done to injure the prospects of their especial favorite. The adherents of General Jackson were few in number, but they sat patiently by, hoping that they might be called in as umpires, in which event they could take the oyster to themselves, and leave the shells for the contentious disputants. The introduction of Mr. Flagg's resolution, set in motion all the stormy elements which had been collecting their energies in anticipation of the approaching struggle. It was vehemently attacked by Wheaton, Tallmadge, Barstow, and Wilkin, and defended with equal warmth by Flagg, Edwards, Ruger, Hosmer, Whiting, and Mullet. The mover of the resolution was charged with an intention to embarrass the proceedings of the Legislature, and to evade, or delay action on the electoral bill. Mr. Flagg defended himself with ability against the weight of talent arrayed on the opposite side, and succeeded in carrying his resolution through the House, by the decisive vote of seventy-six to forty-seven.

After holding several meetings, the committee on the electoral question, which was composed of a majority of Crawford men, agreed to report a bill, giving to the people the power of choosing the electors by a majority of all the votes, and providing that, in case no choice should be had, the election should be made by the Legislature. An animated discussion took place on the merits of the bill, and the provisional clause, authorizing the Legislature to make choice of the electors, where there was a failure to elect by the people, was stricken out. The test question in the existing state of parties, as neither candidate had a majority, was then presented, in the shape of an amendment, substituting the choice *by a plurality,* instead of that *by a majority* of the votes. The amendment was defeated by a vote of sixty-four to fifty-two. This result was produced by a union of the Adams and Clay Bucktails with the Crawford men; the former being apprehensive that Mr. Clinton would be brought forward as a candidate for the presidency, if a plurality vote could secure the electors. The majority feature was therefore retained, and in that shape the bill passed the House.

In the Senate, on the 6th of February, the electoral bill was referred to a committee, of which Charles E. Dudley, afterwards a senator in Congress, was chairman. The whole subject was suffered to rest in quiet, until the 20th of the same month, when a resolution offered by Mr. Ogden, requesting the committee to report, was debated in the Senate. Mr. Ogden, Mr. Burt, and Mr. Cramer, advocated its passage, but it was opposed by Mr. Wright, Mr. Wheeler, and Mr. Sudam. On motion of the last named gentleman, the consideration of the resolution was indefinitely postponed, by a vote of twenty-one to nine, Mr. Wright voting in the affirmative. The object of this postponement may be understood, by a reference to the condition of things at Washington. The breach in the republican party had grown wider and wider. Considerable bitterness of feeling was manifested on the part of the rival interests, and the determination of the opponents of Mr. Crawford not to go into a caucus, where he would be certain to have a much larger vote than either of the opposing candidates, was made known in positive terms. Each faction was fearful that a combination might be formed between the friends of Mr. Crawford, and the adherents of some one of the opposing candidates. If no caucus was held, there would not be an opportunity to accomplish any such purpose, supposing that it was in contemplation, except in the House of Representatives, where the opponents of Mr. Crawford were desirous of having the matter determined, inasmuch as his strength lay principally in the larger states, and the manner of voting in that body would deprive him of every chance of an election. The refusal to go into a caucus was regarded by the Crawford men as an act of bad faith, because it was a departure from the invariable usage of the republican party; and hopes were entertained that a portion of the refractory members, sufficient to constitute a majority, would be willing to attend a meeting, provided one was called. Accordingly, Mr. Forsyth and Mr. Dickerson, on the part of the friends of Mr. Crawford, issued a notice on the 6th of February, calling a meeting of the democratic members of Congress, on the 14th instant, for the purpose of nominating a candidate for President. When Mr. Ogden's resolution was under discussion in the New York Legislature, it was known that such a notice had been issued, but the result of the caucus was not yet ascertained. In a few days, however, it was understood, that but sixty-six, out of two hundred and sixty-one members of Congress, had attended the caucus. Notwithstanding this result, the friends of Mr. Crawford were not disposed to give up the contest. They thought that a great deal of unfairness had been shown on the part of the other candidates; and they then determined absolutely to prevent the passage of an electoral law, in the hope of being able to secure the elec tors if they were chosen by the Legislature. As an abstract proposition, the measure was approved by a majority of Mr. Crawford's friends; but, under the circumstances of the case, as it was evident, in their opinion, that it was the intention of his opponents to force the presidential question into the House of Representatives, and thus reduce New York, Virginia, North Carolina and Georgia, to a level with the smallest state in the Union, they were unwilling to do anything to favor such a project.

On the 26th of February, the committee on the electoral law reported adversely to the passage of the bill. The reasons which they presented in support of their conclusions, may be found in the following extracts from their report:—

"The committee are not apprised that there are at this time any peculiar objections against the present mode of appointing electors, which have not heretofore existed with equal force; but the committee do think that proof in favor of the *policy* of its original adoption, and of its continuance until a uniform mode is adopted throughout the several states, by an amendment to the constitution, is derived from the peculiar circumstances of the present period. There never was before so much distraction of public opinion on the subject of the presidency, nor so many competitors for that exalted station; consequently, the danger that an election may finally devolve upon the House of Representatives was never so imminent. Such an event, the committee are satisfied, must be viewed by every sober-minded and reflecting citizen, as pregnant with the most alarming consequences; intrigue, and, perhaps, corruption, would be called in to compete with the legitimate power, for, perhaps, the most splendid prize ever offered to cupidity and ambition. The established principles of a republican government would be subverted, by putting the power to choose a President into the hands of a small minority; the state of New York, with its thirty-four representatives, would be entitled to only one vote; and the states of Delaware, Mississippi, Illinois, and Missouri, with only one representative each, would be entitled to four votes. * * * * * Such consequences would, probably, be prevented by a choice of electors, in large states, by the Legislature; because, in that case, the danger of a divided vote would, as has been heretofore seen, be avoided. * *

"At this time several propositions to amend the constitution, and to establish a uniform mode, are pending before Congress, and there is every reason to believe that success will speedily attend these efforts, unless opposition is elicited from the smaller states. But if New York, at this most inauspicious moment, should immediately set the example, which may be followed by the other large states, of forbearing to exercise its right in a way to secure a united vote, the small states, duly appreciating their advantage over the others, will be encouraged to withhold their assent to any of the proposed amendments. * * * * * *

"The committee are therefore of opinion, for the reasons set forth in this report, that it would not be expedient to pass the bill from the Assembly, or any other bill changing the present mode of appointing electors of President and Vice-President of the United States; or, at least, until the efforts which are now seriously making in Congress to establish a uniform rule of appointment, by an amendment of the constitution of the United States, by which the people can elect by districts, have either terminated in the adoption or rejection of such amendment by that body."

This report was taken up in the Senate, on the 10th day of March, when Mr. Cramer moved to amend it, by striking out the last clause, and inserting a resolution, declaring that it was expedient to pass a law, "at the present session of the Legislature, giving to the people of this state the choice of electors of President and Vice President." In the discussion which ensued, Mr. Wright took a prominent part. He was already conspicuous as a debater, and his clearness of intellect, and strong reasoning powers, were acknowledged on all sides. Propositions to amend the resolution of Mr. Cramer, by inserting a clause, providing that the choice should be made "by congressional districts," and another requiring "a plurality of votes," were presented by different senators. Mr. Wright opposed both propositions; but voted in favor of an amendment, requiring the election to be made by general ticket. While the question was under consideration, Mr. Wright offered an amendment, providing for the choice of electors by general ticket, and by a majority of votes, except that the state electors were to be chosen by the Legislature, who were also to have the power of filling up all vacancies in the electoral college. But three senators voted with him in favor of this proposition. The resolution of Mr. Cramer, as amended, was then adopted—yeas sixteen, nays fifteen—Mr. Wright voting with the majority. Mr. Ogden then moved to commit the bill and report to a committee of the whole; whereupon, Mr. Livingston moved to postpone "the further consideration of the report and bill to the first Monday of November"—that being a day beyond the extra session; at which, under the existing laws, the electors would be chosen by the Legislature. Before the question was taken, Mr. Wright made some remarks in defence of the vote he was about to give, which were thus summed up in the legislative report of the Albany Argus:—

"Mr. Wright said he had the honor of offering a proposition giving to the people the choice of *electors by general ticket, and by a majority of votes*, which he had supposed the only safe system to be adopted. He had, however, been unfortunate enough not to be able to induce but three members of the Senate to think with him, after all the reasons he could offer in favor of the proposition. A proposition had then been made to make the choice *by districts*, which, after being fully and ably discussed, had received but two votes. And now, said Mr. W., we have rejected the proposition to choose by *general ticket and plurality of votes.* Divisions have been taken upon all these propositions, and the name of every member of the House stands recorded upon our journals, with his vote upon each proposition distinctly given. These, Mr. W. said, were all the propositions he had heard suggested, nor had he ingenuity enough to suggest or devise a fourth. He, therefore, despaired of even a hope that the Senate could agree upon a law, as he did not believe that members trifled with their votes upon this important subject, or were prepared to change their names as they already stood upon the journals. These being his views, Mr. W. said he should vote for the postponement, unless he could hear some reasons to convince him that his conclusions were not correct. The resolution (Mr. Cramer's) just taken could not be made effective, as both the majority and plurality systems, by one of which alone it could be made so, had been deliberately rejected, and he saw no good reason for spending more time on the subject."

The vote on Mr. Livingston's motion was as follows:—

Yeas—Messrs. Bowman, Bowne, Bronson, Dudley,

Earll, Greenly, Keyes, Lefferts, Livingston, Mallory, McCall, Redfield, Stranahan, Sudam, Ward, Wooster, Wright—seventeen.

Nays—Messrs. Burrows, Burt, Clark, Cramer, Gardiner, Green, Haight, Lynde, McIntyre, Morgan, Nelson, Ogden, Thorn, Wheeler—fourteen.

The senators voting in the affirmative, on the motion of Mr. Livingston, were afterwards known in the political history of the state of New York, as the famous "seventeen senators." While their conduct was condemned in the most unequivocal terms, by the party opposed to them, their friends were equally zealous in its defence. A large majority of the electors in the state, however, overlooking the circumstances under which the law was presented, and not yet acquainted with the character of the project, which was subsequently developed in the election of Mr. Adams by the House of Representatives, were in favor of the electoral law, and were highly indignant at the course taken to defeat it in the Senate. A portion of this indignation was visited upon Governor Yates. At the caucus held by the republican members of the Legislature, his re-nomination was urged by his friends, among whom were Mr. Wright and Mr. Flagg, who insisted that he ought not to be sacrificed for aiding to carry a party measure into effect. But it was finally determined to take up a new man for governor, and the nomination was conferred on Colonel Young.

Apprehensions were entertained before the close of the session, that Dewitt Clinton would be nominated by the people's party, as their candidate for governor. Mr. Wheaton, and others, protested that there was no such design in contemplation, and it was then generally understood that Mr. Tallmadge would receive the nomination. In order to test the disposition of the anti-Clintonians in the people's party, a resolution was submitted in the Senate, by Mr. Bowman, removing Mr. Clinton from the office of canal commissioner. The resolution was adopted, with but three dissenting voices,—Messrs. Cramer, Morgan, and McIntyre. In the House, the vote stood sixty-four in favor of the removal, to thirty-four against it. General Tallmadge, Mr. Wheaton, and nearly all the Adams men belonging to the people's party, voted in the affirmative.

When some one remarked to Fouche, that the murder of the Duke d'Enghien, was a foul blot upon the character of Napoleon, he replied, "It was more—it was a mistake!" The removal of Mr. Clinton was something very similar—it was an ill-advised act. It not only opened the way to his nomination, but it often returned to plague the inventors. The act itself was hardly deserving of condemnation, because it proceeded from the avowed political opponents of Mr. Clinton; and it is not uncharitable to him—nor unjust to his memory—to say, that no man encouraged party proscription more than himself. Who that was acquainted with the removal of the Burrites, the Lewisites, and the Livingstons, from office, would regret to see the chalice presented, in its turn, to his own lips? Still, the policy of this movement was most unfortunate for the republican party, and no doubt it was soon regretted by those who were the most active in its accomplishment.

The rejection of Governor Yates by the republican caucus, was by no means agreeable to his feelings; and he seems to have entertained the opinion, after the adjournment of the Legislature, that, should he come out openly in favor of the electoral bill, he might obtain the nomination in the people's convention, which was to be held on the 21st of September. He therefore determined on calling an extra session, that he might have an opportunity to make known the change in his opinions. His proclamation for that purpose, was dated on the 2nd of June, and, after adverting to the fact, that Congress had made no provision for changing the mode of selecting the presidential electors, he went on to say, that "the people were justly alarmed with the apprehension, that their undoubted right of choosing the electors of President and Vice-President would be withheld from them;" and to prevent this result, he thought proper to call the two Houses together.

The Legislature re-assembled on the 2nd of August, in pursuance of the executive proclamation. Immediately after the reading of the governor's message in the House, Mr. Flagg offered the following resolutions:

"Resolved, That since the last adjournment of the Legislature, nothing has transpired within the letter or spirit of the constitution, requiring an extraordinary session at this time; and therefore the proclamation of the governor convening the same is not warranted by the constitution.

"Resolved, That inasmuch as the transaction of legislative business, in obedience to a proclamation thus illegally issued, and especially in relation to a subject which had been repeatedly discussed and acted upon by the Legislature at their last meeting, would sanction a precedent of dangerous tendency; it is due to the members of the Legislature, as well as to the constitution under which they sit, and the oath they have taken to support it, as to the highest and best interests of their constituents, that they should forthwith adjourn. Therefore,

"Resolved, (If the Senate concur,) the two Houses

will immediately adjourn, to meet again pursuant to law."

General Tallmadge opposed the adoption of the resolutions, but the first two were passed by a strong vote, and the third was temporarily postponed. A resolution was also adopted, on the same day, by a vote of seventy-five to forty-four, declaring that an electoral law ought to be enacted. In the Senate a resolution was sustained, by seventeen to fifteen, Mr. Wright voting in its favor, affirming generally that the people ought to have the privilege of choosing their own electors. On the 3rd of August, Mr. Ogden presented a resolution declaring that it was expedient to pass a law at the then session of the Legislature. This was lost, by the same ominous vote of seventeen to fifteen —Mr. Wright being again with the majority. The resolutions of the House, to which was now added the third providing for the adjournment, were then adopted, and after a brief session of four days, the members returned to their several homes.

At the convention held by the friends of the electoral bill, in September, the Clintonians were in the majority, and succeeded in nominating their favorite leader as the candidate for governor. The original people's men in the convention took umbrage at this, and a large number of them withdrew, in a body, and formed a separate organization. General Tallmadge was selected as the candidate for lieutenant-governor, with the unanimous approbation of both organizations, although he had voted for the removal of Mr. Clinton. This completed what was called the Clintonian and People's ticket.

The November election resulted in the complete overthrow of the republican ascendency. The removal of Mr. Clinton had added new fuel to the popular indignation, and his friends eagerly availed themselves of the argument it afforded to promote his election. He received a large majority of the votes, and General Tallmadge was elected by a still larger majority. Six of the eight senators chosen at this election, and more than three-fourths of the members of Assembly, were either Clintonians or People's men.

On the 2nd of November, the Legislature again convened to make choice of presidential electors. On the 10th, the Senate nominated electors friendly to Mr. Crawford, by the votes of the seventeen senators who had postponed the electoral bill. The Adams and Clay electoral tickets received seven votes each. In the House, the choice of electors was attended with more difficulty. On the first ballot, the Adams ticket received fifty votes; the Crawford ticket, forty-three; and the Clay ticket, thirty-two; but an agreement was afterwards entered into between the Adams and Clay men, and a union ticket formed, composed of the friends of both the candidates. Upon a joint ballot of the two Houses, thirty-two of the Adams and Clay electors were declared chosen. A second ballot was then had, and the whole number was completed, by the choice of four Crawford electors. This result was produced by the defection of a portion of the Adams men, which, in all probability, prevented the election of Mr. Clay as President of the United States. It was at that time well known that there would be no choice by the electors, and that General Jackson and Mr. Adams would be the two candidates highest on the list. The contest, therefore, was between the friends of Mr. Crawford and Mr. Clay, as to which should be presented to the

House of Representatives; and the four electoral votes of New York decided it in favor of the former.

Previous to their adjournment, the Legislature passed a law to obtain an expression of opinion from the electors of the state, as to the manner in which an electoral law should be framed. The inspectors of election were required to provide three boxes, at the next annual election, which were to be respectively labelled—"By districts"—"By general ticket, plurality"—"By general ticket, majority"—and in which the ballots of the voters corresponding with the labels were to be deposited. The result of this voting was certified by the secretary of state to the Legislature, at its annual session in 1826; and a law was then passed in accordance with the decision of the people.

The passage of this law terminated the discussion upon a most exciting question; though it was long before the feelings which had been engendered were suffered to die away; and whenever one of the "seventeen senators" came before the people as a candidate for their suffrages, the journals of 1824 were sure to be ransacked in search of electioneering materials. At the time, without doubt, their course was exceedingly unpopular; but it is a somewhat singular fact, that many of them were afterwards repeatedly elected to some of the highest offices in the state, and that, too, by unusually large majorities. The history of the electoral question is here presented in detail, because of its connection with the name of Silas Wright. Upon a calm and dispassionate review of the facts, taken together with the election of Mr. Adams, by the House of Representatives, in the winter of 1825, no fair-minded man will hesitate to acknowledge the correctness of these conclusions:—

1. That the republican party in 1824, was very much divided upon the question of the presidential succession; and that this division resulted in a serious quarrel, and rupture in their ranks.

2. That the electoral project in the state of New York, was originated and proposed for a special political purpose, viz. the defeat of Mr. Crawford; and that its most strenuous advocates in the Legislature, showed most plainly, by their conduct in the fall of 1824, and in the winter of 1825, that they were actuated, rather by selfish impulses, than by any sincere desire to surrender to the people a right which had been improperly withheld from them.

3. That a plan was early formed at Washington, to prevent a choice of President by the electoral colleges, in order that the same might devolve upon the House of Representatives.

4. That the opponents of Mr. Crawford committed the first act of bad faith, in refusing to abide by the established usages of the party to which they claimed to belong; and that the inevitable tendency of their movements was, to produce a result more destructive of popular rights, than anything which transpired in the New York Legislature.

The question still remains, however, whether Mr. Wright was, or was not, deserving of censure for the course he thought proper to pursue? That he was understood to be in favor of the passage of an electoral law, at the time of his election in the fall of 1823, is not doubted. It was a prominent topic of discussion, and his views were likely to be inquired after. At no time in his life was he the man to conceal his opinions, on any subject, from his constituents; and he did not disguise his sentiments in regard to the proposed change in the mode of choosing electors. The strong vote also, that he received in his own county, which had previously given a large Clintonian majority, is evidence that he agreed with the electors, as to the propriety of adopting the proposition which had been suggested. But if he succeeded as the friend of an electoral law, he was also chosen as a decided supporter of Mr. Crawford. The developments made at the capital of the National Government, in the winter of 1824, gave an entirely new aspect to the whole question. At Albany, the opponents of Mr. Crawford were clamorous for the passage of an electoral law; while, at Washington, they were engaged in an attempt to nullify the voice of the larger states in the Union, and were striving night and day, to prevent a choice by the electors, and remove the selection of their chief magistrate still farther from the people. True, this was one of the modes which the constitution provided for the election of a President; but the Crawford-men in the New York Legislature, only proposed to observe the law which they found upon the statute book. The alternative, then, which was presented to Mr. Wright, and the sixteen senators who voted with him, was—either to postpone the subject until the danger they apprehended had passed, or, by carrying the proposition into effect at once, to divide the vote of New York, and thus produce a state of things yet more reprehensible than that which they were called upon to remedy. The fact that the vote of the state was ultimately divided, does not alter this view of the case. Mr. Wright and his associates decided to postpone the question; and if the result of the election in 1825, may be taken as a criterion, which it certainly was, a majority of the electors in the state approved their course. At that election the members of the Legislature were chosen, by which Mr. Flagg, the leader of the Crawford party in the Assembly, when the electoral bill was under discussion, was first appointed secretary of state.

The error committed by Mr. Wright and his friends, and that it was an error he would himself have admitted, consisted in voting, or making any efforts for the passage of an electoral law, after the refusal of the opponents of Mr. Crawford to go into a caucus. Had they come out openly at that time, and pointing to the position of affairs at Washington as their justification, avowed their fixed and unalterable determination not to change the law until the presidential question was decided, there would have been no room for censure. By pursuing a different course, they left that to be inferred, which would have appeared much better, and produced a more powerful impression, if enforced in their speeches, and in the columns of the able journals which had advocated the election of Mr. Crawford.

Soon after the commencement of the session of the Legislature in 1825, it became apparent that General Tallmadge, Messrs. Ogden, Burrows, Gardiner, and other leading members of the people's party, were determined to thwart the wishes of Governor Clinton. The term of service of Rufus King as a senator in Congress, would expire on the 4th of March, 1825. He had declined a re-election, on account of his advanced age, and the Clintonians generally were desirous of bestowing the office on Ambrose Spencer, the late chief justice of the supreme court. His election was defeated by a union of the Crawford and People's men in the Senate, who prevented a nomination by that body. The first day of February was fixed, by law, for the choice of senators in Congress. On that day an attempt was made to nominate a candidate in the Senate, with the following result:—*Ambrose Spencer* was nominated by Messrs. Brayton, Clark, Colden, Cramer, Crary, McIntyre, McMichael, Morgan, Spencer, and Wilkeson; *James Tallmadge*, by Messrs. Burt and Lynde; *Edward P. Livingston*, by Messrs. Dudley and Mallory; *Victory Birdseye*, by Messrs. Earll and Wright; *Samuel Young*, by Messrs. Ellsworth and Haight; and *John W. Taylor*, by Messrs. Gardiner and Ogden. Each of the remaining senators, viz. Messrs. Bowman, Burrows, Greenly, Keyes, Lake, Leferts, McCall, Redfield, Thorn, Ward, and Wooster, voted for a separate candidate. After the result was announced, Mr. Wilkeson offered a resolution, declaring Ambrose Spencer to be duly nominated on the part of the Senate. This was lost—yeas eleven, nays twenty. Similar resolutions, containing the names of James Tallmadge and Samuel Young, were then offered by Mr. Wilkeson, both of which were laid on the table, on motion, respectively, of Mr. Redfield and Mr. Wright. A second attempt was then made to nominate, which also proved ineffectual, Mr. Spencer being nominated by only eight senators, and the others scattering their votes among the various candidates. A resolution was now offered by Mr. Wilkeson, nominating John W. Taylor, which was lost—yeas nine, nays twenty-two. After taking this vote the Senate adjourned.

The Constitution of the United States provides, that "the Senate shall be composed of two senators from each state, chosen by the Legislature thereof;" and by the laws of New York, as they existed in 1828,* it was necessary that the Senate and Assembly should each openly nominate one person for the office of senator

* 1 Revised Laws, 162.

in Congress; after which, the two Houses were to meet and compare nominations. If the nominations agreed, the person so nominated was to be declared appointed; but, if they disagreed, it was provided that the election should be made in joint ballot. This last result, it will be seen, could not be produced until a majority of the Senate had selected a candidate. The effect of the scattering vote of the Crawford and People's men was, to prevent any selection. Mr. Spencer was nominated in the Assembly by a vote of seventy-seven to forty-five; but, as the Senate adjourned without presenting a candidate, no choice was made in the manner provided by law.

It is more than probable that the friends of Judge Spencer would have pursued a similar course with that taken by the majority of the Senate, had the situation of things been reversed, as their feelings towards the Crawford men and General Tallmadge were peculiarly bitter and vindictive; yet this would hardly justify the conduct of those senators who prevented an election The probable causes of the defeat of Mr. Spencer were these: the Crawford men opposed him because he was friendly to Mr. Adams: the adherents of General Tallmadge imagined that he might be appointed, by joint resolution, in case no election was made in the customary manner; a portion of the Adams men would not concur in anything approved by Governor Clinton; and another portion, headed by Thurlow Weed, of Monroe county, also rejoiced at his defeat, because they hoped it might lead to the selection of Albert H. Tracy, of Buffalo. Resolutions were subsequently passed in the Senate, with the vote of Mr. Wright, nominating General Tallmadge, and Mr. Tracy: the House refused to concur, on the ground that that mode of appointment was unknown to the laws of the state;

but it is not unlikely that their legal scruples would never have been heard of, had the name of Judge Spencer been inserted in one of the resolutions.

Acts like this, though unfortunately of frequent occurrence in the history of all parties in the Union, must certainly be regretted. They may admit of palliation, but not of defence. In the fierce contests of opposing interests, and the rivalries among ambitious politicians, such evasions of the law will sometimes take place, but they should not be held up as worthy of imitation. Surely, no one would have more deeply lamented any such attempt, than Mr. Wright. At the time, he and his friends insisted that a majority of the people were opposed to the appointment of Judge Spencer. The result of the fall election showed that this was the case; and it is some little gratification to know, that the electors of the state ratified, in the end, the conduct of their senators in 1825.

At the session of 1826, Nathan Sanford, then chancellor of the state, and a prominent member of the Bucktail party, was almost unanimously appointed to succeed Mr. King in the United States Senate. At this session, also, resolutions amending the constitution, by extending the right of suffrage, and giving the election of justices of the peace to the people, were adopted by large majorities in both Houses. These salutary reforms received the approbation of Mr. Wright.

In the fall of this year, for the first time, conventions were held by the two parties, for the nomination of candidates for governor and lieutenant-governor. The friends of Mr. Van Buren, of whom it is unnecessary to say that Mr. Wright was among the foremost, were already prepared to unite with Mr. Clinton in the support of General Jackson; but they did not think it advisable that the state election should be conducted with any particular reference to the presidential question. The nominations of the Herkimer convention were supported by them, in good faith, though Judge Rochester, the candidate for governor, was known to be an Adams man. A portion of the Crawford men, however, in the city of New York, and in the adjacent counties, came out in favor of Mr. Clinton, who was nominated for re-election, and Mr. Pitcher, the nominee of the Bucktail convention for lieutenant-governor. This movement, in connection with the subject of a state road, which had long been agitated in the south-western tier of counties, and had been approved by those gentlemen, secured their election. The Bucktail party succeeded in electing a large majority of the members of Assembly, and carried seven of the eight senate districts.

The signal ability with which Mr. Wright had filled the office of senator, led to his nomination in 1826, as one of the representatives in Congress from the double district composed of the counties of Jefferson, Lewis, Oswego, and St. Lawrence. His associate on the ticket was Rudolph Bunner. The canvass was active and spirited beyond all precedent. This was the first occasion on which one of "the seventeen" had presented himself before the people as a candidate for office, and a powerful attempt was made to defeat him. The scenes of 1824 were yet fresh in the minds of the electors; but it speaks volumes in favor of Mr. Wright's popularity, and of the general appreciation of his worth and integrity, that he was elected over his competitor by a majority of more than five hundred votes. The candidates supported by the Clintonians, in opposition to Messrs. Wright and Bunner, were Nicoll Fosdick and Elisha Camp.

CHAPTER III.

1827.—Takes his Seat as a Member of Congress—Opposition to Mr. Adams' Administration on the part of Mr. Van Buren and his Friends —The Tariff Question—The Harrisburg Convention—Its Bearing on the Presidential Election—Movements of the Administration—Nomination of General Jackson for the Presidency in the State of New York—Defeat of the Adams Men—The Twentieth Congress—Prominent Members—Election of Speaker—Mr. Wright Appointed a Member of the Committee on Manufactures—Feeling in Favor of a Protective Tariff—Action of the Committee—Resolutions of the New York Legislature—Report of the Committee—Debate in the House—Opposition to the Tariff Bill—Its Defence by Mr. Wright—Amended and Passed—Speech of Mr. Wright in Reply to Mr. Barnard—Proceedings on the Bill in the Senate—Its Final Passage—Objects of the Act of 1828—Approved by Mr. Wright—Subsequent Change in his Opinions—His Declarations to that Effect in the Senate of the United States—Re-nomination and Election—Informality in the Returns—The Certificate delivered to his Opponent—Second Session of the Twentieth Congress—Attempt to Repeal the Tariff Act—Slavery in the District of Columbia—Mr. Wright Appointed Comptroller of the State of New York.—1829.

The term of office of Mr. Wright as a member of the 20th Congress, commenced on the 4th of March, 1827, and he accordingly resigned his seat in the state Senate. His loss was severely felt in that body. His plain but convincing arguments, his apt illustrations, his lucid expositions of the tendency of every measure brought up for consideration, and his never-tiring labors in the committee-room, not less than his frank and manly deportment, and his estimable qualities as a friend and companion, were long missed by those who had admired and esteemed him. He took his seat in the House of Representatives, at the commencement of the session in December, 1827. Previous to that time, however, events had transpired to which it will be both proper and necessary to refer, before alluding to the course pursued by Mr. Wright in the new position he had been called upon to fill.

The strong federal and consolidation doctrines put forth by Mr. Adams in his inaugural address, were far from being palatable to the friends of General Jackson, Mr. Crawford, and Mr. Calhoun. Murmurs of discontent were heard soon after the commencement of his administration, but no serious attempt was made to organize a party in opposition. His favorite measure, the Panama mission, widened the breach; and the manner in which the committees of the 19th Congress were arranged by his friend, John W. Taylor, of New York, the speaker of the House, indicated no disposition to conciliate those politicians who had opposed his elevation to the presidency, but rather afforded the evidence of an intention to exert the official patronage in behalf of his re-election. Early in the winter session of the New York Legislature, in 1827, an attempt was made by the Clintonian Adams-men to secure the election of Stephen Van Rensselaer to the United States Senate, in the place of Martin Van Buren. But two Adams men belonging to the Bucktail party could be prevailed upon to attend the caucus; and on the 6th of February Mr. Van Buren was re-elected by a large majority; he having received the votes of Messrs. Colden, Bogardus, and Viele, of the Senate, and those of several members of the lower House, who were the most zealous and devoted friends of Governor Clinton. The letter of Mr. Van Buren in reply to the official notification of his appointment, intimated a determination on his part to oppose the administration; Mr. Calhoun and the leading politicians at the South, with the exception of Mr. Clay, had taken a decided stand against it; General Jackson was the only prominent candidate for the next presidency, besides the then incumbent of the office; and when it became apparent that a coalition was about to be formed for the purpose of promoting his election, between the leaders of the two great parties in the powerful state of New York, the friends of Mr. Adams began to be seriously alarmed.

No fears were entertained that the eastern states would desert the administration; but it was equally certain that those at the south and south-west would be opposed; and therefore the middle and western states must be the battle-ground of the presidential contest in 1828. The great and controlling interest at the North and West was that of the tariff; but divisions had sprung up among the advocates of a protective system of duties, which were daily growing more marked and serious. The commercial, ship-building, and manufacturing interests of the East, though advocating a high tariff where they would be benefited, were hostile to the protection demanded by the producers of wool, hemp, corn, and rye, in the middle and western states, and the iron manufacturers in Pennsylvania. The act of 1824 was designed to favor the latter, and hence it encountered the opposition of the eastern members of Congress. New York, Pennsylvania, Ohio, and Kentucky, alone gave seventy-five votes for the bill, in the House of Representatives; whilst Maine, New Hampshire, and Massachusetts, gave but a single vote each in its favor. At the session of 1826–27, an act was passed, known as "The Woollens Bill," in the House of

Representatives, which was intended to satisfy both the wool-growers and manufacturers; but neither party approved of its provisions. The project of calling a convention of the friends of a protective tariff, to be held at Harrisburg, in Pennsylvania, was then encouraged by the administration, and received the general assent of all classes and parties in the northern and western states. The convention met on the 30th of July following, and was numerously attended. An elaborate report in favor of the protective system was made, and a tariff of high duties, which met the approbation of the manufacturers, though not entirely satisfactory to the agriculturists, was presented and adopted. It was thought by the friends of Mr. Adams, that if the supporters of General Jackson in the tariff states opposed this measure, his defeat would be certain; and, on the other hand, if they came out in its favor, a breach would be made between his northern and southern adherents, that could not be healed.

Prior to the adjournment of Congress in the spring of 1827, a caucus was held by the Adams' men at Washington, in which John W. Taylor, Henry C. Martindale, and James Strong, of the New York delegation, were appointed as a sort of executive or vigilance committee for that state. The administration were sanguine of success on the national issue, and it was declared in the columns of the New York American, then in the interest of Mr. Adams, prior to the fall election in the state of New York, that "the choice of members of the Legislature should be made with distinct reference to the presidential question." On the 26th of September, the general republican committee of the city of New York adopted a series of resolutions to the same purport, but announcing their intention to sustain General Jackson. This decisive movement was made, it is said, under the advice of Governor Clinton and Mr. Van Buren. All the prominent Bucktail journals in the state took ground at once in its defence and support. The Adams men were not wholly unprepared for this unmasking of the enemy's batteries, but the denouement was more sudden than they anticipated. The election came on before they had time completely to rally their scattered forces, and the new Jackson party obtained a complete triumph; electing nearly all the senators, and three-fourths of the members of Assembly. The majorities in some of the counties were very large, and particularly in those in which Mr Taylor and Mr. Martindale resided.

Such was the condition of political affairs when Mr. Wright took his seat in the 20th Congress, as the leading republican member from New York. Among his colleagues and associates in that body, were some of the most talented and distinguished citizens in the Union. On the side of the administration, there were John Davis, Isaac C. Bates, John W. Taylor, Dudley Marvin, Daniel D. Barnard, Henry R. Storrs, and Elisha Whittlesey. The most prominent Jackson members were John Randolph, George McDuffie, Wm. C. Rives, Churchill C. Cambreleng, Andrew Stevenson, Edward Livingston, James K. Polk, John Bell, James Buchanan, Ralph I. Ingersoll, and Gulian C. Verplanck. Amidst such an array of intellectual strength, it required a mind of more than ordinary capacity, to take, or maintain, a position above mediocrity. But true genius, if it have the opportunity, is sure to find its proper level, and the sequel will show that Mr. Wright soon gained a place in the foremost rank.

At the election of speaker of the House, the party

lines were drawn between the administration and the opposition. On the first ballot, Mr. Stevenson received 104 votes, to 94 for Mr. Taylor, the Adams candidate. This was claimed as a test vote by the republican journals, and admitted to be such on the other side. Every administration member, with the exception of a few anti-tariff Virginians, who scattered their votes, supported Mr. Taylor. Mr. Wright, with seventeen of the other members from New York, voted for Mr. Stevenson. The appointment of the committees, therefore, was in the hands of the opposition, and Mr. Wright was placed upon that on manufactures, of which Mr. Mallary, of Vermont, was chairman. Upon this committee devolved the most important business of the session. Every eye was turned towards it. The whole North and West, save in a few isolated cases, which hardly constituted an exception to the general rule, were avowedly in favor of a tariff for protection. This was neither concealed nor disguised. There could have been no other object in asking the imposition of higher duties. The treasury was abundantly supplied; the public debt was almost liquidated; and no necessity existed for an increase of revenue. This question, in itself, had become one of vast importance; but there were still more momentous considerations connected with it, in the estimation of the politician—for, upon its decision, the issue of the presidential election must depend. The votes of the southern states, except those of Maryland and Delaware, were irreparably lost to Mr. Adams. But the tariff strength was sufficient to re-elect him, provided it could be united—if it remained divided, he could not succeed.

The proceedings of the Harrisburg convention, and the various propositions for the amendment of the tariff laws, were laid before the committee on manufactures, at an early day. Mr. Wright, and a majority of his associates, soon came to the conclusion that they required more information upon certain points, than was in possession of the committee. It had been alleged, that the bill passed at the previous session favored the manufacturer, at the expense of the wool-grower; and they desired to ascertain what degree of protection would afford the former a fair remunerating profit. Application was accordingly made to the House, on the 31st of December, for leave to send for persons and papers. The motion was resisted by a portion of the Adams men, and was advocated by Mr. Wright, who frankly stated his inability to prepare a bill that would be satisfactory, with the light he had; but if the House directed a report, without waiting for further information, he was prepared to obey their commands. The resolution granting leave was amended, so as to require the committee to report the minutes of their examinations, and in that shape it passed the House by the votes of the republican members. The delay rendered necessary in order to procure the attendance of witnesses, and take their testimony, was attempted to be turned to advantage by the friends of the administration; and it was asserted in the New York Commercial Advertiser, that the committee were opposed to protective duties; that they would not meet, and sought delay. The chairman of the committee, himself an Adams man, corrected these impressions, by stating before the House that they had met thirteen times within the month following their appointment, and that the members were more punctual in their attendance than those of any other committee.

While the subject was still pending before the committee, the New York Legislature assembled for its winter session. On the 30th of January, 1828, the following resolutions were introduced in the Assembly, by a member from one of the counties in Mr. Wright's congressional district, and passed that body by a vote of ninety-seven to three:—

"Resolved, (if the Senate concur herein,) That the senators of this state in the Congress of the United States be, and they are hereby instructed, and the representatives of this state are requested, to make every proper exertion to effect such a revision of the tariff as will afford a sufficient protection to the growers of wool, hemp, and flax, and the manufacturers of iron, woollens, and every other article, so far as the same may be connected with the interests of manufactures, agriculture, and commerce.

"Resolved, (as the sense of this Legislature,) That the provisions of the woollens bill which passed the House of Representatives, at the last session of Congress, whatever advantages they may have promised the manufacturer of woollens, did not afford adequate encouragement to the agriculturist and growers of wool."

The first resolution passed the Senate of the state, on the 31st of January, without a dissenting voice; on the second, the vote stood twenty-seven to three. By a singular coincidence, which, whether designed or otherwise, was not without its effect in other tariff states, General Jackson was nominated at a caucus of the republican members of the Legislature, held on the evening of the same day, as their candidate for President.

Upon a comparison of views in the committee on manufactures of the House of Representatives, it was ascertained that they would not be able to make a unanimous report. Mr. Wright, and a majority of the committee, were in favor of adhering, very nearly, to the tariff of rates proposed by the Harrisburg convention, in regard to wool in its raw state; but they wished to make the duties on the manufactured article, and especially the finer qualities, considerably less than had been recommended. Mr. Mallary, who expressed, more authoritatively, the sentiments of the manufacturers, thought a bill formed on such a basis, would afford little or no protection to the woollen interest, and desired to reduce the duty on the raw material, and increase it on woollen goods. Such being the opinions of the chairman, Mr. Wright was selected to draw up the report. Taking the testimony of the persons engaged in manufactures, who had been examined before the committee, as his guide, the report was prepared, and the details of the accompanying bill perfected. This duty was discharged with so much fidelity and ability, that Mr. Mallary availed himself of an opportunity presented in the progress of the debate on the bill, to say, that "as a statement of the proceedings of the committee in the performance of a most laborious duty, the report met his approbation; and, as an argument in favor of the provisions of the bill, he saw nothing in it unfair or uncandid."

The report of the committee, and the bill which accompanied it, were presented to the House by Mr. Wright, on the 31st of January, 1828. The principal articles upon which higher duties were imposed by the provisions of this bill, were iron, wool, hemp, flax, molasses, spirits, glass, and cotton and woollen goods. The debate that ensued on the merits of the question, was ably conducted, and possessed an unusual degree of interest. The main issue to be determined, was that between the wool-growers and the manufacturers. The eastern members declared that the bill would ruin the latter class, and insisted that adequate protection must be shown to them, though corresponding duties could not be laid for the benefit of the producer. The bill as reported imposed a specific duty of seven cents per pound, on wool costing eight cents or less, and forty per cent. ad valorem, to be increased annually five per cent., until it amounted to fifty per cent. Mr. Mallary proposed to strike out the whole specific, and retain the ad valorem duty, which would then be merely nominal; and to increase the duty on manufactured goods. His views were enforced by himself, and by Messrs. Storrs, Davis, and Barnard, in several speeches of great merit and power. The defence of the bill necessarily devolved upon Mr. Wright. On the 6th and 10th of March, he spoke at length in support of the views presented in the report. The subject was an abstruse one, but he handled it with clearness and force. His speech imbodied the facts elicited on the examinations before the committee; it was elaborate, argumentative, and logical; and attracted attention throughout the state and nation.

The Harrisburg scheme, the leading features of which were advocated by Mr. Mallary, and other Adams members, was voted down—there being but eighty votes in its favor, to one hundred and fifteen opposed. Mr. Sutherland then offered a medium proposition, reducing the specific duty on wool to four and a half cents, subsequently modified to four cents, and increasing the duty on manufactured woollens, the value of which was under fifty cents per square yard, from sixteen cents, as proposed by the committee, to twenty cents, the rate fixed by the Harrisburg convention.

This proposition retained the minimum principle in part. for which the manufacturers contended so earnestly, and was adopted by a vote of one hundred and eighty-three to seventeen—Mr. Wright voting in favor of the amendment. But there were other features of the bill equally objectionable to the eastern members. The increased duties on hemp and flax, designed to encourage the production in Kentucky and other western states, did not meet with the approbation of those who represented the ship-building interests; and the friends of commerce were dissatisfied with the provisions in regard to manufactures of iron and other articles, of which large quantities were imported. The additional duty on spirits was also opposed; and that on molasses, without allowing a drawback on the exportation of spirits distilled therefrom, was resisted with much warmth. The two last mentioned provisions were successfully defended by Mr. Wright and Mr. Buchanan, who contended that every gallon of New England rum took the place of one bushel of corn or rye, and that every cent laid on molasses, operated to give the farmer two or three cents a bushel on his grain.

The bill was ordered to a third reading on the 15th of April. The fate which awaited it had been for some time in doubt, and the friends of the administration appeared undecided as to what course they should pursue. If the bill passed, the dominant party in the House were sure to reap the advantage. At one time, it was asserted that "all the views and votes of Mr. Wright were supported by the southern members," and at another, the bill was declared to be worse and more objectionable than the act of 1824. But the Adams men from the middle states, were unwilling to disregard the wishes of their constituents, though disapproving of some of the provisions of the bill; and the friends of Mr. Clay from the West, were determined to support it. The vote on its final passage was one hundred and five to ninety-four. Of the New England delegation, fifteen voted in favor of the bill, Mr. Mallary among the number, and twenty-eight against it The members from the middle states stood fifty-six to eleven. There were thirty-three of the New York delegation present, twenty-seven of whom voted for the bill; those who opposed it were Messrs. Cambreleng, Hallock, Johnson, Oakley, Verplanck, and Ward With a single exception, all the western members, including those from Kentucky, supported the bill. But three representatives from the southern states voted with the majority.

Besides the principal speech made by Mr. Wright, he addressed the House several times during the progress of the debate, in answer to different speakers. In the course of the discussion, while in committee, Mr. Barnard advocated a protective duty to favor the manufacturer, amounting to a monopoly, and made use of some remarks in reference to the arguments of Mr. Wright, which drew from him a most pertinent and effective reply. The following is an extract from his speech on that occasion:—

"But, Mr. Chairman, are we to enter upon this doctrine of monopoly? Am I to agree, that this is the only and correct stopping point in the protective system? I had supposed, that when I put the American manufacturer upon a par with the foreigner, and not only so, but left against the foreigner the whole of the expense and charges of bringing his goods to our markets, I had granted a fair protection to our manufacturer, but not that I had thereby granted to him a monopoly. Such protection, and more, is furnished by the bill as reported by the committee. But, sir, it is not monopoly; and hence denunciations against that bill. Hence, too, I suppose, the arguments of the gentleman from Vermont (Mr. Mallary) have been heard against the proposition of the member from Pennsylvania, (Mr. Buchanan,) because that proposition will not effect the desired monopoly.

"I must here be permitted, Mr. Chairman, to correct a misrepresentation of one of my own arguments used upon a former occasion. I was represented by my colleague (Mr. Barnard) as having urged the protection of the *native* wool of this country, in preference to, if not to the exclusion of, other kinds and qualities of wool. Sir, I used no such argument. The bill makes no such provision; nor has any such distinction been suggested by me. But the terms, and language of my colleague, in making this representation, deserve a moment's notice. After he had given this turn to my argument, he informed the House that I was a lawyer; and then appealed to me in that character, and in a strain of eloquence, to which he was aided by a draft upon the poets, to inform him how far removed from the blood of the merino a sheep must be, to entitle it to protection upon my principles. When at home, sir, I bear the appellation of a lawyer; and whether my colleague intended to apply it to me here reproachfully, or not, I know not; but I have not considered a place in that respectable profession disgraceful. I have already said that my colleague misrepresented my argument. He equally mistook my information. I will assure that honorable gentleman, that I have never inquired into the *degrees of blood* of sheep or men. No part of my education has led me to these inquiries. No branch of the profession of the law, which I have studied, whatever may have been the fact with my honorable colleague, has furnished *me* with the information he asks. None of my ambition is drawn from considerations of blood, and it therefore never has been any part of my business to trace the blood of men or beasts. It never shall be any part of my business, sir, until that system of monopoly is established in this country which my colleague so ardently wishes, and so loudly and so boldly calls for from this committee. When that time shall arrive, *his blood* may rate him among the monopolists. Then too, sir, the *degrees of blood*, of *my* kindred, of *my* friends, may determine whether they are to labor in the factories, or to be ranked among the monopolists; and then, if my honorable colleague will make this appeal to me, as to the degrees of blood of these relatives and these friends, it shall be my duty carefully and accurately and distinctly to answer him."

When the tariff bill was presented to the Senate, Mr. Webster opposed the duties on hemp, flax, molasses, distilled spirits, and other articles; and it was ascertained that the bill could not pass, until it was made acceptable to the administration senators from New England. It was accordingly modified, and passed the Senate on the 13th of May, by a vote of twenty-six to twenty-one; Mr. Webster voting in its favor. The House concurred in the amendments, and it became the law of the land.

The act of 1828 has been often referred to, in our legislative halls and political assemblages, as "the bill of abominations." The term was not altogether inappropriate; as the authors of the measure themselves subsequently admitted. The tariff of duties established by the law was exorbitant. The act of 1824 averaged thirty-eight per cent., but the former averaged over forty-one per cent. But it was notoriously intended for protection, without even discriminating for the sake of revenue, because that was unnecessary. The object of the bill was not disguised. Mr. Wright stated it distinctly. He was in favor of its principles; and never sheltered himself behind the instructions of the Legislature. There were scarcely two opinions upon the subject in the state of New York, out of the city and its vicinity; but he did not ask, or desire, any part or portion of his constituents to assume the responsibility of his vote. Political considerations may have been connected with the passage of the bill; yet they did not influence his action, for his support of the measure was cordial and voluntary. At the time, it received his approbation, and he voted in accordance with the dictates of his judgment. But, short as was his life, he lived long enough to regret that vote, and to express his regret, not privately to a few confidential friends, that it might be whispered about in his praise, in particular localities of the country; it was done manfully and openly, upon the great theatre of his usefulness and fame. It is to acts like this, that we may point for the exhibition of a true magnanimity—that magnanimity which does not consist in never changing, but in being willing to renounce an error; which is not made up of professions of consistency, but is tempered and subdued by the frankness that conceals nothing from those who have the right to know.

In the Senate of the United States, during the discussion on the compromise act, Mr. Wright avowed different sentiments from those he had previously entertained;* and on the memorable passage of the tariff law of 1842, he referred, in more explicit terms, to his vote in 1828. In announcing the conclusion of his mind, slowly and reluctantly formed, to support the measure then under consideration, he said: "His first service in Congress was as a member of the committee on manufactures of the House of Representatives, during the session of 1827 and 1828, when he assisted to form, and voted for, the tariff bill of 1828, which has been so extensively denominated 'the bill of abominations.' He was then wholly without experience in legislation of this class and character; but his experience from that action had taught him the truth of the adage, that 'mens' evil deeds follow them.' He became very soon convinced that he had committed a great error upon that occasion, and it was possible he was about to commit another as great now. It grieved him to know and feel, that many friends within the reach of his voice, whose judgment he most highly respected, and whose good opinions were most valuable to him, would so look upon his present vote. He could not. The occasions appeared to him to be wholly dissimilar. The tariff of 1828 was avowedly passed for protection; and if considerations of revenue had any connection with it, they were only incidental to the main object of protection. There was no complaint of want at the treasury; no alleged necessity for increased revenues; and no blemish upon the public credit, so far as his recollection served him."

Besides the tariff bill, there were few questions of special moment determined at the first session of the 20th Congress. On the 10th of May, a bill was passed for the relief of revolutionary officers and soldiers, which

* Niles' Register, Vol. XLIV. p. 24.

received the vote of Mr. Wright. The internal improvement bill also obtained his approbation and support.

In the fall of 1828, Mr. Wright was re-nominated, with great unanimity, by the congressional convention held in his district. He was also a delegate from the county of St. Lawrence to the democratic state convention, at which Martin Van Buren was nominated for governor, and Enos T. Throop for lieutenant-governor. The excitement in the state of New York, which had grown out of the abduction of William Morgan by a number of persons connected with the masonic fraternity, was, at this time, at its height; and had a complete union been formed between the national republicans, as the Adams men were termed, and the anti-masons, Mr. Van Buren would have been defeated. But there were a large number of masons in the ranks of the national republicans, and hence such an event was out of the question. The sudden death of Governor Clinton left him, without a rival, at the head of the Jackson, or democratic party; and its whole strength was rallied in his support. The November election resulted in the general success of the democratic ticket. Mr. Wright encountered a violent opposition in his district, on the part of the national republicans and anti-masons, who united their forces, in many instances, upon the local candidates. The vote was exceedingly close, and for a long time the issue remained in doubt. Joseph Hawkins, one of the persons on the Adams ticket, was elected; Mr. Wright also received a majority of the votes, but the certificate was given to his opponent, George Fisher, for the reason that the word "junior" was omitted on several tickets evidently intended for him, and because a slight informality had been made in the return from one of the towns.

At the session of Congress commencing in December, 1828, Mr. Wright was again appointed on the committee on manufactures. The opponents of the tariff law enacted at the previous session, were not yet disposed to give up the contest; and on the 10th of December, a resolution was offered by Mr. Weeks, of New Hampshire, instructing the committee on ways and means to bring in a bill repealing the act. The subject of the repeal was discussed by several speakers, and on taking the question, but twenty-two members voted in favor of the resolution, to one hundred and fifty-one against it. Among the latter was Mr. Wright. This vote was so decisive, that no further efforts were made to procure the repeal at that session; nor was any attempt to change or modify the law successful, until the passage of the act of 1832.

On the 9th of January, 1829, two resolutions were adopted in the House of Representatives, providing, respectively, for the appointment of a committee to inquire into the condition of the slave trade in the district of Columbia, and the laws in relation thereto; and to consider and report upon the propriety and expediency of the abolition of slavery in said district. The vote on the first resolution was one hundred and twenty to fifty-nine; on the second, one hundred and fourteen to sixty-six. Mr. Wright voted for the resolutions. On the 13th, a resolution presented by Mr. Wickliffe, of Kentucky, requiring all votes taken on the election of the officers of the House to be given *viva voce*, was laid upon the table by a vote of ninety-seven to ninety-two; Mr. Wright voting in the minority.

The election of Mr. Van Buren as governor of the state of New York, rendered it necessary for him to resign his seat in the Senate. His successor was Charles

E. Dudley. Although not a candidate for the office, Mr. Wright had become so well known throughout the state, and had obtained so high a reputation for ability, that he received a number of votes in the caucus. But his constituents were not unmindful of one whom they believed had served them so faithfully and well, and on the 27th of January he was elected Comptroller of the state, to fill the vacancy occasioned by the appointment of William L. Marcy as one of the justices of the supreme court.

CHAPTER IV.

1829. Mr. Wright leaves Washington, and enters upon the duties of the Office of Comptroller—His Skill and Ability as a Financier—Careful Regard for the Interests of the State—His Course as a Legislator—The Lateral Canals—Application to the Legislature—The Black River, Genesee Valley, and Chenango Canals—Views of Colonel Young, Mr. Marcy, and the Canal Board—Sentiments of Mr. Wright—Opposition of his Party Friends—Justice to the Dead—Legislation in regard to the Chemung and Chenango Canals—Mr. Van Buren and Mr. Throop—Provisional Act to Construct the Chenango Canal—The Chemung and Crooked Lake Canals Authorized—Mr. Wright Claims his Seat in Congress—Unanimously awarded to him—Resignation—Message of Governor Throop—Report of Mr. Wright as Comptroller—Extract—Report of the Canal Commissioners in regard to the Chenango Canal—Mr. Granger—The Bill Defeated—General Election in 1830—Determination of the Chenango Interest to persevere in their efforts—Legislation in 1831 and 1832—Governor Throop Recommends a Direct Tax—Defeat of the Bill—Re-elected Comptroller—The State Election in November 1832—The Georgia Missionaries—Letter of Messrs. Wright, Dix, and Flagg, to Governor Lumpkin—Mr. Marcy Resigns his Seat in the Senate—Election of Mr. Wright as his Successor.—1833.

While engaged in the discharge of his official duties at Washington, Mr. Wright received the intelligence of the new honor which had been conferred upon him, and he immediately returned to Albany, having procured leave of absence for the remainder of the session. The office to which he had been appointed was one of great importance. The comptroller bears the same relation to the state, that the secretary of the treasury does to the nation. Patience, industry, promptitude, and fidelity, united to a capacity for arrangement and organization, are the qualifications necessary in that office. Mr. Wright possessed these executive talents in an eminent degree. Exact, methodical, and business-like, in the performance of every duty, he found little difficulty in conducting the affairs of the department intrusted to nis charge. The funds of the state were divided into so many classes, and the revenues distributed among such a variety of objects, that great care and accuracy were required in their management. He proved himself equal to the task, and soon displayed those financial abilities which afterwards placed him in the front rank of American statesmen. While he watched with faithful care over the interests of the state, and examined with jealous scrutiny the accounts of the public creditor, he was courteous and attentive, kind and obliging; though rigid on the one hand, he was impartial on the other.

Shortly after the completion of the Erie and Champlain canals, various sectional interests sprang up in the state of New York, having in view the construction of lateral works of the same character. The most important of these were subsequently known in the legislation of the state, as the Black River, Genesee Valley, and Chenango canals. The citizens of the counties likely to be benefited, were warmly enlisted in favor of these projects. The Legislature was beset every winter with importunities, either to grant an appropriation to construct a work, or to provide for the survey of the different routes which had been suggested. Mr. Wright's views and feelings in relation to these questions, had been made known while he occupied a seat in the Senate. He was ready to support any object affording even the most distant hope of remuneration to the state; but no work of doubtful utility could receive his sanction. Appropriations for surveys, and for the purpose of procuring information, where the money voted was not to be lavishly expended, he cheerfully supported, both for the sake of enlightening the minds of his constituents and of the people of the state at large, and to enable the Legislature to act understandingly upon these questions. It was not in his nature to offer a factious opposition to any measure. He deliberated slowly and carefully; but when he had determined in his own mind, as to what duty, and a regard to the welfare of his constituents, required at his hands, his vote was given without hesitation. If he felt bound to oppose a proposition, which was warmly urged by any particular section of the state, or advocated by those for whose opinions he entertained a sincere deference and respect; or originating with the party to which he belonged, and with which it was always a pleasure for him to vote; he did what he conceived to be right—firmly, it is true—yet with reluctance.

At the session of the Legislature in 1825, provision was made for surveying several routes, along which it was proposed to construct the contemplated tributaries of the great thoroughfare between the Hudson and Lake Erie. Mr. Wright, with a large majority of the senators and members of the lower House, voted for these surveys. In his annual message at the commencement of the session of 1827, Governor Clinton urgently recommended the extinguishment of the public debt of the state, and insisted that "the precedent would be more beneficial in itself, and more animating in all its aspects and consequences, than any fugitive, or even permanent advantages, that could emanate from another course;" yet, at the same time, he advised the construction of a number of new roads and canals, which would have increased the debt several millions of dollars. In accordance with the suggestions of the governor, applications were made early in the session, in behalf of the Black River, Genesee Valley, and Chenango canals. The counties of Broome, Chenango, and Madison, were deeply interested in the last named project; and its proposed termination at Utica enlisted in its favor the influence and sympathies of the citizens of the large and populous county of Oneida, then wielding, through her able and talented representatives in the democratic party, a great degree of power and control over the politics of the state. There being so many interests combined in support of this measure, it was thought advisable to make it the pioneer of the other lateral canals in contemplation. The surveys made in pursuance of the action of the Legislature in 1825, had demonstrated, in the opinion of the canal board, the inutility of undertaking the construction of those works in the existing condition of the treasury; when the deficit in the revenues of the state was annually increasing, and provision was to be made for the ultimate payment of the large debt already created. Mr. Marcy, (the comptroller,) Colonel Young, and a majority of the board, opposed the Chenengo canal project, at that time, on the ground that the public debt ought first to be extinguished; and that, if improvements of that character were to be made, they should not be commenced until the surplus revenue from the canals was sufficient to furnish the means of discharging all the liabilities that it would become necessary to incur. Mr. Wright entertained similar opinions with the board.

This opposition to the Chenango canal, laid the foundation of subsequent divisions in the democratic party, the effect of which was often visible in the state elections. Mr. Wright himself occasionally suffered from its exhibition; but it is unnecessary for the sake of his defence, to impute selfish, unworthy, or dishonorable motives, to those who differed from him in opinion. Whatever may have been his sentiments with regard to the justice or propriety of the course pursued by others, there was no feeling of personal bitterness or animosity buried in his grave. And that man would do injustice to his memory, who should disturb the ashes of the dead, to gather the materials for reviving past differences, or enkindling new feuds and contentions. Those who opposed his nomination, or election, to the high offices for which he was a candidate, will not do him or themselves so much wrong, as to deny that he was a manly and honorable opponent. This, of itself, should content those who adhered to him through weal and through woe. To ask for more, would be to wound the pride and self-respect of the living, and to mar his character, in the judgment of posterity, with a stain of selfishness that was never suffered to dim its purity.

The persevering and untiring efforts of the friends of the Chenango canal secured a favorable vote for their project, in the Assembly, at the legislative session of 1827. In the Senate, the bill met with a determined and effectual resistance, and failed in its passage by a vote of fourteen to ten. The same result was witnessed at the winter session in 1828. Bills for constructing the Chemung and Chenango canals, were passed in the Assembly, but defeated in the Senate. In 1829, Mr. Van Buren, though understood as concurring in the views of the canal board, expressed no definite opinion in regard to the financial policy of the state. Mr. Throop maintained the same cautious reserve, in his farewell address to the Senate, when about to take his place in the executive chair, made vacant by the resignation of Mr. Van Buren. When Mr. Wright reached Albany, bills were pending before the Legislature in regard to those works, the construction of which had been pressed with so much pertinacity; and it has been thought proper to present, as briefly as possible, a review of what had transpired in former years, in order to show how he became connected with these questions, and what was the origin of the hostile interests frequently opposed to him, even after the occasion had passed by that called them into existence. From his position as a member of the canal board, his influence was necessarily felt upon all the measures connected with the system of internal improvements of the state, which were discussed in the Legislature while he remained in office.

On the 24th of March, 1829, an act was finally passed, authorizing the construction of the Chenango canal, coupled, however, with the conditions, that the canal commissioners should not proceed with the work, unless they should be first satisfied that there would be an adequate supply of water, without using the water of either the Oriskany, or Sauquoit creeks; that the cost should not exceed one million of dollars; and also, that the canal would produce to the state, within the first ten years after its construction, an amount of tolls equal to the interest on its cost, besides repairs and expenses. This proviso was esteemed unnecessarily harsh and severe, by the friends of the project, though based on their own representations; and its incorpora-

4

tion in the bill was attributed to the counsels of the comptroller and Colonel Young. The Chemung and Crooked Lane canals were also authorized to be constructed at this session; but as those works were esteemed more feasible, and as promising a more speedy return to the state, on the moneys to be invested in their construction, there were no conditions or limitations, to hinder or delay their completion.

At the commencement of the session of Congress in December, 1829, Mr. Fisher, the candidate supported in opposition to Mr. Wright, at the election in 1828, took his seat in the House of Representatives. A petition was immediately presented on behalf of Mr. Wright, setting forth the facts and circumstances under which the certificate had been delivered to the incumbent, and claiming that the seat should be awarded to him. The petition was referred to the committee on elections, who reported a resolution giving the contested seat to the claimant. The resolution passed the House unanimously; the sitting member himself acquiescing in the justice of the decision. Mr. Wright then forwarded his letter of resignation, which was laid before the House on the 9th of March, 1830.

In his annual message delivered to the two houses of the Legislature at the session of 1830, Governor Throop did not recommend any additional improvements, either by roads or canals; but stated that, in his opinion, a direct tax would soon become necessary to defray the ordinary expenses of the government, in consequence of the diminution of the general fund. The views of the executive were founded upon the financial condition of the state, as made known to him by the comptroller. The report of that officer was ably drawn, and presented a clear and distinct statement of the monetary concerns under his supervision and control. It appeared that the general fund had diminished, to the amount of nearly four hundred thousand dollars, within the three previous years, during which time no state tax had been collected ; and that a deficit of more than one hundred thousand dollars, beyond the means of the year, existed on the 1st day of December, 1829, notwithstanding the sale of canal stock, and the other large expenditures during the year, to meet the demands upon the treasury. The deficit for the ensuing year was estimated at seventy-five thousand dollars.

"In the estimate of receipts for the present year," says the report, "are included the ordinary receipts of principal from the general fund, amounting to $40,000, and also the anticipated receipts from the tax sales to take place in the spring, amounting to $150,000; so that from neither of these sources can anything be expected to meet the above deficiency. The receipts of this year will be increased at least $120,000, by the tax sales, beyond what they can be calculated at for several future years, and until another sale occurs. No hope, therefore, can be entertained, that the next year will be better able to make up for the deficiencies of the last, than is the present, unless new sources of income are supplied ; but, on the contrary, the certainty now exists, that the ordinary revenue and the ordinary receipts of principal from the general fund, for the next year, must fall short of the ordinary expenses of the government."

After this positive and unequivocal statement of the resources and liabilities of the state, no member of the Legislature could have complained that he was not forewarned in time to meet the emergency which was likely to arise. The reports of Mr. Wright, while he filled the office of comptroller, were, in like manner, distinguished for their plain and straightforward exhibition of the condition of the treasury. He was no alarmist, but he did not attempt to conceal anything that required correction. He was a faithful and accurate accountant, keeping his books posted up, and his balance-sheet ready to show, at any moment, the situation of the important interests committed to his charge.

The canal commissioners made their annual report on the 21st of January. They stated that they had examined, and again surveyed and explored, the proposed route of the Chenango canal, and that from the result of that examination they could not, consistent with the terms of the law, commence the construction of the work. They also expressed their opinion, that it would cost more than a million of dollars, and that "in regard to its revenue, it would not produce an amount of tolls, in connection with the increased tolls on the Erie canal, that would be equal to the interest of its cost, and the expense of its repairs and superintendence, or of either of them." This portion of the report was attributed to Colonel Young, then one of the canal commissioners; and when it was taken in connection with the exhibit of the financial condition of the state made by the comptroller, it presented a very strong argument against going on with the work. But the facts and conclusions of the state officers were not satisfactory to the citizens interested in the construction of the canal, though subsequent experience demonstrated their fidelity. A bill was introduced into the Assembly peremptorily ordering the commissioners to commence the work without delay. The bill was strenuously advocated by Francis Granger, a member of the House from Ontario county, and the candidate of the anti-masonic party for governor at the ensuing November election. The democratic members generally opposed the bill, and it did not receive a favorable vote at this session.

Mr. Wright was one of the delegates to the democratic state convention which met in September, and warmly urged the nomination of Mr. Throop for the office of governor. The friends of General Root, in connection with the Chenango canal interest, endeavored to prevent this result; but the attempt was unsuccessful. Mr. Throop was nominated and elected, notwithstanding a large portion of the democratic electors residing in the Chenango valley, gave their votes to Mr. Granger, the opposition candidate.

Early in the session of the Legislature, commencing on the 4th of January, 1831, a bill for the construction of the Chenango canal was introduced into the Senate. After considerable discussion, it was lost, by a vote of sixteen to fourteen. But five democratic senators voted in its favor. At this session Judge Marcy was elected to the Senate of the United States, as the successor of Mr. Sanford, whose term expired in March.

The message of Governor Throop in 1832, advised the imposition of a state tax, in conformity with the recommendations of the comptroller, Mr. Wright, in order to supply the deficiency in the general fund. A bill was soon after reported in the Senate, authorizing a tax of one mill on the dollar, to be levied annually, for three years, on all real and personal property. A similar tax had been collected, for the same purpose, from 1819 to 1825, when it was reduced to one-half of a mill, and, in 1827, it was entirely removed. The fund immediately began to diminish, and the comptroller was of the opinion that measures should be taken to arrest that diminution. His views were presented in his annual report with his accustomed ability. The governor also, who was much indebted to Mr. Wright, for the clearness and force with which he exhibited the financial condition of the state, expressed his decided approbation of the measure. But the friends of the Chenango canal would not give their assent to any proposition that might jeopard the success of their own project; and a number of the senators were inclined to believe, that before the general fund could be exhausted, there would be a sufficient surplus revenue from the canals, after paying all the cost of construction, to defray the ordinary expenses of the state government; which was the object had in view in the creation of that fund. The tax bill, therefore, failed to secure a majority vote in the Senate. The deficiency in the fund was afterwards made up by temporary loans from the common school and other specific funds, and it was ultimately found necessary to resort to a direct tax. The Chenango canal bill, containing very severe restrictions, was passed in the Senate at this session, by a vote of sixteen to fifteen, but was defeated in the Assembly. Mr. Wright was re-elected in the month of February to the office of comptroller. Some little opposition was manifested at one time, by those whose measures he considered it his duty to oppose, to his remaining in the office he held; but his acknowledged abilities, and his conceded fitness for the station, prevented any formidable effort to defeat his re-appointment.

The excitement and agitation growing out of the veto of the bill to re-charter the Bank of the United

States, by President Jackson, in July 1832, though almost unanimously approved by the democratic party in the state of New York, rendered it desirable that unusual care should be taken in the choice of candidates for the fall election. The advocates of the Chenango canal were as urgent and pertinacious in pressing their claims, as ever. Mr. Granger, who was certain to be the candidate of the opposition party, had been long known for the friendly interest he took in behalf of the work. The re-nomination of Governor Throop, under such circumstances, was deemed unadvisable; and he addressed a letter to the state convention which assembled at Herkimer, respectfully declining a nomination. Mr. Marcy was then selected as the candidate for governor. The fact, that the positions he had occupied for several years previous, had kept him, in a great measure, aloof from state politics, was a strong argument in favor of his nomination, and the vote was nearly unanimous. John Tracy, of Chenango county, was nominated for lieutenant-governor. Mr. Wright was a member of the convention from the county of Albany, and participated in its proceedings. The state nominations were entirely acceptable to the friends of the Chenango canal; and they were given to understand, that the bill they had urged, so far in vain, would be favorably considered at the next session of the Legislature. The democratic ticket succeeded; and in the winter of 1833 a bill was passed, authorizing the immediate construction of the canal.

On the 18th of December, 1832, Mr. Wright, together with Azariah C. Flagg, and John A. Dix, addressed a letter to Governor Lumpkin, of Georgia, recommending the pardon of certain missionaries among the Cherokee Indians, who had been convicted and imprisoned for alleged violations of the state laws. The jurisdiction of Georgia had been called in question; and as the controversy was likely to lead to collisions with the General Government, they asked the release of the imprisoned persons, as an act of magnanimity on the part of the state. Their interposition proved effectual, and the missionaries were restored to liberty.

The election of Mr. Marcy as governor of the state produced a vacancy in the Senate of the United States. The general choice of the party centred at once on Mr. Wright. The friends of the Chenango canal did not favor his appointment, but he was elected by a large majority early in the session of 1833.

CHAPTER V.

1833.—The Anxiety of Mr. Wright's friends for his Success—Enters the Senate—Talent in that Body—His Course and Character as a Senator early formed—Mental Qualities—Condition of the Country—Nullification—The Force Bill—The Compromise Act—His Objections to the Bill—Vote on its Passage—His Remarks—Mr. Clay's Land Bill—Distribution—The Bank of the United States—Removal of the Deposits—Derangement of the Currency and Pecuniary Distress—Firmness of General Jackson—Marriage of Mr. Wright—Meeting of Congress—Presentation of Petitions—Resolutions of the New York Legislature—Speech of Mr. Wright—Regarded as the Organ of the Administration—Motion of Mr. Webster for leave to Introduce a Bill to Re-charter the Bank—Speech of Mr. Wright on the Motion—Resolutions of Mr. Clay Censuring the President and Secretary of the Treasury—Debate thereon—Defence of the Executive by Mr. Wright—Protest of the President—Difficulty in the Post Office Department—Vote in the House of Representatives on the Resolutions of Mr. Clay—Bill for the Improvement of the Wabash—Indemnity for French Spoliations prior to 1800—Invitation to a Public Dinner at Albany—Ill Health—Executive Patronage—Regulation of the Deposits—Appropriation Bills—Anticipated Rupture with France—The Fortification Bill—Mr. Wright's Speech.—1835.

At the time Mr. Wright took his seat in the Senate, there were those who distrusted his abilities; who feared that he would be unable to maintain his own reputation, and the high character of the state he represented, in the fierce intellectual contests which must inevitably take place. They did not stop to consider how often it is, that "honor pauseth in the meanest habit;" they did not appreciate, at its proper value, the strong and powerful genius concealed beneath his plain and unassuming manner; and they trembled for the senator, still young in years, as he crossed the threshold of the chamber where the sages and statesmen of the past had so often assembled in council, and enrolled his name as a member of the ablest body in the nation—perhaps in the world. But those who knew him intimately and well, had no fears or apprehensions. They had caught some glimpses of the sterling metal in his composition, and they were willing that it should be submitted to the ordeal, satisfied in their own minds that, like the gold of the refiner, it could but come the purer from the trial. They were anxious, very anxious; but they doubted not Remembering that

> "Peace hath her victories,
> No less renowned than war,"

they were content to see him enter the arena, in the full confidence that he would gather new laurels to adorn his brows, and confer new honor upon those who had promised so much in his behalf.

It was, indeed, a critical time in his history. There were hosts of friends to cheer and encourage him; he was the representative of one of the largest and most important members of the confederacy; it was conceded that he possessed talents of a high order; but his character as a statesman was yet to be formed. Everything was expected from him, and those expectations must not be disappointed. There was a great deal in the past to incite him to renewed exertion, and, like Alexander on the shores of the Hellespont, before him lay "Hope and the world!" Had he faltered then—had he hesitated but for one moment—who can say what his destiny might have been? The country was agitated from one extremity to the other. The best talent in the land was collected in the Senate. Opposed to the administration he would be called upon to sustain, at the head of his compeers, stood the gallant and chivalrous Clay—captivating the heart, and enchaining the imagination, by the magic bursts of his thrilling eloquence; Calhoun, the fearless champion of the sovereignty of the states, with his chaste diction, and analytical mind—every sentence that he uttered a whole chapter of argument, and every word a political text; Webster, calm, profound, and argumentative—powerful in stature, and gigantic in mind; the smooth and plausible Clayton; and Preston, fervid and impassioned, as the rays of the southern sun which had warmed his genius into life. On the opposite side, there was Benton, industrious, determined, and unyielding—with his pockets overflowing with statistics, and his head full of historical lore; Forsyth, easy and graceful in his address, but an able and experienced debater; Rives, the eloquent and talented senator from the Old Dominion, seeking to give vent to the inspiration he had caught in the groves of Monticello; White, with his metaphysical and sententious apothegms; and the shrewd and cautious Grundy, familiar with parliamentary tactics, watching for the weak points in his adversary's argument, and never caring to conceal his gratification when he saw the fabric, reared with so much labor, toppling down in the dust.

Such were the statesmen among whom Mr. Wright had taken a place, and against and with whom he was obliged to compete for the brilliant honors he acquired in his senatorial career. At the outset, the course was marked out which he subsequently pursued. Courteous and affable—dignified and respectful—he never suffered himself, in the midst of the stormiest debate, to forget the character he had assumed. Cool, thoughtful, and deliberative, every word was weighed before he gave it utterance, and not one of his opponents ever obtained an advantage that he voluntarily surrendered. There were none of those impulsive features in his character, which would have induced him to dash heedlessly forward, in the hope of outstripping every competitor at the start; and, if he failed, to console himself with the reflection that he had dared something beyond the power of human skill to accomplish.* His advances were slow and steady, but sure. He did not thrust himself forward. He did not assume too much. Not even when the bold and independent Jackson was willing to lean upon him for support, and he became known as the confidential friend of Mr. Van Buren, was there anything like assumption, or dictatorial harshness, in his tone or manner. The efforts of his discriminating and logical mind were directed to the enforcement of the positions he laid down, and the principles he advocated, for the sake of the argument; for the sake of what he believed to be just and right; and not to compel those who listened to adopt the conclusions at which he had arrived. If successful, he never advanced too hastily, but was content to wait until he had secured what was gained. He did not peril everything by attempting to grasp more than could be reached. And when he was defeated, when dark and portentous clouds hung around the political horizon, and the omens for the future were fearful and threatening, he did not lose his confidence in the ultimate triumph of the truths he labored to establish; but he calmly seated himself down, prepared patiently to bide

* "Magnis tamen excidit ausis," was the consolation of the unfortunate Phaeton.

his time, "with his feet to the foe," and his breast bared for the shock, ready alike to resist an attack, or to advance and secure the victory.

Mr. Wright entered the Senate as a member of that body on the 14th of January, 1833. The second session of the 22nd Congress, though short, was a memorable one. The internal improvement question had been settled for the time, by the Maysville veto; the difficulties with the Creek and Cherokee Indians were temporarily laid aside; and the excitement growing out of the refusal of the President to affix his name to the bill providing for the re-charter of the Bank of the United States, had partially subsided. But a still more important subject was now agitated—the dissolution of the American Confederacy. The inconsiderable reduction made in the tariff act of 1832, which had been designed to modify the objectionable features of the law of 1828—and, especially, the continuance of the high protective duties on the protected articles, and the admission, duty free, of those consumed by the manufacturers—were regarded in the southern states as tampering with their rights, as independent parties to the original compact between the members of the Union. The state of South Carolina assumed an attitude of hostility to the General Government, and declared that the revenue laws should not be enforced within her borders. On the 11th of December, 1832, the President issued his celebrated proclamation, which elicited such a general feeling of approbation at the North, and caused every heart to beat high with patriotic hope and devotion, as the sentiment was repeated, "The Union, it must be preserved!"

On the 16th of January, 1833, the nullification message of General Jackson was communicated to Congress, and on the 18th of February following, Mr. Wright was called upon to give his vote for the "force bill," as it was termed, intended to secure the prompt collection of the revenue in the state of South Carolina. The bill passed the Senate by the decisive vote of thirty-two to eight. In the meantime, a tariff bill had been prepared by Mr. Clay and others, called "The Compromise Act," and presented to the Senate. This act surrendered the protective principle, and established the ad valorem: a gradual reduction of the duties on all protected articles was also to be made, until the 30th of June, 1842, when no duty was to be imposed above twenty per cent. The general object of the bill was approved by Mr. Wright, but he was opposed to certain of its features, and endeavored to procure its amendment. On the 22nd of February, he voted to strike out the clause requiring a home valuation, believing that it would be impossible ever to establish such a system; that it would be constantly fluctuating, and could never be relied upon. The act of 1832 had reduced the duty on coarse wool, in accordance with the wishes of the manufacturers, and he made an unsuccessful attempt to restore it. Mr. Dallas moved to strike out the "revenue feature" of Mr. Clay's bill, declaring that after the minimum standard of duties had been reached, no more revenue should be collected than was "necessary to an economical administration of the government." The vote on the motion was fourteen in favor, to twenty-two against it. Mr. Wright, with Mr. Benton and Mr. Webster, supported the motion; and it was opposed by Messrs. Clay, Calhoun, Forsyth, and Rives. Mr. Wright likewise disapproved of the abolition of all specific and discriminating duties, and predicted the very evils from the adoption of the measure, which were witnessed in 1842, and which led to the passage of a law completely at variance with the compromise act, and that, too, in those features that he had opposed. Having attempted, in vain, to make the bill conform to his views, he gave his vote in its favor. The details of the act were not satisfactory; but he felt that the state of the country required its passage, as nothing better could be obtained. His feelings may be gathered from the following report of his remarks delivered previous to the final vote on the bill:—

"Mr. Wright then rose, and stated the defects he found in the bill. He objected to the proposed rate of reduction for the eight years, and to the want of a uniform rule of valuation. He objected to the inequality of the protection given by this bill. His next objection was, that while the duty on negro cloth exists, it refuses to impose any duty on the material which enters into that fabric, and which is grown in abundance in this country. He also objected to the system of home valuation, which he deemed to be impracticable, or if practicable, most unequal; and he objected further to the abolition of all specific and discriminating duties, and substituting a mode unjust and oppressive [the ad valorem principle.] He would not discuss the power of Congress to protect our manufactures by imposing duties on foreign articles, but he thought that this bill did not sufficiently recognize that power. On this point he quoted the language of the address of the free trade convention, which met last year. He expressed his own opinion to be in favor of laying imposts for the purpose of raising sufficient revenue for the wants of the country. So far, he was assured that the power to impose duties was vested in Congress.

"His strongest objection to the bill was, that it endeavors to bind the action of future Congresses. He considered this as a provision which was puerile in itself, and one which would never be considered as binding. He then viewed the circumstances under which Congress was called upon to act on this bill, imperfect as it is. He knew that he should be charged with legislating under the influence of his fears. He could not suffer his fears to govern his conclusions. But he would not disregard them. There had been a deep and settled discontent in a certain portion of the country, against our legislation, and he could not bring himself to regard that discontent lightly.

"Under the expression of that feeling, Congress had done what, if they had not done, would have left the Union dissolved. The operation of that discontent was against the whole body of laws for the collection of the revenue; and would, if carried on, have destroyed all the means of the government, and without the purse, no government could exist. He had, therefore, come to the question, deeply impressed with the conviction, that it was his duty to give his vote to prevent such an evil. He had been long of the opinion that the revenue ought to be reduced. He had also been long impressed with a sense of the inequality of the tariff system. No one had questioned the principle on which this bill was founded; it was only in reference to the details that difference of opinion existed. A part of the country is deeply excited, deeply exasperated; by what means, it was not for him to inquire; but the condition of things was such as to render it uncertain whether the Union can exist even until the month of December, unless something shall be done."*

How prophetic were these words—how lamentably the predictions of Mr. Wright were verified, the legislation of 1842 will bear witness! The passage of the bill, however, quieted the agitation; and the state of South Carolina expressed herself satisfied with its provisions. The only prominent measure discussed at this session of Congress, besides the compromise act, was the famous land bill of Mr. Clay, which passed the Senate on the 25th of January. The bill authorized the distribution of the proceeds of the public lands among the states for a limited time. Mr. Wright opposed the measure, on this occasion, as he did whenever it was again brought forward. His opinions were; that the public lands constituted a fund set apart for national purposes; that the avails were necessary to the General Government; and that the distribution was only an indirect mode of paying the debts of the several states. The bill was retained by the President after the adjournment of Congress, and returned to the Senate, with his objections, at the ensuing session.

In the summer of 1833, General Jackson determined upon the removal of the national deposits from the Bank of the United States. He had previously advised Congress that he considered the Government funds insecure; but that body had taken no action in the premises. Under the impression that the bank was pursuing a reckless and improvident course, in order to create a panic in the monetary affairs of the country,—which opinion was shown to be not entirely without foundation, by the developments made on the winding up of the affairs of that institution,—he read to his

* Niles' Register, Vol. XLIV. p. 24.

cabinet, on the 18th of September, his reasons for desiring the removal; which received the approbation of a majority of his constitutional advisers. The secretary of the treasury, Mr. Duane, refused to carry out the wishes of the President, and he was displaced, to make room for Mr. Taney, by whom the removal was made, early in October. This proceeding was followed by an immediate derangement of the currency of the country, and a general depression in business—attributed, on the one hand, to the removal, and on the other, to the struggles of the bank to perpetuate its existence. The act was denounced in the bitterest terms by the friends of the bank, as an arbitrary exercise of power, demanding the impeachment of the President, and his removal from office. He was alternately entreated and threatened, to induce him to restore the deposits; but he remained firm in his determination to carry into effect what had been decided upon with care and deliberation. Many of the most influential politicians in the country, who had previously given him their support, united with the opposition; every danger that the imagination could suggest was forcibly depicted, to move him from his purpose; the panic became, for the time, visible and real; and the whole land was thrown into commotion, from the St. Croix to the Sabine. Still the President could not be induced to forego his conclusions. He believed himself in the right. He was aware that embarrassment must be produced, but he thought it could only be temporary in its duration. The measure was, indeed, as rigorous as it was unexpected; yet he trusted to his countrymen to sustain him, when they came to know the reasons which had influenced his conduct.

In the fall of 1833, Mr. Wright was married to a

Miss Moody, the daughter of a gentleman at Canton, in whose family he had always boarded. This connection was not only productive of sincere and unalloyed happiness to those more immediately interested, but it afforded much pleasure and gratification to the friends who witnessed and participated in it. Both parties resembled each other in that kindness of heart, and amiability of disposition, which are sure to produce harmony and contentment; and it has been said that an unkind word, or look, never passed between them. This is a sufficient commentary upon the association formed under such happy auspices, which death has so rudely severed.

But the absorbing topics to be presented to the Congress of the Union, summoned Mr. Wright to Washington in the midst of his felicity. The course of the President was in accordance with his own views, and he was prepared to sustain him with all the ability he possessed. The administration, too, counted upon his aid, and it could not have found a more zealous defender. The opinions he entertained on the exciting questions brought before Congress, may be summed up in a few words: He believed, with the President, that the deposits were unsafe with the bank of the United States, and that the circumstances of the case required their removal; that the executive was responsible to the country for the proper discharge of the official duties of every member of his cabinet; and that the power of removal necessarily belonged to him, in order to effect that object. In regard to the existing pecuniary distress, he thought the bank had produced it for the purpose of creating an impression favorable to its re-charter; and that if it would confine itself to closing its affairs, confidence would be restored, and the country become prosperous. Upon these general views, his speeches and votes were founded, at the session commencing in December, 1833.

At the opening of the session, Mr. White, the president pro tem., declined to appoint the committees of the Senate. It had been customary, since the year 1828, for the presiding officer to discharge that duty; but the Senate thought proper to take the power from the Vice-President, and appoint the committees by ballot. Mr. Wright was placed on the committees on agriculture and on commerce. With the organization of the Senate commenced the warfare between the friends of the administration and the opposition. The latter had a majority in the Senate; but in the House the preponderance was in favor of the executive. Petitions of every class and character were presented. The prayer of all was, that relief should be afforded to the monetary interests of the nation, which, it was said, were now threatened with a complete prostration. Some thought the restoration of the deposits would be sufficient—others asked for the re-charter of the bank. But the main questions put, in and out of Congress, were—What does the government propose?—what will the administration do in this emergency? On the presentation of petitions, it was usual for senators to express their opinions in regard to the financial distresses which all admitted to exist, and which all deplored. On the 30th of January, Mr. Wright presented a series of resolutions approving of the removal of the deposits, adopted by the Legislature of the state of New York, and availed himself of the occasion to express his views at some length.* He disclaimed to speak as the organ of the administration, but every one felt that he

* See Appendix.

uttered the sentiments, not only of himself, but of the President and Vice-President. He defended the removal of the deposits, and declared that he was opposed to their restoration. He also assumed a position adverse to the re-charter of the bank, or the incorporation of any similar institution; on the broad ground that the constitution had not conferred the power upon Congress. He acknowledged that the pecuniary affairs of the country were deranged, but assumed that they would soon return to a healthy condition, provided the bank would adhere to its legitimate business, and prepare to bring its concerns to a close. The speech was able and eloquent. It was listened to with deep interest; and those who knew the inflexible nature of President Jackson, and the uncompromising character of the speaker, saw that there could be no hesitation, or change, in the course of the administration.

On the 20th of March, Mr. Wright addressed the Senate again, upon a motion made by Mr. Webster, for leave to introduce a bill re-chartering the Bank of the United States for a limited period. This speech, like the previous one, was expressive of his views upon the currency questions, and attracted attention, on the part of the friends, as well as of the opponents of the administration. No one now denied him the possession of commanding talents—Mr. Webster paid him a high compliment for the ability he had displayed—and he was afterwards regarded as the leader of the democratic party in the Senate. The following extracts from the concluding portion of the speech on Mr. Webster's resolution, present Mr. Wright's opinions in regard to the course of the bank, and the propriety of its re-charter, in a clear and forcible manner:—

"I cannot, then, be mistaken when I say, that if the

Bank of the United States would cease its efforts for, and its hopes of, a re-existence, and would endeavor to perform its duty to the country, by closing its affairs with as little injury as possible to any individual or public interest, the state banks would be able to extend their loans, confidence would be restored, and the pressure upon the money market would soon cease. Apprehension,—a just apprehension of the hostile movements of this great institution, is the most powerful cause of the present scarcity of money. This scarcity must exist so long as this apprehension continues. How, then, is it to be allayed? would seem to be the pertinent inquiry. The honorable senator from Massachusetts answers us by the bill upon your table. Recharter the bank; appease the monster by prolonging its existence, and increasing its power. I say, no, sir; but act promptly and refuse its wish; destroy its hope of a re-charter, and you destroy its inducement to be hostile to the state institutions. A different interest—the interest of its stockholders—to wind up its affairs as profitably to themselves as possible, becomes its ruling object, and will direct its policy. The more prosperous the country, the more plenty the money of other institutions, the more easily and safely can this object be accomplished; and every hope of a continued existence being destroyed, that this will be the object of the bank is as certain as that its moneyed interest governs a moneyed incorporation. Mr. President, this is unquestionably the opinion of the country. Look, sir, at the files of memorials upon your table, and however widely they may differ as to their views of the bank, they all hold to you this language, 'act speedily, and finally settle the question.'

"But we are told, sir, that the country cannot sustain the winding up of the affairs of this bank. Is this so? What does experience teach us upon this subject? The old Bank of the United States, within four months of the close of its charter, was more extended in proportion to the amount of its capital than the present bank is at this moment, and still it is almost two years to the close of its charter. The old bank struggled as this does for a re-existence; the country was then alarmed; memorials in favor of the bank were then, as now, piled upon the tables of the members of Congress; the cries of distress rung through these halls then, as distinctly as they now do;—nay, more, gentlemen were then sent here from the commercial cities to be examined upon oath, before the committees of Congress, to prove the existence and the extent of the distress; business was then in a state of the utmost depression in all parts of the Union; commerce was literally suspended by the restrictive measures of the government; trade was dull beyond any former example; property of all kinds was unusually depressed in price; and the country was on the eve of a war with the most powerful nation in the world. Still, Congress was unmoved, and the old bank was not re-chartered. Such is the history of that period, and, with the final action of Congress, all knowledge of the distress ceased. Who has ever heard of disasters to the business of the country, proceeding from the winding up of the old bank? I, sir, can find no trace of any such consequences. I do find that, in a period of about eighteen months after the expiration of the charter, the bank disposed of its obligations, and divided to its stockholders about eighty-eight per cent. upon their stock.

"It is now admitted, on all hands, that the country

is rich and prosperous in an unusual degree; property of all kinds is abundant; commerce is free, and extensive, and flourishing, and business of every description is healthful and vigorous. If then, we cannot, in this condition of things, sustain the closing of the affairs of this great moneyed incorporation, it is safe to assume that the country will never see the time when it can do it. Grant it longer life and deeper root, and in vain shall we try in future to shake it from us. It will dictate its own terms, and command its own existence. Indeed, Mr. President, the whole tendency of the honorable senator's argument seemed to me to be, to prove the necessity of a perpetual bank of this description; and we have been repeatedly told, during the debate of the last three months, that this free, and rich, and prosperous country, cannot get on without a great moneyed power of this description to regulate its affairs. The bill before the Senate proposes to repeal the monopolizing provision in the existing charter, and the honorable senator tells us that this is to be done that Congress may, within the six years over which this is to extend the life of the present bank, establish a new bank to take its place, and into which the affairs of the old may be transferred, so as to be finally closed without a shock to the country. Sir, this is not the relief I seek. My object is the entire discontinuance and eradication of this or any similar institution. We are told the distresses of the country will not permit this now. When, sir, will it ever permit it better? When will the time come, that this odious institution can be finally closed with less distress than now? Never, while cupidity obeys its fixed laws; never, sir, never!

"This distress, Mr. President, did not exist when we left our homes; we heard not of it then; it commenced with the commencement of our debates here; and I doubt not it will end when our debates end, and our final action is known, whatever may be the result to which we shall arrive. It must necessarily be temporary, and it does not prove to my mind the necessity of a bank, but the mischiefs a bank may produce. I care not whether it be or be not in the power of the bank to ameliorate the evils now complained of. That it can cause them in any manner, is proof that, if the disposition exist, it can cause them at pleasure; and this very fact is the strongest evidence, to my mind, that no institution, with such a power, ought to exist in this country.

"Sir, the subject of our present action involves two great first principles: one of constitutional power, and one of governmental expediency. Upon neither should our action be governed solely by considerations of temporary derangement and distress in the money market. Revulsions in trade and business, and pecuniary affairs, will happen. They must be temporary; the country will restore itself, and money will again be plenty; but the settlement of important principles must involve consequences of an enduring character,—consequences which will exert an influence for good or for evil, through all time."

Early in the session, Mr. Clay introduced in the Senate two resolutions—the one declaring that the reasons given by the secretary of the treasury for the removal of the deposits, in his report to Congress, were insufficient and unsatisfactory; and the other, having reference to the President of the United States, which was modified previous to the final vote thereon, so as to read as follows:—

"Resolved, That the President, in the late executive

5

proceedings in relation to the public revenue, has assumed upon himself authority and power not conferred by the constitution and laws, but in derogation of both."

The debate on these resolutions was protracted to a late day in the session, and called out the most powerful talent in the Senate. All the prominent members of that body spoke on the subject. The clashing and collision of so much intellect in the fiery debate, it was terrible to witness. The relation which the bank sustained to the government as its fiscal agent; the extent of the discretionary authority of the secretary to control the funds; the power of removal and appointment to office; and the right to censure or impeach the President; were reviewed at length. It was a severe school to a new member like Mr. Wright; but he sustained himself, even above the expectations of his friends. On the 26th of March, 1834, he delivered one of the most touching and forcible speeches that was made upon the resolutions, and which elicited the highest encomiums from those who heard it.* "Mr. Wright," said the correspondent of an opposition paper in the city of New York, "argued long in defence of the full and complete power of removal from office given to the President; and, taking the ground as formerly by Mr. Benton, that the President was amenable criminally, and subject, if guilty, to impeachment by the House of Representatives, the Senate, he concluded, as his judges, ought not to entertain the resolutions; that the resolutions were not relevant, and if relevant, there was nothing in the facts to support them. After arguing upon all these, and urging much in deprecation of the proceedings the Senate was about to take, to blast the character of one whose actions, commencing in the

* See Appendix.

revolutionary annals of the country, had closed by his victory at New Orleans, with a blaze of glory which time would not extinguish; he concluded, after a well-delivered and feeling eulogy and appeal, by hoping that it was not such a person they were about to condemn, without trial, without that which was given to every other individual. He besought them to consider that in his career he had done the state some service; that age was creeping fast upon him; that his gray hairs were without a stain; and that they would permit him to enjoy the rights guaranteed by the constitution which he had gallantly defended from the attack of its enemies in the field, and let conviction precede their sentence. This defence and peroration were given by Mr. Wright, in a manner which is creditable to his head and heart."

In spite of the efforts of the administration senators, the resolutions of Mr. Clay were passed on the 28th of March, by large majorities; and on the 15th of April following, the President communicated to the Senate his protest against their proceedings. The passage of the resolutions had been followed by a season of calm and quiet; but the appearance of the protest aroused the fires of excitement and passion which had only been smothered, and not subdued. The right of the executive to communicate such a paper to the Senate was positively denied, and the act denounced as a breach of privilege. The war of words was fiercer than ever; and Messrs. Clay, Calhoun, and Webster, delivered most effective speeches in opposition to the reception of the protest. Mr. Wright, and the administration senators, manfully defended the course of the President, but they were overborne by the resistless power of numbers. The Senate refused to enter the protest on their journals, as was requested by its author, and the controversy soon after terminated. It is a remarkable fact, in connection with the debate on this subject, and the other exciting discussions of the session, that Mr. Wright always preserved his self-possession, and was never known to be ruffled in temper. While other senators around him, older in years and in experience, occasionally gave way to the impulses they were unable to restrain, he was never wanting in courtesy or respect. It is honorable, also, to the distinguished statesmen at the head of the opposition, who found in him an antagonist whom it required all their strength to encounter, that they ever paid him the most marked deference and regard.

Mr. Wright endeavored to procure the passage of a bill at this session regulating the deposits in the safety-fund banks; but was unsuccessful. Mr. Clay offered resolutions requiring the deposits to be restored to the Bank of the United States, which were adopted by a party vote. The affairs of the Post-office department were also made the subject of investigation. It appeared that the postmaster-general had made loans for the purpose of discharging the liabilities of the department, without authority of law, and a resolution, pronouncing such loans illegal and void, was unanimously passed in the Senate—Mr. Wright being present and voting in its favor. It was not alleged against the officer whose conduct was censured by this vote, that he had committed any intentional wrong; and hence no further proceedings were instituted.

The resolutions of Mr. Clay in regard to the secretary of the treasury, and the restoration of the deposits, were laid on the table in the House of Representatives. A resolution, declaring that the Bank of the United States ought not to be re-chartered, was carried, by a vote of 132 to 82. The session closed on the 30th of June—many of the members of both branches of Congress having completely exhausted their energies and strength, with the incessant labor and excitement. Mr. Wright, at all times assiduous in the discharge of his public duties, was never more so than during the winter and spring of 1834. After his return home, he was attacked by a severe fit of sickness, but recovered in time to set out for Washington prior to the meeting of Congress in December. While on his way to the seat of government, he stopped for a few days in the city of Albany, where he had formerly resided; and, during his stay, he was invited to a public dinner by the republican general committee. He declined the invitation in polite terms, acknowledging his indebtedness to his friends in that city, and to the democratic citizens of the state, "for everything of character and standing he possessed as a public servant," and avowing his willingness at all times to acknowledge their claims upon him. "You will believe me, gentlemen," he said, in his letter declining the invitation, "when I say that from no quarter could such a mark of friendship and confidence come to me more acceptably, than from the democratic citizens of Albany. With them for my associates and counsellors, and under their personal observation, has much the largest portion of my public duties been discharged; and this evidence that I have been so fortunate as to secure their approbation, is most gratifying, as it permits me to hope that my efforts to be faithful to the public have not been wholly unsuccessful. A proper attention to the same duties compels me to ask you, and those whom you represent, to excuse me from meeting you and them as you request. My short stay in the city must be wholly devoted to public business and public interests of great importance, a necessary attention to which brought me here thus early, on my way to the seat of government; and while I will not attempt to express my regret that I cannot enjoy the social meeting to which you invite me, I am consoled by the reflection that the loss will be mine—not that of the friends who are thus partial to me."

At the second session of the 23rd Congress, commencing in December 1834, Mr. Wright was elected a member of the committees on finance and on commerce. One of the most important questions discussed at this session, was that of the reduction of the executive patronage. The design of the bill introduced on this subject was, to limit the power of the President in making removals from office, and to require a vote of the Senate in certain cases. The bill was opposed by Mr. Wright in an able speech, in which he proved most conclusively, that the first Congress had decided that the power of removal belonged to the President, under the constitution, and that every executive from Washington downwards had exercised it. The bill passed the Senate by a vote of thirty-one to sixteen, but failed in the House. At the session of 1833–34 an act was passed for the improvement of the Wabash river, which the President had refused to sanction, on the ground that it could not be considered a national work, as there was no port of entry on that river. In 1835 an attempt was made to pass a bill establishing a port of entry on the Wabash, in order to evade the constitutional difficulty. Mr. Wright regarded such legislation as trifling with the constitution, and gave his vote against the bill.

At this session Mr. Wright opposed the passage of the bill providing for the payment of French spoliations prior to 1800. He also took a prominent part in perfecting the bill to regulate the deposits in the state banks, which was lost in the House, and the annual appropriation bills.

In his message to Congress, at the commencement of the session, the President had stated his apprehensions of a termination of the friendly intercourse existing between the government of the United States and the French nation, growing out of the refusal or neglect of the latter to fulfil the stipulations of the treaty of 1831. He also recommended that measures should be taken to provide for the defence of the country. The Senate were of the opinion that it would be more advisable to delay action, until it was known what had been the proceedings of the French Chambers, and therefore passed a resolution declaring that any legislation at that time was inexpedient. But as Congress was about to adjourn, intelligence of the most alarming character was received, and both Houses unanimously resolved to insist upon the execution of the treaty. It was feared that hostilities might commence before the new Congress could be summoned together, and on the evening of the last day of the session, at the request of the President, an amendment was inserted in the fortification bill, then before the House of Representatives, appropriating the sum of three millions of dollars, to be expended under his directions, in preparations for war, if it should be necessary. The opposition members of the Senate refused to concur in this amendment, on the ground that it was placing too much power in the hands of the President. After several senators had spoken, Mr. Wright made a most eloquent and patriotic speech in reply, which is reported as follows:—*

* Niles' Register, Vol. XLVIII. p. 52.

"Mr. Wright hoped the Senate would not adhere to their disagreement. He felt himself bound to state that he did not know that he had heard of the constitution being broken down—destroyed—and the liberties of the country overthrown, so frequently in that Senate, as to render him callous to the real state of things. For the last sixteen months these fears and forebodings had been so strongly and often expressed on that floor, that they had been forcibly impressed upon him; yet, he must say, that he was incapable of perceiving a particle of their effects. No evidence had he seen of them; nor could he now partake of the alarm which some gentlemen pretended to feel, when he saw that the asseverations made at this time came from the same source. What had the Senate now before it? A bill from the House of Representatives—from the immediate representatives of the people, proposing to provide for the defence of the country. What had honorable senators debated? The danger of executive power. Were, he would ask, those representatives, sitting at the other end of the capitol, the most likely to contribute to that danger? Was that the source from which senators were compelled to look for danger in that respect? Such an idea had never occurred to his mind. Under what circumstances did the members of the other body permit the appropriation? He believed, and he spoke on good authority, that our minister at the court of France had informed this government that it was problematical that the French might strike the first blow against us by detaining our fleet, now in the Mediterranean. Congress were on the point of adjourning; and being in possession of such advices from our minister, they had thought proper to act as they had done in regard to this appropriation; and he would inquire, by what notion it was, that the Senate were to be impressed with the danger of putting this power into the hands of the executive—that our liberties were to be destroyed, and the constitution trampled upon? Ay, in making an appropriation for the defence and safety of the country from a foreign enemy!

"The honorable senator," (Mr. Leigh) said Mr. Wright in continuation, "has exhibited to us the dangers—of what? Not a *foreign* enemy, for he would hardly dread the landing of a foreign foe at our doors—but a *domestic* enemy is to ruin us! I remember, though it was at a period when I was very young, that a certain portion of the country held the same opinion as the honorable senator, and, when a *foreign* enemy did land in it, no alarm was shown, but the people there were alarmed at the *domestic* enemy. How was the foreign enemy met? As the honorable senator has most eloquently said—'breast to breast?' No; that enemy was seen holding a Bible in his hand, and the American citizen putting his hand upon it, and swearing allegiance to the British government. Such is not *my* feeling in regard to a foreign enemy. I would prepare to repulse him at the first step; I would prepare to prevent him from touching my native soil, if I had it in my power."

The earnest appeal of Mr. Wright was not without its effect. The Senate appointed a committee of conference, of which Messrs. Webster, Frelinghuysen, and Wright, were members, to meet a similar committee from the House. The result was, the reduction of the amount to be appropriated, to eight hundred thousand dollars. The Senate concurred in the amendment, but when the subject was again presented to the House, there was not a quorum of members in attendance, and the whole bill failed. With the adjournment, the twenty-third Congress, one of the most important in the history of the country, terminated its existence.

CHAPTER VI.

1835.—Nomination of Mr. Van Buren for the Presidency—Standing of Mr. Wright in the Senate—The Land Bill—Abolition of Slavery in the District of Columbia—The Surplus Revenue—Speculations—Remedies for the Financial Evils of the Country—Distribution—Opposition of Mr. Wright and others—The Specie Circular—Election of Mr. Van Buren—Act to Repeal—Abolition Petitions—Acknowledgment of Texan Independence—Expunging Resolution—Re-election of Mr. Wright—Visit to Vermont—The Pressure—Differences of Opinion—Views of Mr. Wright—Extra Session—The Independent Treasury—United States Bank—Special Deposit System—The Conservatives—Slavery in the District—North Eastern Boundary Question—The Bankrupt Bill of 1840—Renomination of Mr. Van Buren—His Administration—Expenses—Extra Session called by President Harrison—Repeal of the Independent Treasury—Loan Bill—Bankrupt Law—Land Distribution Bill of Mr. Clay—Vetoes of the Bank Bills—Provisional Tariff Bill and Vetoes of the President—Mr. Clay's Resolutions—Apportionment Bill—Tariff Law of 1842—Bill to Refund the Fine Paid by General Jackson at New Orleans—Mr. Wright Re-elected for a Third Term.—1843.

In May 1835, a national democratic convention was held at Baltimore, of which Mr. Wright was a member. Public opinion had for a long time been fixed upon Mr. Van Buren as the successor of General Jackson in the chair of state, and he received the unanimous nomination of the convention for the presidency. The conspicuous position occupied by Mr. Wright during the stormy session of the twenty-third Congress, as one of the ablest supporters of the administration; the reliance of the President on his counsel and advice; and the high estimation in which his practical good sense and sound judgment were held by his party friends, had contributed to place him prominently before the nation. The selection of Mr. Van Buren, as the presidential candidate, and its undoubted confirmation by the electors of the country, attracted still greater attention to his movements. Possessing the unlimited confidence of the President and Vice President, it was generally thought that in all he said or did, he was prompted more or less by a regard for their views and interests. This sudden elevation to a high place among the ablest statesmen of the day might well have dazzled one less fixed and unchanging in his principles. He was surrounded by men who were active participants in the political contests of a past generation. Many of them he had distanced, and all were willing to acknowledge him as an equal. But no one remarked a change in his bearing. He was the same upon the floor of the Senate, when he was looked upon as the confidential representative of the executive, that he had been while administering justice, and reconciling differences, between his fellow-citizens in a quiet country village. Substantial, enduring merit was his, and a clear, well-balanced mind. He was not elated at his success, but calmly pursued the straightforward, undeviating track, along which his footsteps had been directed. The purity of his motives was never questioned, nor his integrity doubted, upon the floor of the Senate. Had any dared to whisper aught against him—all, even the most zealous and determined partisan in the ranks of the opposition, would have shrunk from the calumniator, as if there had been poison in the touch.

Congress convened in December 1835, and Mr. Wright was again placed on the committee on finance.

having been supported by the administration senators for chairman, in opposition to Mr. Webster. He was also a member of the committee on agriculture. At this session he advocated the passage of the prospective pre-emption bill, the admission of Arkansas and Michigan into the Union, and the bill for the relief of the sufferers at the fire in New York. The land distribution bill of Mr. Clay was again brought forward, and again passed the Senate. Mr. Wright, with Mr. Calhoun and Mr. Benton, voted against it. During the session, a petition was presented from the Society of Friends in the city of Philadelphia, praying for the abolition of slavery in the District of Columbia. On Mr. Buchanan's motion to reject the prayer of the petition, Mr Clay, Mr, Benton, Mr. Calhoun, and Mr. Wright, voted in the affirmative. But six members of the Senate opposed the motion. On the 2nd of June 1836, a bill was passed to prevent the transmission through the mail of printed matter calculated to excite the prejudices of the citizens of the southern states, in regard to the question of slavery. Mr. Wright voted for the bill. A resolution was unanimously passed in the Senate on the 1st of July, declaring that the Independence of Texas ought to be acknowledged, so soon as it was ascertained that it had an established government in successful operation.

But the most important question presented for the consideration of the national legislature at this session was, that of the disposition of the surplus revenue and the regulation of the deposits. It was important, not merely so far as the safety of the government funds was concerned, but in the influence it exerted upon the administration of Mr. Van Buren, and the commercial and mercantile interests of the country. The amount deposited in the state banks selected as the fiscal agents of the treasury, exceeded forty millions of dollars. This large sum formed the basis of a most gigantic system of speculation. The amount of credit resting upon this actual capital could hardly be estimated with exactness, but it is supposed to have been several hundred millions of dollars. Heavy loans were made by the deposit banks upon the government funds in their vaults. Money, or the representative of money, became plenty; and the dreams which had haunted the early Spanish adventurers, of an El Dorado in the West, seemed about to be realized. City lots, and real estate of every description, were converted into mines of wealth. The prices of all articles of value rose as if by magic. The fever—for it was but a fever, as fitful and exciting in its progress, as terrible when at its height, and as slow and painful in its convalescence—the fever of speculation, raged in the city, in the town, and in the country. The ledger of the merchant, or the banker, was laid aside; the briefs of the lawyer were left untouched upon his table; the tools of the mechanic rested in their places; and the plough of the farmer remained idle in its furrow. One engrossing sentiment occupied every mind—the desire for gain.

Among the many objects of speculation, were the western lands belonging to the Government. The loans made by the deposit banks were employed in purchasing up large tracts, whose descriptions had for years cumbered the files of the land office, and the moneys paid to the receivers were returned to the banks, as new deposits, to form the basis of new loans. The able statesmen in Congress, of both parties, foresaw the evils which must ensue, and began seriously to reflect upon a remedy. The administration proposed to expend such portion of the surplus revenue as could be advantageously used, upon the military defences of the nation. Mr. Benton offered a resolution having that object in view, which was supported by Mr. Wright. The opposition senators voted for striking out the word "surplus" in the resolution, and succeeded in carrying the motion. As amended, the resolution was unanimously passed. But it was shorn of its strength, and a disposition of the surplus was yet to be made. The idea of investing it in state stocks was then suggested on the part of the administration, and it was proposed on the other side to deposit it with the several states. It was objected to the plan of the administration, that the secretary of the treasury would have too much power and patronage at his disposal, under such a regulation, and that the funds would be less reliable and secure than if deposited with the states. Subsequent events have shown that the last argument was of little weight, though it was warmly urged when the subject was under discussion. The stocks of the states would have enabled the government, in some degree, to sustain itself in its embarrassments; but the mere indebtedness proved to be wholly nominal. The first objection of the opposition would have been removed, by the adoption of restrictions more severe than those which had been proposed; but the friends of the distribution of the surplus among the states, had a commanding majority in Congress, and were determined to carry the measure into effect. Both parties were desirous of regulating the deposits, and of preventing their use as the basis of loans to speculators. But the opposition, with a large proportion of the administration members, thought proper to couple the two projects together. Mr. Van Buren was decidedly opposed to the distribution. Mr. Wright and Mr. Benton labored to prevent its adoption. The former delivered an elaborate and argumentative speech, in which he predicted the financial difficulties that afterwards crippled the government and the energies of its citizens, as the inevitable results of this disposition of the surplus. His warnings were not heeded, and the bill became the law of the land. Mr. Wright, and the senators who thought with him, persisted in their opposition to the last, and recorded their votes against the bill. To the latest hour of his life, he was prouder of that vote, than of any other given during the time he was a member of the Senate. In the course of the debate on the bill, Mr. Tallmadge, the colleague of Mr. Wright, intimated that the latter had disregarded the wishes of his constituents, and that his opposition to the measure under consideration would be visited with their displeasure. Mr. Wright made but a few remarks in reply, but those were uttered with so much manliness and dignity, that no one envied the position of his colleague.

On the 11th of July, subsequent to the adjournment of Congress, President Jackson issued his celebrated "Specie Circular," requiring all payments for the public lands to be made in gold and silver. The design of this movement was, both to check the spirit of speculation, which continued to increase until the distribution act went into operation; and also to guard the treasury against loss, when the catastrophe, which was now confidently predicted by himself and the opponents of that measure, had come to pass. While the country was still apparently prosperous, the presidential election was held, and resulted in the choice of Mr. Van

Buren, by a large majority of the electoral votes. In December, 1836, the administration party had a majority in the Senate, in consequence of several changes which had taken place. Mr. Wright was then appointed chairman of the committee on finance, a position which he continued to occupy until the whigs came into power in 1841, adding every year to his previous reputation for industry and ability.

The specie circular was the main topic of discussion at this session. It no doubt operated harshly and rigorously in many instances, and while it was thought to close up a source of inexhaustible wealth, which, in fact, was but transitory in its duration, and delusive in its character, it was felt to be oppressive. A portion of the administration members of Congress, most of whom afterwards opposed the Independent Treasury bill, united with the opposition in passing a law repealing the circular. The President declined carrying it into effect, on the ground that it was uncertain and indefinite, and, for the present, the currency question remained in its former position. At this session, Mr. Wright procured the passage of a bill reducing the duty on certain articles. It was opposed by Mr. Clay, on the ground that it violated the compromise act; but it was carried in the Senate by a vote of twenty-seven to eighteen. The question of the reception of abolition petitions was again discussed, and the subject disposed of, by the informal adoption of a rule among the senators, of laying the motion to refer, or the motion to receive, on the table. This course was approved by Mr. Clay, Mr. Benton, Mr. Calhoun, and Mr. Wright. On the 1st of March, 1837, a vote was taken on a resolution previously introduced in the Senate, acknowledging the Independence of Texas. Mr. Wright, and nearly all the administration senators from the northern states, were of the opinion that it would be unwise, inasmuch as a proposition for the annexation of Texas to this government was in contemplation, or a wish to that effect had been expressed, to pass the resolution, while negotiations were understood to be pending between the Texan government and Santa Anna, the President of the Mexican republic; and therefore they opposed its adoption. At this session also, the resolution censuring General Jackson for the removal of the deposits, passed in 1834, was ordered to be expunged from the journal, by a vote of twenty-nine to fourteen—Mr. Wright voting in its favor.

At the annual session of the Legislature of New York in the winter of 1837, Mr. Wright was re-elected for the full term of six years. At the caucus to nominate a candidate, some opposition was manifested to his selection. The friends of the lateral canals were not unmindful of his opposition to their projects, and the banking interest of the state had become in a measure hostile to Mr. Van Buren and himself. There were older politicians, too, who were jealous of his increasing popularity—even in spite of their respect for the man, and their admiration of his talents. The opposing candidate was Samuel Beardsley, then attorney-general of the state. The caucus decided by a large vote in favor of Mr. Wright, and on the following day he was elected by the Legislature.

Immediately after the adjournment of Congress, Mr. Wright visited the state of Vermont. At Burlington, he received an invitation to a public dinner, which, in accordance with his invariable rule, he respectfully declined. Everywhere throughout the state, where his early years had been passed, he was regarded with especial favor, and received many evidences of the respect and esteem of its inhabitants. He returned from his journey in time to witness the explosion which he had anticipated. The distribution act had not prevented the evil which its friends declared would be averted. The crisis came—came too, with crushing force—bearing everything before it; and crumbling into dust the whole fabric of the credit system, which had depended on the surplus revenue for its strength and support. The measures of the administration doubtless hastened this catastrophe, but how could the result have been avoided? The system was an unsound one in its origin. The surplus was not designed to furnish the means for banking facilities or operations; nor should it have been considered as so much actual capital on which a permanent credit could be based. But laying this argument aside; there was another reason why such a state of things could not long have endured. A large amount of individual capital was invested in unproductive real estate, or in that which possessed a fictitious value. Nominal wealth was made to take the place of what should have been real, and when the day for payment came to those who relied upon such means, as it could not but eventually come, however long it might have been postponed, no human agency could have prevented just such results as were witnessed in 1837. The feelings growing out of the political contests of that day, are still cherished by those who participated in the struggle; and while some may condemn the administration and its friends, as it is but natural that they should if they were then honest in their opinions, others will defend them. It must not be expected, that those who suffered from the blow could so easily forget the causes which they believed had produced it. Many, many bright hopes, depended upon the speculations of that period—oh, how bright were they, and gorgeous—and how painful must it have been, to see them scattered forever, like the leaves of the Sibyl, before the breath of the tempest!

The views of Mr. Wright in regard to the objects of the specie circular, and its propriety and expediency, were often expressed on the floor of the Senate. It was designed to prevent the speculation in western lands; to save the government from loss; and check the over-issues of the banks. The avowed intention of the distribution policy was to accomplish the same purposes. Its advocates declared themselves desirous of preventing the use of the surplus as the basis for bank loans; and no more effectual mode could have been devised to secure that object, than its deposit with the states. But that was not the only result, as Mr. Wright contended, that was produced by the measure. While remaining on deposit, it had formed the foundation of the most stupendous banking system, in the aggregate, that ever existed in the country. Its withdrawal from the eastern cities left the system without prop or support. The specie circular, in his opinion, would have prevented the extravagant speculations which all desired to correct, and the investment of the surplus in state stocks, as proposed by him in Congress, have relieved the pressure by retaining the surplus in the large commercial towns.

The removal of the government deposits from the banks, for the purposes of distribution, was followed by a heavy demand for specie to be shipped to Europe. Large importations of foreign goods had been made in 1836. The financial condition of the European states, towards the close of that year, was such, that a commercial revulsion was apprehended—abroad as well as at home. The Bank of England curtailed its operations, and refused to discount for the houses engaged in the American trade. Bills drawn on them were protested, and returned in the spring of 1837. Specie funds were required for their payment, which the banks were expected to furnish. The pressure began to be felt in March, and rapidly progressed, until alarm and consternation pervaded every department of business. Early in May, the President was waited upon by a committee from the city of New York, who requested him to rescind the specie circular, to delay the collection of the bonds given for duties, and to call an extra session of Congress. The delay asked for was immediately assented to; but the other requests were not granted. Two days after the decision of the President was made known in New York, the banks in that city suspended specie payments. Their example was soon followed throughout the whole Union. An extra session was now rendered absolutely necessary. Public officers were prohibited by law, from receiving or paying out bank notes not convertible into current coin, on the demand of the holder, at the place where they were received, and from making deposits in banks not paying specie. The funds of the government previously received were deposited with the banks, and therefore entirely unavailable. On the 15th of May, therefore, the proclamation of Mr. Van Buren was issued, summoning Congress to meet on the ensuing 4th day of September.

In 1835, a proposition for the entire separation of the government from the banks was presented in Congress, but did not meet the approbation of members. At that early day, both Mr. Van Buren and Mr. Wright were deeply impressed with the belief that there was no necessity for the connection which had formerly existed. Yet the business relations of the country were such, and public opinion was so firmly fixed in its favor, that it was not then thought expedient to propose a change. But now that the failure of the banks to fulfil their functions as the fiscal agents of the treasury, had dissolved the connection, the question arose—whether it should be renewed? After the proclamation of the President appeared, the desire to know what were the views and plans of the administration was increased. The suspense daily grew more painful and exciting. Fear and uncertainty prevailed on every hand. Rumor was busy with her thousand tongues, devising strange tales and inventions. In the midst of the anxiety, the plan of an Independent Treasury was shadowed forth in the columns of a leading democratic paper in the vicinity of Mr. Wright's residence. None doubted from whence that voice proceeded. The tone and the manner were recognized far and near. Some approved; while others feared, and condemned. The few who had long thought the separation inevitable, hailed the project as the omen of hope and encouragement; but the many looked upon it as the darkling cloud, ready to burst in its fury, over the angry waters now surging and tossing in madness and rage.

The extra session of Congress was awaited with intense interest. The whig party, by which name the opponents of the administration were then known, had evinced their decided hostility to the financial scheme in contemplation. A large number of the supporters of Mr. Van Buren also, and especially those connected with mercantile and banking operations, who felt—honestly felt—that their interests would be endangered, were opposed to the measure. Others, too timid to strike out in advance of public sentiment, but waiting to be borne along on the wave, hoped that it would not be urged. The message appeared; and the President distinctly and explicitly announced his opposition to the establishment of a national bank, and to the renewal of the connection between the government and the banks. Mr. Wright was indefatigable in preparing the several bills upon which it was desired to obtain the action of Congress, in order that the session might not be unduly protracted. On the 11th of September, he reported from the committee on finance, a bill to postpone the payment to the states of the fourth instalment of the surplus placed on deposit, which was subsequently passed by Congress, with an amendment, changing the time to which the postponement was made. On the following day he introduced bills to authorize the issue of treasury notes; to provide for the adjustment of the claims against the deposit banks; and to postpone the collection of duty bonds. The bill in relation to treasury notes authorized the issue of an amount not exceeding ten millions of dollars. It encountered a vehement opposition from the whig members of Congress, who preferred a direct loan in its stead. On the part of the administration it was urged, as being more convenient for the temporary purpose it was designed to serve, and as furnishing at all times the means of paying the obligations of the government in such sums as were desired. A majority approved of the bill, and it was passed during the session.

On the 14th of September Mr. Wright reported the great measure of Mr. Van Buren's administration—the bill providing for the divorce of bank and state. As originally presented by him, the bill contained no provision in regard to the character of the funds which should be received in payment of government dues. In the course of the debate on the treasury note bill, Mr. Calhoun, who had indicated a disposition to offer that support to the administration which was afterwards rendered, expressed his fears that there existed a design to restore the connection with the banks. Mr. Wright, though never assuming to speak for others besides himself, positively and unequivocally disavowed any such intention on his part; and on the third of October the bill was amended, with his vote, by adding the specie clause proposed by Mr. Calhoun. The amendment contemplated the gradual collection of government duties, in what Mr. Wright, Mr. Benton, and Mr. Calhoun, insisted was the only constitutional currency of the country; and was adopted by a vote of twenty-four to twenty-three. Mr. Wright was in favor of requiring payments to be made in specie, from the beginning; but he desired to have the subject brought up as a separate proposition, yet cheerfully waived his own preferences, when his friends offered to incorporate the feature with the independent treasury bill.

The opponents of the separation denounced the bill, as originating in a design to overthrow the banking institutions of the country; to unite the purse and the sword in the hands of the President; and to establish a hard-money government. Its advocates supported it, as the best and most feasible mode of collecting and disbursing the public revenues, and as placing the funds of the government beyond the reach of danger from the convulsions and exigencies of trade, which had recently proved so disastrous. While Congress was in session, a number of memorials were presented in favor of chartering a national bank. A resolution was reported by Mr. Wright, from the committee on finance, declaring that "the prayer of the memorialists ought not to be granted;" which passed the Senate by a vote of thirty-one to fourteen. The House of Representatives also decided against a bank, by the strong vote of one hundred and twenty-three to ninety-one. These votes decided the question as to the re-charter of a national institution; but a proposition offered by Mr. Rives, and advocated by himself, Mr. Tallmadge, and the other members of Congress who had before supported the administration, but were opposed to the independent treasury, providing for the establishment of a special deposit system, was regarded with more favor. This plan contemplated a return to that which had just failed, but with such modifications and restrictions as, it was alleged, would prevent any improper use of the government funds. The democratic members of Congress who favored this project were styled conservatives, and a large portion of them afterwards united with the opposition. The vote in the Senate on Mr. Rives' project was twenty-two in favor, to twenty-six against it. The independent treasury bill was then passed, on the 4th of October—yeas twenty-six, nays twenty. On the 14th of the same month the bill was laid on the table in the House by a vote of one hundred and nineteen to one hundred and seven; and Congress soon after adjourned.

At the regular session commencing in December 1837, Mr. Wright again reported the independent treasury bill, with the specie clause. The act which he had drawn up was also more complete in its details, than that presented at the extra session. The one previously introduced, had constituted each officer a receiver;

but this proposed the appointment of persons, to be charged with the special duty of keeping and paying out the public funds. This provision was intended to obviate the objection which had been raised, that the administration was desirous of establishing an army of office-holders, who would have the means of the government at their disposal. Severe penalties were also prescribed, for any neglect of duty, or breach of trust; and every precaution taken to provide against losses. The opponents of the measure were free to admit that, waiving the principle upon which the bill was founded, nothing could be better calculated to carry into effect the object had in view. Mr. Wright made several able speeches while this question was agitated in Congress; but that delivered on the 31st of January, 1838, probably exceeded them all. In his speech on that occasion, he reviewed the whole subject of the collection, keeping, and disbursement of the public revenue. He avowed it as his firm and settled conviction, that the state banks could not be relied upon as the fiscal agents of the government; for the reason that, as state institutions, Congress would be unable to exercise that control over them which was absolutely requisite. He also declared that there could be no middle ground—that a system based on the principles of the bill before the Senate must be established, or they would be compelled to resort to a national bank. The bill reported by Mr. Wright was discussed for a long time in the Senate, and on the 24th of March the specie clause was stricken out—yeas thirty-one, nays fourteen. Several of the democratic senators voted for the motion, in obedience to the instructions of their state Legislatures. Mr. Wright, with Mr. Benton and Mr. Calhoun, resisted it to the end. On the 26th the bill passed the

Senate by a vote of twenty-seven to twenty-five. Like its predecessor, this bill was laid upon the table in the House—yeas one hundred and six, nays ninety-eight—the whigs and conservatives voting for the motion. At the next session, in 1838–39, Mr. Wright again brought forward the independent treasury project, without the specie clause, in the hope of securing a favorable vote, as some law on the subject was deemed necessary; but it was a third time defeated. The elections for members of the twenty-sixth Congress, however, terminated in the choice of a reliable majority for the administration, in the House of Representatives; and soon after the commencement of its first session, Mr. Wright brought forward a bill establishing the system which he had so earnestly advocated since the extra session in 1837. The specie clause was added, with his vote, and in that shape it passed the Senate. On the 1st of July, 1840, a final vote was taken on the bill in the House, which resulted in its passage—yeas one hundred and twenty-four, nays one hundred and seven. The law thus enacted was known, by its title, as "An act to provide for the collection, safe-keeping, transfer and disbursement, of the public revenue."

The various bills introduced in the Senate, during the administration of Mr. Van Buren, which were designed to protect the settlers on the public lands; to graduate the prices of the latter; and to secure the rights of pre-emption, received the cordial and hearty support of Mr. Wright. At the session of Congress commencing in December 1837, the subject of slavery in the District of Columbia, was brought up in the Senate. On the 10th of January, 1838, Mr. Wright voted, with Mr. Clay and others, in favor of a resolution, declaring that any interference, on the part of the citizens of other states, with slavery in the district, endangered the rights of the citizens of such district, violated the implied faith in which the cession was made by Maryland and Virginia, and would disturb and endanger the Union. Mr. Rives offered a similar resolution, on the 11th of the same month, in regard to slavery in the territories, which also declared that the people of those territories, when applying for admission, would have the exclusive right to determine the question for themselves. Mr. Wright voted against this resolution; but supported one offered by Mr. Clay, affirming that it would be injudicious to interfere with slavery in the territories; that such interference would be a violation of faith towards those who had been permitted to settle, and hold slaves there; and that the inhabitants would be exclusively entitled to decide the question, when admitted into the Union. Mr. Preston, of South Carolina, offered a resolution, at this session, asserting that the original boundary of Texas was the Rio Grande, previous to its cession to Spain; that it was unwise to cede it; and that it was desirable to re-annex it, when it could be done with the consent of Texas, and consistent with the treaties, stipulations, and faith of the United States. The resolution was taken up for consideration on the 14th of June, and finally disposed of by a motion to lay it upon the table. The vote stood twenty-four for the motion, and fourteen against it. Mr. Wright voted with Mr. Clay, Mr. Buchanan, and Mr. Webster, for the motion. It was opposed by Mr. Benton, Mr. Calhoun, and Mr. Preston.

In 1838, Mr. Wright warmly urged the passage of a bill, which he had introduced, to revoke the charters of the banks in the District of Columbia, provided they did not resume specie payments by the 1st of May in that year. He also proposed to prohibit the issue and circulation of small bills in the district—believing that stringent measures of that character were required, in order to protect the people from imposition and fraud. On the 16th of May, 1838, he delivered one of his most elaborate speeches in the Senate, on a joint resolution prescribing the funds to be received for government dues, and advocated a return to a specie currency, as the only one known to the constitution.

At the close of the session in the spring of 1839, the difficulties on the northern frontier growing out of the unsettled state of the boundary question, assumed a threatening aspect. A general feeling prevailed in Congress in favor of maintaining the cautious and decided stand of the administration. The task of its defence, therefore, on the part of the democratic senators, was comparatively light and easy. The unanimity of feeling that existed, may be understood by referring to the fact, that in March, 1839, Congress placed a large sum of money at the disposal of the President, and authorized him to call out fifty thousand volunteers, if he judged it expedient for the defence of the country, without scarcely a show of opposition. The vote in the Senate was unanimous, and there were but six nays in the House.

On his route home in March, 1839, Mr. Wright passed through Harrisburg, and was invited to a public dinner by the democratic members of the Legislature of Pennsylvania. A similar invitation was tendered to him in the city of New York. Both invitations were declined. It was very grateful to his feelings to be singled out as the object of attention and regard, on the part of his fellow-citizens; though the opinions he entertained forbade his acceptance of the civilities thus tendered.

The commercial disasters of 1837, had reduced a large number of persons throughout the Union, to what they regarded as hopeless and irretrievable insolvency. Relief was earnestly besought for them, by the passage of a law to enable them to have outstanding debts entirely cancelled. Petitions for the enactment of a bankrupt law were presented to Congress, and at the session of 1839–40, a bill was introduced in the Senate. Mr. Van Buren had formerly recommended the passage of a law of that character, applicable to banks and bankers. Mr. Wright was in favor of that proposition, and he also supported the bill before the Senate; which contained both the compulsory and the voluntary feature, or, in other words, combined the principles of an insolvent with a bankrupt law. Mr. Clay made a motion to strike out the compulsory clause, which Mr. Wright opposed. The bill passed the Senate on the 25th of June, 1840, but was laid on the table in the House.

Mr. Van Buren was unanimously nominated in 1840, as the democratic candidate for President, and General Harrison, of Ohio, was selected as his opponent. The canvass was animated and exciting, but the ultimate result did not long remain in doubt. Mr. Wright made a number of powerful and effective speeches, at New York and other places, during the electioneering campaign, and was everywhere listened to with interest and delight. But all the efforts of the able and talented men who gallantly defended the administration, proved unavailing. The pecuniary reverses of 1837, were still seriously felt; confidence was not entirely restored; and a change afforded some hope of relief.

A majority of the conservatives united with the opposition; of the remainder, some stood aloof from the contest; others yielded a lukewarm and reluctant support to Mr. Van Buren; and others again, generously and manfully aided to secure his re-election. The severe measures which it had been found necessary to employ in order to preserve the neutrality of the country, during the outbreak and insurrection in Canada, had alienated many of the citizens along the northern frontier from the administration which they had once supported. The banking institutions of the country, too, were far from being friendly to the President. The measures he had recommended, and which Mr. Wright and others had advocated in Congress, were believed to indicate a feeling of hostility towards them; and the remarks of many of the most prominent administration journals, had the tendency to strengthen that impression. This feeling was, to a great extent, erroneous, although Mr. Wright most certainly believed that there were many defects in the banking system which required correction. To banks, as such, he was not opposed—but he did not hesitate to condemn the abuses which had been committed, under the cover and protection of chartered rights and privileges.

Mr. Van Buren was defeated. Notwithstanding every effort, his opponent was elected by an unusually large majority. The people had spoken, and it but remained to register their decree. When Congress met in December, little was to be done, except to render an account of the manner in which the government had been administered, during a season of continued excitement, of constant agitation in the money market, and embarrassment in all the business relations of the country. The friends of the in-coming administration, however, began to discover that it was much easier to criticize, than to correct—to point out an evil, than to provide a remedy. They had the power in their hands, and knew that they could overturn and destroy; but it was for the future to determine whether they would be able to build up and restore. They foresaw the difficulties in their way, and were anxious to avoid them. The feeling in favor of exorbitant appropriations, which had originated in a large surplus, and which had proved so disastrous to Mr. Van Buren, who attempted in vain to control it, might prove equally as unfortunate to his successors. It was then rumored that a large debt would be left upon their hands, for which they must provide the means of payment. Inquiries were made in the Senate, and among others, Mr. Webster demanded to know the condition of the treasury and the amount of the debt. On the 17th of December, Mr. Wright replied, by pointing out the erroneous character of the estimates which had been made, and showing that a large mass of claims, never recognized by Congress or the Government, and the treasury notes issued to supply those which had been returned and cancelled, were added to the actual debt of five millions of dollars, including the notes originally put in circulation, in order to make up the array of figures which had excited so much alarm. He also referred to the alleged necessity of calling an extra session of Congress, for which the existing administration would be held responsible; and said, that, so far as he was concerned, "he should do everything in his power to obviate any such necessity; and to accomplish that object with the greatest certainty, he should use his utmost endeavors to keep the appropriations of this session within the anticipated means of the year 1841.

He believed the estimates supplied all the necessary wants, and he intended to adhere to them strictly. Having done so, he should cheerfully leave it to those who had been placed in power by a triumphant expression of the popular voice, to call a Congress when they pleased, and to recommend such measures as they pleased." This pledge, thus publicly made, was religiously fulfilled on the part of Mr. Wright. But a portion of his political friends thought proper to unite with the opposition, in voting appropriations which he believed were both unnecessary and unwise. By connecting them with the regular supply bills, the President was compelled either to approve, or to leave the government entirely without the means of support. Mr. Wright was still of the opinion, that an extra session was uncalled for, except it were to adopt measures and projects not connected with the payment of the public debt. The successor of Mr. Van Buren thought differently, and soon after his inauguration a proclamation was issued, requiring Congress to convene on the 31st of May.

At the election in 1840, the whig party had chosen a large majority of the members of Congress, and they never doubted their ability to enact such laws as would be agreeable to their wishes. But how delusive are human expectations—how transitory all the things of this world! On the 4th of March, 1841, General Harrison stood uncovered, in the capitol of the nation, with thousands upon thousands of his fellow-citizens around him, and took that solemn oath to administer the government in accordance with the constitution and the laws. On the 4th of April, he lay cold and lifeless in the executive mansion. The period of his administration was over. The same streets along which he had passed, but a few days before, receiving the voluntary homage of a free people welcoming the Chief Magistrate of their choice, witnessed another and a sadder pageant. The shouts of the multitude, the swelling notes of martial music, the waving plumes, and the gay trappings, gave place to the mournful lamentation, the low tones of the muffled drum, the black pall, and the funeral hearse. The opening of the month was bright and cheering—its close was dark and dreary. It was like a day in the early spring. The sun rose in joy and gladness, in its unclouded majesty and splendor—it set in sorrow and gloom!

The national Congress assembled at Washington. The objects of the extra session were now made known. Four prominent measures were brought forward—a bill authorizing a loan of twelve millions of dollars; a bankrupt law divested of the severe compulsory provisions which Mr. Wright had advocated; the distribution of the proceeds of the public lands; and the incorporation of a national bank. Mr. Wright was succeeded in the committee on finance by Mr. Clay, and placed upon those on commerce and claims. The whigs had a gallant and fearless leader at their head, in whom all confidence was placed. The plans he recommended were instantly adopted. The independent treasury law was repealed on the 9th of June. On the 18th of August a bankrupt law was passed, in opposition to the vote of Mr. Wright; only to be repealed by the same Congress, in less than two years from the date of its enactment. The loan bill also became a law, though Mr. Wright and others earnestly recommended a temporary resort to treasury notes. The project of Mr. Clay for the distribution of the proceeds of the public lands was then taken up. The democratic senators opposed it, on the ground that it was the assumption of the debts of the several states in a disguised form; that it was impolitic in the existing condition of the treasury, to surrender so large a portion of the annual revenue; and that the bill was designed to create a necessity for a high protective tariff. The last objection was so evident, that a number of the whigs united with Mr. Wright and his friends in inserting a provision, declaring that the distribution should cease whenever the average rate of duties collected exceeded twenty per cent. This clause prevented the bill from ever being carried into effect. A bill for the incorporation of a national bank also passed the Senate; the democratic members remaining firm in their opposition. It received a favorable vote in the House, and was presented to Mr. Tyler, who, as Vice President, had succeeded General Harrison in the executive chair. A suspicion had for some time been gaining ground, that the state rights doctrines of the President, and the views entertained by the leading politicians of the state of Virginia, which he had been known to favor when in Congress, might produce a division in the ranks of the whig party. The bill was vetoed, and the fears of its advocates were increased. But the manly form of their distinguished champion was still recognized by its proud bearing amid the surrounding confusion. He was a host in himself, and so long as he was disposed to struggle, they hoped that all would yet be well. A second bill was presented to Congress, and adopted by the votes of the whig members. Great care had been taken to avoid what were said to be the constitutional objections of Mr. Tyler; and the apparent object was only to establish a fiscal agent for the treasury, and provide a moneyed circulation of uniform value throughout the states. Another veto followed, and the whig party was thrust out of power, by the very hand they had raised to protect and defend it. They possessed a numerical majority in the National Legislature—but they had no President.

Congress adjourned in confusion, and the cabinet was dissolved. At the regular session in December, 1841, Mr. Clay again appeared; but was unwilling to assume the position he had occupied on the committee on finance. He was succeeded by Mr. Evans, of Maine. The experience, industry, and ability of Mr. Wright, in examining, arranging, and determining, the large number of claims presented to Congress, were so universally conceded, that he was retained on that committee. He was also re-appointed a member of the committee on commerce. Early in the session, Mr. Clay introduced a series of resolutions, declaratory of his views in regard to the revenues and expenditures of the government. He avowed himself friendly to the general principles of the compromise act; but he desired that a sufficient amount of revenue should be raised from the customs, to support the government; that the land fund should be surrendered to the states; and that the proviso in the distribution act should be repealed. His friends in the Senate supported the resolutions, but Mr. Wright and the democratic senators opposed them, for the same reasons which had influenced them in resisting the policy of distribution, from the outset. For several years, Mr. Clay and Mr. Wright had been placed as competitors against each other, in all the prominent debates in the Senate. But during all that time, each had preserved towards the other the most marked courtesy and respect. Mr. Clay resigned his seat on the 31st of March, to retire to private life. The leave-taking with his old associates was painful and affecting:—but how much more sad would it have been, had he known that it was his last parting for this world with his friend—for they were friends in the midst of violent party excitement—with his friend Silas Wright.

The depression in trade had reduced the imports of 1841 to such an extent, that the public revenues had materially diminished, and it became necessary to provide means for the relief of the treasury. The loan authorized at the extra session had not been made, on account of the difficulty of disposing of the stock upon the conditions prescribed in the bill; which contained a proviso forbidding any sales below par. The difficulty, as alleged by the democratic senators, originated in the general impression entertained among capitalists, that the government had unwisely yielded up the land revenues, in prospective, when they would be needed for its support; but Mr. Evans reported a bill from the committee on finance, authorizing, among other things, the stock "to be disposed of at the highest price" which the secretary of the treasury could obtain for the same. On the 5th of April, Mr. Wright gave his views, at length, in opposition to the bill. He stated his willingness to vote for the necessary supplies, but he could not approve of the measure under consideration, and it should not receive his vote. The foreign relations of the country were far from being peaceful, and he did not think that such was the time to offer "the very standard of American credit for sale in the markets of the world." He advised the government to call back the land fund; to increase it by pre-emption and graduation bills; and to offer new lands for sale. "If," said he, "these things cannot be done, follow the noble example of New York; lay taxes, direct or indirect, or both; stop expenditure beyond the means which the lands and the customs will supply; fund the outstanding treasury notes as you propose to do, in this bill, and wait until the money market shall improve, or until you can realize an adequacy of means from your improved revenues. Again I say, do anything, do nothing, rather than propose to sell your credit in the open market, *for what it may bring*."

At this session, a bill was proposed, which proved unsuccessful, to restore the fine of one thousand dollars imposed on General Jackson at New Orleans in 1815, together with the interest from the time of its payment. During the debate, Mr. Conrad, of Louisiana, who had opposed the bill, recommended the passage of a resolution to procure a painting representing the scene, and hang it in the capitol, in which the victorious general should appear bowing himself to the majesty of the law, that the exigency of the case had compelled him to violate. Mr. Wright advocated the passage of the bill, and in his speech alluded to the suggestion of the senator from Louisiana, in a strain of manly eloquence He said:—

"Sir, such a picture would be a proud one for the country, and especially for that distinguished general; and I should rejoice to see it gracing the capitol of the nation. But will you write beneath it, 'We gained a thousand dollars to the public treasury by this operation, which has paid for this picture?' Will you hang the proud national emblem aloft in this marble palace, and invoke towards it the attention and admiration of all succeeding ages; and, in the very moment when you do so, make up a record upon your journal here, which must either disgrace the general, whose gallant services and patriotic forbearance gave the sketch for the painting, or must disgrace the country he so faithfully and disinterestedly served? The general, by his wisdom and valor, defended, with a handful of undisciplined militia, one of your proudest cities against a veteran enemy of many times his numbers. In doing so, he had, in the opinion of a judge and a lawyer, committed a technical breach of the law, and been guilty of a technical contempt of court. He was arraigned by the precise judge for his offence; and within the very bounds of his military camp, in the hour of his proud victory, and in the presence of his gallant companions in arms, and of thousands of his indignant countrymen, he unresistingly permitted himself to be led to the bar of the court as a criminal, and there received the sentence of the law, and paid this thousand dollars as the penalty for the offence charged against him; not a human being then, or since, questioning the purity of his intentions, or the wisdom of his acts. This is the event, it is said, we should commemorate by a national painting; and yet we are urged to refuse to refund the penalty thus incurred in our service; or, if we do refund it, to say, as part of the act, that it was worthily imposed. Will we, can we, do this? No, sir, no. The heart of every man who occupies a seat here will tell him that he cannot do it; that he cannot vote for such a memorial to national honor and private merit, and place his vote at the foot of such a record."

The subject of the division of the several states into single congressional districts was also brought forward in the session of 1841-42, and a provision inserted in the apportionment bill which passed both Houses of Congress. Mr. Wright opposed the bill, on the ground that it was subversive of the rights of the states, and assumed to control and dictate the action of their Legislatures.

He addressed the Senate at various stages of the bill, and in his final speech presented the following summary of his positions:—

"Passing the other arguments by which this novel enactment is attempted to be sustained, I wish to bring the Senate, for one moment, to the consideration of the great interests—I may almost say, in a political sense, estates—involved in this action.

"The first in the constitutional order, was the people of the respective states, to whom the right of electing representatives to the Congress was expressly reserved.

"The second was the Legislatures of the states, upon which the duty was devolved, in the absence of any action on the part of Congress, to prescribe the regulations necessary to enable the people to exercise this great constitutional right.

"The third was, Congress, upon which a discretionary power was conferred to make these regulations, if the states did not, or to alter the regulations which the states might have made.

"The first (the people) have thus far enjoyed their great right under the regulations of the states—and that, too, without injury or complaint.

"The second (the states) have acted under the constitution, and performed the duty enjoined upon them, in a way to preserve the right of the people and its practical and beneficial exercise.

"The third (Congress) now comes in, and proposes, not to make regulations by its own action—not by its own action to alter the regulations which the states have made—but to prescribe certain rules by which the Legislatures of the states shall alter their own regulations.

"Congress admits its want of power to compel the

state Legislatures to comply with its prescription, and alter their regulations to conform to it. And how does it propose to attempt coercion upon them? By abridging any of their powers or privileges? No; but by forfeiting this great right of the people of the state to elect representatives, if their Legislature do not comply.

"Thus the fault is to be either in Congress, or in the state Legislature. The people can coerce neither; and yet the forfeiture for the fault is to be visited upon the only innocent party of the three—the people, who cannot make the regulations, and whose most essential right is to be forfeited if they are not made. Was such action, on the part of Congress, constitutional, or wise, or expedient? To his mind, it was neither."

By the provisions of the apportionment bill, the state Legislatures were required to district their respective states; and if not so districted, it was contended that they should not be represented. Mr. Wright conceded the power in Congress of making any division it saw fit, or of altering such as might be made by any state Legislature; but he denied the right to prescribe to the states what laws they should enact. In one of his speeches he stated, that he was ignorant as to what would be the course of the Legislature of New York under such an enactment. His colleague, Mr. Tallmadge, who had been re-elected in 1840, by the then whig Legislature, referred to this admission of Mr. Wright, in his remarks on the bill, as casting a "blot upon the escutcheon of the state." After the separation of the former gentleman from the democratic party, Mr. Wright studiously avoided any collision or dispute with him upon the floor of the Senate in regard to the state they represented. But to such an attack he felt bound to reply. He said that "he would not undertake to say whether it was his fault, or his misfortune, that he could not look into futurity and tell what would be the actions of men hereafter; but the fact was so. He did not know, and therefore could not tell; and if that was to be charged against him as an offence, or a dishonor to the state, he could only say that it proceeded from the mistake of his respected and intelligent constituents in sending so ignorant a representative there. The same senator," he continued, "had assumed that by his declaration, he had dishonored the memories of the Hamiltons, and Livingstons, and Clintons, and Tompkinses of their state. The memories of all the patriots and statesmen of New York, of the present and of former days, ought to be dear to him, and he thought they were so; and while he could scarcely hope to avoid reflecting dishonor upon them, by the inadequacy of his powers to discharge in a manner worthy of their memories the high and responsible duties pertaining to his present station, he would say to his colleague, that to a man who had drunk less deeply from the political doctrines of the Hamiltons of New York, and more deeply from those of her Livingstons, and Clintons, and Tompkinses, the idea would never have occurred that opposition to this provision of this bill was placing a blot upon the clear escutcheon of that proud democratic state."

Another important question presented to the twenty-seventh Congress, at its first regular session, was that of revising the compromise act. On the 30th day of June, 1842, the minimum was to be reached. No duty exceeding twenty per cent. was to be collected after that date; and then, unless Congress should make some different provision, the distribution act would go into effect. It was doubted, whether duties could be collected subsequent to that day, unless a law was passed authorizing it to be done; and whether the compromise act would have any force whatsoever, except as fixing a maximum standard to govern the legislation of Congress. A provisional tariff bill was therefore passed, extending the compromise act to the 1st of August, 1842, and requiring duties to be collected at the same rates as were collectable on the 1st of June. The bill also postponed the distribution of the proceeds of the public lands; but the principle was not surrendered, and Mr. Wright therefore voted against it. The President did not approve it, and it was returned with his objections. A general bill was then framed, with increased rates of duties, averaging nearly forty per cent., but containing a section repealing the proviso in the distribution act. Mr. Wright voted to strike out the objectionable clause; but it was retained, and a second veto was the consequence. A great deal of confusion existed in Congress, and much angry feeling was manifested towards the President. But it was necessary to have some revenue law, and it was satisfactorily demonstrated that a tariff averaging twenty per cent. would not be sufficient to meet the expenses of the government. The whigs had the control in Congress, and they were expected to devise a plan to supply the treasury. They were unwilling to yield the principle of distribution, and Mr. Tyler refused to sign any bill that contained it. Efforts were then made to prepare a tariff not exceeding twenty per cent., by taxing tea, coffee, and other articles, which it was supposed would yield a large amount of revenue. By enacting such a law the proviso of the distribution act would have been satisfied, and the law be permitted to go into operation. The duty on tea and coffee was opposed by a large majority of the democratic members of Congress, and by a sufficient number of the whigs to prevent its insertion. Mr. Wright was uniformly opposed to this duty, and voted against a bill proposed by Mr. Rives in the Senate, which he preferred in other respects, because it contained that provision.

The law, known as the tariff act of 1842, was finally prepared. The average rate of duties fixed by this bill was about thirty-two per cent. Many of its provisions Mr. Wright believed to be unjust and unequal, and he subsequently pointed them out, in an able speech on the subject, delivered in the Senate in 1844.* But the country was rapidly augmenting her debt, and Congress was about to adjourn without providing the means for its support. The principle of distribution, after a long struggle to retain it, was surrendered; and that was something gained. The bill came to a final vote in the Senate on the 27th of August. It had passed the House by one majority. The senators were known to be nearly divided in their opinions, and everything depended on a single vote. That vote—the vote of Mr. Wright—saved the bill. He gave it with reluctance, and before announcing it, he stated the reasons which had induced him to separate himself, on this occasion, from his party friends; all of whom, with the exception of Mr. Buchanan and Mr. Sturgeon, of Pennsylvania, and Mr. Williams, of Maine, voted against the bill. The government was in a perilous condition, and he was not willing to adjourn without affording relief. The bill was objectionable, but he trusted to see it amended under more favorable auspices. "The treasury," said he, "is empty; and almost daily the public creditors are turned away from

* See Appendix.

it without payment. This very Congress has increased, and is daily increasing the public expenditures, and thus creating the necessity for increased revenues. And the public credit is not sinking, but sunken; so that loans, at high interest and at long time, cannot be negotiated at home or abroad, upon the declared reason that we have not revenues to meet the payment of the public liabilities. These changes of circumstances constituted, in his mind, the highest necessity for a revenue law, and forced upon him, under the most solemn sense of public duty, the course of action which he proposed to pursue. All he could ask of the friends who should differ from him, and believe him to be still in error, was, that they would believe him to be governed by pure motives; and if in error, to be honestly so. He owed it to those friends, as well as to himself, to make another remark; which was, that the consequences of his action, if evil, should be visited upon himself alone; as no friend, here or elsewhere, had interfered to bring him to the conclusion he had pronounced. Many very dear friends, whose judgments, upon almost all occasions, he valued more highly than his own, had kindly attempted to convince him that he was in error —not one to urge him to give the vote."

Several of the democratic senators, who spoke previous to the passage of the bill, expressed their regret that Mr. Wright was about to give his vote in its favor. But not one doubted the purity of his motives, or reproached him for supporting it. They saw that the sacrifice pained him deeply; that if the bill could have passed without his vote, he would have remained with them in the opposition; and they honored him for his manliness and independence, and respected the mora greatness which had dictated his course.

Congress re-assembled in December. But little business of importance was transacted at this session The elections in the fall had proved disastrous to the whig party, and they cared not to propose any new measures, for their successors to modify or overturn. The bankrupt law was repealed. The bill to refund the fine imposed on General Jackson was again discussed, but did not become a law. Mr. Benton offered a series of resolutions against the assumption of the debts of the states by the General Government, for which Mr. Wright cheerfully voted. In the month of February, 1843, the latter was re-elected, for another term of six years, by the Legislature of New York. In the caucus at which he was nominated, the vote was unanimous in his favor. The idea of returning another person to fill the place of Silas Wright in the Senate was entertained by no one.

CHAPTER VII.

1843.—Bill Passed to Refund the Fine Imposed on General Jackson at New Orleans—Reduction of Postage—Notice to Terminate Joint Occupancy of Oregon—Tariff Bill of Mr. McDuffie—Able Speech of Mr. Wright—Mr. Tyler's Treaty of Annexation—Original Boundaries of Texas—Cession to Spain—Efforts to Recover it—Mr. Wright Declines the Office of Associate Justice of the Supreme Court—Letters of Mr. Van Buren and Mr. Clay on Annexation—Democratic National Convention—Nomination of Mr. Polk—Mr. Wright Nominated as the Candidate for Vice-President—Letter of Declension—Reasons for the Same—Objections to the Treaty of Annexation——Opinions of Mr. Wright—Rejection of the Treaty—Subsequent Project of Annexation—Failure of the Tariff Bill in the House—Adjournment of Congress—Divisions in the Democratic Party in New York—Legislation of the State in regard to Internal Improvements—Stop and Tax Law of 1842—The People's Resolution—Different Factions and Interests—Attempt to bring Mr. Wright forward as a Candidate for Governor—His Refusal to be considered as such—The State Convention—Nomination of Mr. Wright—Address and Resolutions of the Convention—Letter of Acceptance—Letter on unfinished Canals—1844.

In December, 1843, the new Congress assembled. The Senate was still composed of a majority of whigs, but in the House the position of things was reversed. Almost the first business of the session was the passage of the bill to refund the fine paid by General Jackson. On the 8th day of January, 1844, being the twenty-ninth anniversary of the victory at New Orleans, the bill was finally passed in the House of Representatives, and on the 14th of February, it received the concurrence of the Senate. The subject of reducing the postage on letters and newspapers had been agitated for a long time, and at this session a law was enacted effecting a considerable reduction. When the bill was before the Senate, Mr. Wright endeavored to have it amended, by limiting the franking privilege beyond what was proposed; but failing in that, he nevertheless gave his vote cordially in its favor. On the 21st of March, he voted for the joint resolution directing the President to communicate to the government of Great Britain the notice required by the existing treaty, of the termination of the common occupancy of the Oregon territory. He was always favorable to this measure, and anxiously desired to see the power and jurisdiction of the nation extended over the inhabitants of that remote portion of the country, for their protection and security.

The subject of a revision of the tariff of 1842 was early agitated in Congress. Mr. McDuffie introduced a bill proposing to reduce all duties under the law, which were above the rate of 20 per cent., to that rate, by a gradual reduction. The design of bringing forward this bill was to provoke discussion upon the subject, and to test the feelings of senators in regard to the modification of the act of 1842, rather than with any hope of its passage. The committee on finance, to whom it was referred, reported it back to the Senate, without amendment, but accompanied with a resolution recommending its indefinite postponement, upon the ground that the constitution required that all such bills should originate in the House of Representatives. Upon this resolution a lengthy discussion arose, involving the principles of the whole tariff question. Among the speakers was Mr. Wright. His speech occupied two days in its delivery, and is important, not only because it was the last great effort of its author on the floor of the Senate, but for the reason that it contains the matured and enlightened opinions of an able statesman—opinions not formed in the heyday of youth, or the heat of excitement, but pondered long in the closet, and subjected to the rigid, and thorough examination, of a mind peculiarly calculated for the investigation of the subject to which they relate.* Men may differ with him in sentiment, but they must concede the ability with which his positions are maintained. Had he never uttered another syllable, there is in this one speech merit sufficient to secure him a proud place in the estimation of his countrymen. To single out any one part of it would be to mar the whole. It is a labored and complete argument, in defence, as he expresses it, of "that degree of protection which is incident to revenue, and consistent with it," and opposed to the "prohibition destroying revenue, and creating monopoly."

The project of annexing Texas to the United States was presented to the Senate, in a definite form, by a treaty submitted for its approbation, which had been concluded under the advice and direction of President Tyler on the 12th of April, 1844. The original Province of Texas, as described on the Atlas of Humboldt, and the maps of all the old geographers and travellers, lay between the Sabine and the lower Rio del Norte, or Rio Grande, and between the Gulf of Mexico and the Red River. This province was included in the purchase of Louisiana from France, and was ceded to Spain by treaty, in 1819, under the administration of Mr. Monroe, but in opposition to the views of Mr. Adams, then a member of his cabinet, and to those of Mr. Clay, who denounced the cession in the House of

* See Appendix.

Representatives. When Mr. Adams was elected to the presidency, and Mr. Clay appointed secretary of state, an effort was made to recover back the territory, but the terms they offered were not satisfactory, and the negotiation failed. Mr. Van Buren repeated the attempt, as secretary during General Jackson's administration, which was in like manner unsuccessful. The next proposition for the annexation came from Texas herself, after the battle of San Jacinto. Mr. Van Buren was then President, but declined the proposal. Though she had already given evidence of her disposition and ability to maintain her independence, a state of war still existed, and it was thought the annexation could not be effected without a breach with Mexico. At the session of Congress in 1837–38, Mr. Preston offered a resolution in the Senate in favor of recovering the country unwisely ceded to Spain, which was laid upon the table, as has been stated. In 1842, the subject was again revived by individuals owning lands in Texas, but resident within the United States, and by others who viewed with alarm the efforts in England to abolish slavery in that republic, for the purpose, as it was alleged, of injuring the cotton growers in the southern states belonging to the American Union. There were many, also, connected by the ties of kindred, or friendship, with the citizens of that country, who were anxious to see those for whom they entertained so much regard, sheltered with them beneath the same protecting ægis. The agitation of the subject led to the treaty of 1844.

While the question of the annexation was being discussed in Congress, and in the political circles at Washington, the office of associate justice of the supreme court of the United States, made vacant by the death of Smith Thompson, of New York, in December 1843, was tendered to Mr. Wright, but declined. The motives which prompted this offer have often been made the subject of comment, yet it is unnecessary to speak of them here, except it be to remark, that no one who knew Mr. Wright, would have dared to encounter the indignation with which any proposition affecting his political integrity, or his character as a senator, in the remotest degree, would have been met on his part. Almost every act of his life was a refutation of the infamous maxim of the corrupt Walpole. He had no price. Value was not attached to his honor, for it was beyond the wealth of worlds to purchase. A high judicial position might not, under some circumstances, have been unwelcome to him; but to receive anything, from one occupying an equivocal relation towards the party of which he was a member, at a time when a favorite measure required votes in Congress to sustain it, and without the known consent and approbation of the constituents to whom he felt so deeply indebted, was entirely out of the question.

The subject of annexation was also brought to bear upon the presidential nominations in the spring of 1844. Mr. Van Buren and Mr. Clay were the most prominent candidates of the two great parties, and both gentlemen were asked to make known their opinions. The positions assumed in their respective letters were nearly identical. Neither avowed any hostility to the immediate or ultimate annexation, provided it could be done in a proper manner; but they believed its re-union at that juncture would, in all probability, result in a war with Mexico. Mr. Clay was nominated by his party friends, at their national convention. The democratic convention met at Baltimore, in May. The letter of Mr. Van Buren on the annexation question had excited considerable feeling among the friends of the measure, and by means of the two-third rule, which had been adopted in making nominations, he was defeated. After several ballotings Mr. Polk was brought forward as a new candidate, and received the nomination. The nomination for Vice President was then bestowed upon Mr. Wright by the unanimous voice of the convention, but entirely without his consent or approbation. Immediately upon receiving the intelligence, he addressed the following letter to his friend, Mr. Butler, by whom its contents were made known to the convention still in session :—

WASHINGTON, May 29th, 1844.

My dear sir :—Being advised that the convention of which you are a member has conferred upon me the unmerited honor of nominating me as a candidate for the office of Vice President, will you, if this information be correct, present my profound thanks to the convention for this mark of its confidence and favor; and say for me, that circumstances, which I do not think it necessary to detail, but which I very briefly hint at to you [in another letter,] render it impossible that I should, consistently with my sense of public duty and private obligations, accept this nomination.

I am, with great respect, your obedient servant,

SILAS WRIGHT.

Hon. B. F. Butler.

The declension of Mr. Wright was followed by the selection of Mr. Dallas. When it was understood that he positively refused to accept the nomination, a feeling of deep regret was manifested in the convention. His immediate friends in that body expected nothing less from him. The democratic electors of New York through their representatives in the Legislature and in the state convention, had unanimously presented the name of Mr. Van Buren for the presidency. Was he the man then to appropriate to himself an inferior position, when the higher one had been refused to the candidate offered in the name of his constituents? Could he accept a nomination for such an office, without having first consulted the citizens of the state he represented? In his view it was utterly impossible. Justice to them, justice to himself, required that such an honor should be sought, if sought at all, not covertly, but openly, and in the face of day.

But there was still another reason which forbade his acceptance. The nomination had been withheld from Mr. Van Buren, because of his opposition to the immediate annexation of Texas. This was not denied; and had it been, the truth was so apparent as to defy contradiction. Yet he was asked to place his name upon the ticket, when it was known that he entertained similar views and opinions, and was prepared to vote against the treaty then lying before him in the Senate. The same objection that operated in the one case had equal weight in the other. He felt the importance of conciliation and harmony—the peace-offering was appreciated as it deserved—his party obligations were ever sacredly regarded—but there were considerations that rose far above them all. He had shown in his senatorial career that, "if he loved Cæsar less, he oved Rome more"—that when his country required his vote, in opposition to the friends with whom he acted, he did not hesitate. It remained for him to prove, how much dearer was the preservation of his own independence and self-respect, than the honor that seemed a mockery, when it was purchased by the sacrifice of a friend for whom he entertained the affection of a brother; whose banner he had borne aloft in sunshine and in storm, in prosperity and adversity; and to whom he had adhered, when others were false and faithless—never doubting, never yielding, true and steadfast to the last.

The treaty concluded by Mr. Tyler, was the leading topic of discussion in the Senate for several weeks. Its ratification was opposed by Mr. Wright and Mr. Benton. The main objections urged by them were;—the want of a proper regard for the claims, and the honor and character of Mexico, in the manner in which the negotiation had been conducted, without making any attempt to procure her consent—the uncertainty in relation to the boundary line of Texas, which was claimed by her to extend beyond the original limits of the province, and tacitly recognized in the treaty—and the assumption by Mr. Calhoun, in his official correspondence as secretary of state, that the acquisition of the territory was necessary for the protection of the institution of slavery. The question of the liability for the payment of the debt of Texas, was also raised; but it was thought that her public lands would be amply sufficient to discharge it. This objection was renewed after the treaty was disposed of, and shown to be of more weight.

Neither before nor during the pendency of the negotiations for the annexation, was there any effort to secure an amicable arrangement of the claims of Mexico. Whether founded in truth, or otherwise—they were known to exist. They had been made openly and publicly; but it was deemed advisable by the administration not to notice them, while the project itself was being discussed between the representatives of Texas and the United States. Seven days after the treaty was signed, and after the Mexican minister had withdrawn from Washington, instructions were sent to the United States Charge in Mexico, directing him to communicate the fact to the Mexican government; and, at the same time, to assure it, that no "disrespect or indifference to the honor or dignity of Mexico," was designed, and that the measure was adopted under circumstances of great emergency.

By an act of the Texan Congress, approved on the 19th of December, 1836, the boundaries of the republic were defined as follows: "Beginning at the mouth of the Rio Grande, thence up the principal stream of said river to its source; thence along the boundary line, as defined in the treaty between the United States and Spain, to the beginning." This line, established by Texas, not only included the original province which extended along the left bank of the Rio Grande, from its mouth to the mountainous barriers of the Passo, and thence northerly to the Red River, but it embraced one-half of the province of New Mexico, and large portions of the provinces of Chihuahua, Coahuila, and Tamaulipas. The treaty communicated to the Senate, by Mr. Tyler, proposed, on the part of the republic of Texas, to cede "to the United States all of its territories, to be held by them in full property and sovereignty" —thus adopting in almost unequivocal terms, the claims of the Texan Congress.

The principal argument, and the most important reason, urged by the administration of Mr. Tyler for the immediate annexation, as appears from the correspondence between Mr. Calhoun, and the Texan commissioners and the British minister, was the necessity of protecting the domestic institutions of the South, the security and perpetuity of which were endangered by a design, said to be in contemplation, having for its object the abolition of slavery in Texas. In his letter to the United States Charge in Mexico, to which reference has been made, he stated explicitly, that "the step was forced on the government of the United States, in self-defence, in consequence of the policy adopted by Great Britain in reference to the abolition of slavery in Texas. It was impossible," he added, "for the United States to witness, with indifference, the efforts of Great Britain to abolish slavery there. They could not but see that she had the means in her power, in the actual condition of Texas, to accomplish the objects of her policy, unless prevented by the most efficient measures; and that, if accomplished, it would lead to a state of things dangerous in the extreme to the adjacent states, and the Union itself."

Mr. Wright believed that justice to Mexico required that overtures should have been made to her for the settlement of all difficulties and questions in dispute, boundaries included, growing out of the separation of Texas from the Mexican Confederacy, and the subsequent war, prior to entertaining the proposition for the annexation; that the boundary line established by the Texan Congress, was not the true line, and should not have been either directly or indirectly acknowledged; and that the perpetuity and security of slavery ought not to constitute, and did not constitute, a sufficient reason for the annexation, but that there were other arguments in favor of the acquisition, provided it could be obtained without injustice. As for the interference of Great Britain, he deemed that feature of the argument set at rest, by the express disclaimer of her minister; and if any portion of her citizens, as individuals, were concerned in an effort to abolish slavery in Texas, it was nothing more than they were constantly attempting to do in the southern states already belonging to the Union. These general views were repeated by him on several occasions, in addressing the meetings of his fellow-citizens in New York, during the summer of 1844. In his speech at Watertown, he said:—

"There is another subject on which I feel bound to speak a word—a question which sprung up during the last session of Congress. I allude to the proposition to annex Texas to the territory of this republic. I was called on officially to act on that great national proposition. It is not my purpose to discuss the matter before you, because one who is to follow me, and who has paid more attention to the subject than I have, will do it ample justice. But to you am I bound to account for my official action on that great question. I felt it my duty to vote as a senator, and did vote, against the ratification of the treaty for the annexation. It has been supposed by some, that I gave that vote from an unyielding opinion that annexation should never take place. That is not so. I have made up no such opinion. For the treaty I could not vote, and one of the reasons was, that I believed then, as now, if we proposed to take that country into our confederacy, at the time and under the then existing relations between Mexico and Texas, it was our duty as one of the civilized nations of the earth, to go frankly, honestly, and openly to Mexico, and avow our wishes and designs—to offer to negotiate with her in reference to any claim she might have, and to make to her character, honor, and interest, all proper and honorable tenders. I believe the honor, the faith, and standing of this Union, imperiously demanded this course. Again, I believed that the treaty, from the boundaries that must be implied from it, if Mexico would not treat with us, embraced a country to which Texas had no claim—over which she had never asserted jurisdiction, and which she had no right to cede. On this point I should give you a brief explanation.

"The treaty ceded Texas by name, without any effort to describe a boundary. The Congress of Texas had passed an act declaring by metes and bounds what was Texas within their power and jurisdiction. It appeared to me then, if Mexico should tell us, 'we don't know you—we have no treaty to make with you;'—and we were left to take possession of it by force, we must take the country as Texas had ceded it to us—and in doing that, or forfeiting our own honor, we must do injustice to Mexico, and take a large portion of New-Mexico, the people of which have never been under the jurisdiction of Texas. This, to me, was an insupportable barrier. I could not place the country in that position. Again, the record sent with the treaty—the correspondence between our negotiators, and the Texan commissioners, and the British minister—was anything but acceptable to me. That correspondence did not present the true reason why that country should be annexed to the Union, if it should be annexed. It was, as all recollect, put on the assumed ground that it was necessary to strengthen, defend and perpetuate the institution of slavery in the country. On this subject I speak with entire frankness. To say that I am not a friend to the institution of slavery as an individual, would be to offend you; for no man living here in our society, can in his heart cherish an institution of that sort as a matter of principle. It is a libel on man to suppose so."

The final vote in the Senate on the ratification of the treaty, was taken on the 8th of June; sixteen senators voted in favor of the ratification, and thirty-five against it—Mr. Wright, as stated in the foregoing extract from his speech at Watertown, voting with the latter. Before dismissing the subject, it cannot be out of place to refer to an inquiry often made, as to what would have been Mr. Wright's course, had he remained in the Senate, upon the joint resolutions for the annexation of Texas, adopted in Congress on the 1st of March, 1845. It is not difficult to answer this question. The only thing to be determined is—whether his objections were removed. If so, his vote would have been given for the resolutions.

The resolutions adopted by Congress embraced two propositions—the one positive, and the other alternative. It needs no argument to show, that Mr. Wright would have voted for the latter; because it provided for the very thing he desired; a fair and full negotiation—with Texas alone, it is true—but, in such negotiation, all vexed questions might have been disposed of to the satisfaction of the parties concerned. Yet this may be regarded immaterial, since the positive proposition was the one under which Texas was in fact annexed. The election of Mr. Polk by the people of the Union, as the avowed friend of immediate annexation, removed, in a great degree, the objection, that Mexico had not been consulted, inasmuch as the evil, if one, was beyond the reach of remedy—the administration could not retrace its course upon that point without compromising the national honor—and it was fairly to be presumed that a majority of the electors desired the annexation as speedily as possible. Besides, a concession was made in behalf of the claims of Mexico, in that part of the first resolution having reference to the boundaries of Texas; to which, mainly, "the claims of Mexico," as the term was used in connection with this question, had reference. The separate and sovereign character of Texas was recognized by the acknowledgment of her independence. The rights of Mexico in the matter, so far as the United States was concerned, were those connected with the division line and not the original separation. The first clause of the joint resolutions gave the consent of Congress to the annexation of "the territory properly included within, and rightfully belonging to, the Republic of Texas;" and in the second section it was provided, that "all questions of boundary that might arise with other Governments," should be "subject to adjustment" by the Government of the United States. These two features disposed of the boundary objection; they did not recognize the enactment of the Texan Congress, but admitted, in express terms, that there were questions in relation to the boundary that remained yet to be adjusted. The objection in regard to slavery was no longer of force, as an entirely new proposition had been adopted; and although the friends of that institution might not have changed their views, others were left at liberty to support the measure upon different grounds. Moreover, a provision was inserted applying the principle of the Missouri compromise to the territory about to be annexed. A question has recently been raised, as to whether the compromise was not violated by the ratification of the Texan constitution; but this has no necessary connection with the vote on the resolutions, and need not be considered here. Mr. Wright did not oppose the admission of states into the Union, in which slavery existed, on the ground of its existence; but he was in favor of firmly adhering to the Missouri compromise line. The existence of slavery in Texas did not constitute, in his opinion, a valid objection to the annexation; but he never approved of the acquisition of territory, for the purpose of extending that institution. The objection concerning the liability for the payment of the debts of Texas was settled, by the positive declaration in the resolutions that "in no event" were they "to become a charge upon the Government of the United States." If, therefore, these views are correct, Mr. Wright would most certainly have voted, as did his friend and successor, Mr. Dix, for the joint resolutions.

A strong effort was made in the House of Representatives, previous to the adjournment in the summer of 1844, to pass a bill reducing and modifying the tariff law of 1842. But the opinions of members were found to be so conflicting and so various, that nothing definite was accomplished. The last day of the session came, and, with it, Mr. Wright's career as a senator was closed. Had he,—had his associates foreseen, as they took him by the hand at parting, what was so soon to transpire, sadder thoughts would have been cherished than those which accompanied them from the capitol. Though he and they knew it not, he left the seat of government never to return. The separation was final—forever.

On his way home from Washington, and after his return, Mr. Wright addressed his fellow-citizens in different sections of the state, upon what he regarded as the great questions involved in the approaching presidential election. Although he had refused to suffer his name to be put upon the ticket, he gave the candidates nominated, a frank, manly, and honorable support. The influence and exertions of the intimate friends of Mr. Van Buren were requisite to the success of the democratic party. The least appearance of lukewarmness, or hesitation on their part, and the state of New York would give her electoral vote for Mr. Clay. They could not remain indifferent. They desired to see the Independent Treasury re-established, the tariff law modified, the title to Oregon maintained, and the distribution of the land fund prevented; and they were willing that Texas should be annexed, if the people desired it, upon fair and proper terms, and in a careful and judicious manner. Mr. Van Buren himself wrote a letter to his friends in the city of New York, exhorting them "to merge all minor considerations," and sustain the nominations. The letter was published in all the democratic papers of the state, and produced a powerful impression upon the minds of the electors. Mr. Wright and Mr. Butler also tendered their services in addressing the people whenever and wherever they were required. But the issue of the election was still doubtful. Dissensions existed in the democratic ranks, growing out of questions of state policy, and the management of the state finances. The party was divided into two factions, each bitter and unsparing in its denunciations of the other. Personal animosities, private piques and prejudices, served to give a more marked and decided character to the division. At the aucus held by the democratic members of the Legisature, in the spring of 1844, for the first time since the e-organization of the party in support of General Jackon and Mr. Van Buren, a strong effort was made to revent the passage of resolutions approving of the course of the state administration. This had always been customary when they were in power, as was then the case; but a number of the persons present absolutely refused to vote for the resolutions, and directed their names not to be attached to the proceedings.

After the adjournment of the Legislature, the democratic newspapers in the state took up the quarrel which had commenced at Albany. The conduct of the dissenting members of the caucus was vehemently condemned by one portion, and warmly approved by another. William C. Bouck and Daniel S. Dickinson, the governor and lieutenant-governor, were considered as heading one faction, and Colonel Young, the secretary of state, and Azariah C. Flagg, the comptroller, represented the other. The latter was in favor of sustaining and continuing the financial policy advocated and supported by Governor Throop and Mr. Wright, and the former preferred more liberal appropriations, and were less cautious in regard to increasing the state debt. This division line had long existed in the party. It was perhaps derived originally from the opposition of the Bucktails to the numerous projects for the construction of roads and canals brought forward by the Clintonians. After the union of the Bucktail and Clintonian Jackson men in 1827, the feelings which had been entertained seemed temporarily to be forgotten, and when they were revived, many of the leading politicians assumed different positions in relation to the question than they had before occupied. Some of the Bucktails approved of a liberal use of the public credit, while a portion of the Clintonians became decided advocates of economy and prudence in the management and disposition of the resources and revenues of the state.

Mr. Van Buren retired from the office of governor

in time to avoid, in a great measure, the injurious effect upon his own prospects which the agitation of this subject must have produced. The legislation of the state, for several years subsequent to his resignation, has been previously noticed.* The opposition of Governor Throop to the construction of the lateral canals occasioned so much ill-feeling, that he was compelled to decline a re-nomination. Governor Marcy, though yielding to the urgent entreaties of the friends of the Chenango canal, adhered generally to the policy of the previous administration. The veto of the bill to re-charter the Bank of the United States, and the removal of the deposits, occasioned numerous applications to the Legislature of New York for the incorporation of state institutions. This new interest united with the friends of the lateral canals, and those who advocated the immediate enlargement of the Erie canal, in carrying the measures they desired. The gradual enlargement was approved by all parties, but a majority of the Legislature, in 1835, passed a bill conferring almost unlimited power upon the canal board. At this session a great number of banks were chartered. In his annual message to the Legislature in 1836, Governor Marcy pointed out the evils to which this rage for speculation and new enterprises would lead, and earnestly protested "against pledging the credit of the state for further improvements, until ample means had been provided for the prompt payment of the interest." But scores of applications for bank-charters were presented, a large portion of which were granted; heavy loans were made to railroad companies; and acts were passed authorizing the construction of the Black River and Genesee Valley canals. The governor resisted the

* Chapter III.

current for the time, but finally gave way so far as to let the Legislature take its course without his interference. The commercial disasters of 1837 put an end to legislation of this character. A strong faction was formed adverse to bank-charters. Mr. Van Buren and Mr. Wright were known to be in favor of adopting stringent measures where these institutions failed to fulfil their obligations. The specie circular, and the independent treasury plan, were not satisfactory to the chartered banks, and their influence to a great extent became hostile to the national administration. Governor Marcy endeavored to pursue a course which would meet with the approbation of all. The banking interest did not unite in any opposition to his administration, nor was his course in regard to internal improvements calculated to make either faction unfriendly towards him. He signified his approbation of the independent treasury, though at first, like many others, not inclined to favor it. But the ultraists on both sides disapproved of his moderation, and he was defeated in 1838. The whigs came into power, and continued with more freedom the lavish expenditures begun under the former administration, in accordance with the policy they avowed.

Those who thought with Mr. Wright, had warned their party friends to be more cautious in prosecuting the public works, and increasing the state debt, and witnessed with regret the incorporation of such a large number of banks. A sound, judicious system of banking, he and they always desired to see established; but the legislation of 1835 and 1836 did not appear to them very well calculated to promote that object. In 1840, his name was suggested in connection with the nomination for governor; but he was aware that the interests which had opposed his election to the Senate, would not be entirely content to see his name upon the ticket; and, although they might give him their support, the success of Mr. Van Buren would be placed in jeopardy. Upon national questions, the party was well united at this time, except that those who disapproved of the independent treasury were not friendly to the administration at Washington; and he did not desire to introduce new causes for ill-feeling and division. He therefore declined being a candidate for the nomination, and Mr. Bouck was selected by the convention. The whig ticket succeeded, however, and the financial policy continued nearly the same as before. In 1841, the election resulted favorably to the democratic party. Most of their candidates and journals had advocated greater care and caution in managing the finances of the state, the suspension of the public works, and the adoption of immediate measures for the payment of the rapidly increasing debt. The Legislature assembled in January, 1842, and elected Colonel Young secretary of state, and restored Mr. Flagg to the office of comptroller, from which he had been removed by the whigs. The other members of the canal board, appointed at the same time, with one or two exceptions, entertained similar views with those gentlemen. On the recommendation of Mr. Flagg, a law was passed, entitled "an act to provide for paying the debt and preserving the credit of the state." By this act, a tax was authorized to be raised of one mill on every dollar of the valuation of real and personal property; the revenues of the state were pledged for the payment of the debt, variously estimated at from twenty to thirty millions of dollars; and all further expenditures on the public works were suspended, except where the completion of any particular contract would be an act of economy. The vote on this bill was a strict party one; the democratic members uniting in the passage of the bill. This act was termed the "stop and tax law of 1842," referred to by Mr. Wright in the Senate of the United States, when he spoke of "the noble example of New York," and commended it to the advocates of the loan bill.

But apprehensions were entertained by a portion of those who were opposed to the increase of the state debt, that moderate counsels might not always prevail in the Legislature. In 1841, an amendment of the constitution had been urged, forbidding the creation of any debt exceeding a certain specified sum for contingencies, without first submitting the question to the electors of the state. The resolution providing for the amendment was called "The People's Resolution." It was discussed in the Legislature, but did not receive its approval. In 1842, it was again introduced, but the whig members, and the friends of a more liberal policy in regard to works of improvement, opposed its adoption, and insisted that the law passed at that session was sufficiently rigid in its provisions. At the fall election, Mr. Bouck was chosen governor, and Mr. Dickinson lieutenant-governor; the convention by which they were nominated having passed a resolution in favor of a strict adherence to the requirements of the law of 1842. In 1843, "the people's resolution" was connected with another amendment, making the pledges and guarantees of the law of 1842 also, a part of the state constitution. The same influences that had defeated the amendment offered at the preceding session of the Legislature, were again successful. Previous to the fall election, these amendments were extensively discussed before the people and in the public newspapers; and at the session of the Legislature in 1844, they were approved by a majority of the members, in order to be presented to the succeeding Legislature, when, if they received a vote of two-thirds, they were to be submitted to the people for their final ratification. The friends of the governor and lieutenant-governor did not originally approve of the adoption of the amendments; but a portion of them voted to present them to the next Legislature. The principles sought to be ingrafted upon the constitution by these amendments, were those which formed the main points of difference between the two factions in the democratic party. They had assumed various forms and modifications during the successive stages of legislation; but the great question involved in them remained the same. There were also minor shades of opinion, which caused a great many persons to be regarded either as neutral or moderate in their views. The immense interests connected with the public works, gave those who favored their prosecution considerable power and influence, and this naturally occasioned a more determined feeling to spring up on the other side. Personal considerations, appointments to office, and other questions of subordinate importance, were connected with the dispute in regard to the financial policy which should be observed; but when the real ground and origin of the controversy and division was sought after, it was found to consist in the question: Whether or not the debt of the state should be increased at any time, without providing the means for its payment, and relying merely upon anticipated revenues to discharge it.

While these agitating subjects were discussed in the

New York Legislature, and in the newspapers and conventions of the party, upon national subjects the factions remained united. The feeling at one time existing against Mr. Wright had nearly subsided. His course on the Texas question occasioned some remark, but it was mostly confined to those who were enjoying the patronage of Mr. Tyler's administration, and not even they wholly disapproved of his vote. All had the most perfect and entire confidence in the purity of his motives, and this universal feeling in his favor was manifested in the unanimity with which he was re-elected in 1843. This popularity, however, which he had acquired by his course in the Senate, and by remaining almost entirely separated from state politics, furnished the most powerful argument to remove him from the position he had adorned by his high character and conceded talents, and connect his name with the dissensions and differences of the democratic party at home. Soon after his return from Washington, his name was mentioned as that of a suitable candidate for governor, and one upon whom both factions would cheerfully unite. The suggestion originated with those who were opposed to the re-nomination of Governor Bouck; but it was afterwards adopted, not only by them, but also by those who were considered moderate or indifferent in their views as to state questions. From the first it did not receive his approbation. He foresaw that however much he might disapprove of the personal animosities which had been engendered, they would be certain to affect him, provided he adhered to the opinions he had ever maintained in regard to the financial policy of the state; and these were too firmly fixed to be either compromised or waived, under any circumstances. The line between the factions was drawn; he could not satisfy both without a sacrifice of principle; and he entreated his friends to spare him from mingling in the contention and strife which had distracted and divided them. But the feeling in favor of his nomination extended farther and wider. He saw that something must be done to prevent it, and he addressed a letter to a friend in Albany, the substance of which was made public through the columns of a leading paper in that city, stating expressly that he was not a candidate for governor, and that he should not, knowingly, make himself the means of difficulties, or divisions, in the democratic party of the state, to which he was so deeply indebted, at any time, upon any question, or for any object; and certainly not at a time like the present, when a vital national question demanded perfect harmony, and the united and patriotic exertions of the whole party."

This announcement did not check the expressions of public sentiment demanding his nomination. Every day more positive demonstrations were made. The great majority of the party seemed to desire it, and the opinion was generally entertained, that the national ticket would be defeated unless he came forward as a candidate. Still he hesitated. He had ambition; but it was of a high and lofty character. The Senate of the nation was his appropriate sphere, and he did desire to maintain, and, if possible, increase the reputation he had acquired as a member of that body. But he would not peremptorily decline the gubernatorial nomination; for, had he done so, Mr. Polk would have been defeated, and the consequences of that defeat attributed to him. He was also unwilling to disregard the wishes of those who had placed him in the Senate, and whose right to recall him he had always acknowledged. He then determined to leave the matter to the democratic party of the state. If their delegates in the convention brought forward his name; if all concurred in the selection; and the resolutions were in accordance with his opinions upon the financial policy of the state; he would not decline the nomination.

The convention met on the 4th of September. Upon the informal ballot, three-fourths of its members voted for Mr. Wright. Without taking another vote, on motion of one of the leading friends of Governor Bouck, who had been supported in opposition, he was nominated by acclamation. The members of the convention, and the citizens in attendance, were enthusiastic in their approval. The address adopted took firm and decided ground in support of the principles of the constitutional amendments approved by the Legislature at its session during the previous winter; and among the resolutions which received the unanimous concurrence of the members of the convention, was one, containing the following expression of their sentiments: "We proclaim our uncompromising adherence to the debt-paying policy of 1842. It is the policy of integrity, patriotism, and public faith. It is the policy which is to redeem the state from her heavy debt and her financial embarrassments, to give her hereafter the control of her now crippled resources, and to enable her to fulfil her high and glorious destiny. We commend, therefore, to the favorable consideration of the people, and of those whom they shall elect to office, the constitutional amendments adopted at the last session of the Legislature and now in course of publication throughout the state. By them the pledges and guarantees of the act entitled 'an act to provide for paying the debts and preserving the credit of the state' passed March 29,

1842, are confirmed; and a salutary restriction upon the power of the Legislature to involve the state in ex cessive debts or liabilities is imposed."

The feelings which prompted Mr. Wright in accepting the gubernatorial nomination, may be gathered from his letter addressed to the committee appointed on the part of the convention to notify him of the selection they had made. "My strong personal reluctance," he says in the letter, "against being made a candidate for this office, and my settled conviction that I had no right to become a competitor for the nomination, were made public long before the meeting of the convention, and were doubtless known to all the members of that body. My nomination, under these circumstances, is a decision by the convention, that my personal wishes in relation to the office should yield to my obligations to the democratic party of the state, whose representatives the members of the convention were; and the unanimity of the expression leaves me no alternative but to yield to the call made upon me. Much of my personal reluctance upon this subject has arisen from a just apprehension, deeply entertained, that, if elected to the office of governor, I should find myself inadequate to the discharge of its responsible duties in a manner acceptable to those friends who should give me their support for it, or creditable to myself and the state. Still, the obligation upon me to yield every personal preference, and even personal distrust, to the unanimous wish and judgment of that great and patriotic party, which has so liberally bestowed its honors and its confidence upon me, is too plain to allow of hesitation; and if it shall be the pleasure of the people of the state to confirm this nomination by an election, my earnest efforts shall be devoted to the faithful discharge, according to my best ability and judgment, of the high duties which will thus be devolved upon me."

On the 8th of September, a gentleman residing upon the line of the Black River canal, wrote to Mr. Wright, for the purpose of obtaining a declaration of his views and feelings in relation to the unfinished canals and improvements of the state. He had nothing to conceal from those for whose suffrages he was a candidate; and he immediately replied, in a letter containing the most positive assurances that he should adhere strictly to the principles of the law of 1842, and giving his free consent to its publication. In the letter he says:—

"The state convention which has placed me in nomination for the office of governor, has, in the address and resolutions adopted by it, discussed very fully the points upon which your inquiries rest, and very distinctly declared the course of policy which it intends shall govern the action of the candidates it has placed before the electors of the state, and recommended for their support. In accepting the nomination tendered to me by the convention, according to my understanding of the good faith of the case, I substantially adopt the great principles, and measures, and course of policy, which that body has assured the common constituency will be advanced and secured by the election of the candidates it has placed in nomination; and could I not conscientiously do that, it would have been my duty, as I think, to decline the nomination; and if not that, certainly in my letter of acceptance, to have pointed out to the electors wherein, upon questions so important and so directly interesting to them, my course would differ from that marked out and recommended by the nominating convention; less than this would not enable the elector to act understandingly in giving his vote, the very object for which conventions intrusted with the naming of candidates, adopt and publish addresses and resolutions.

"Since the perusal of your letter, I have re-read carefully these portions of the address and resolutions of the state convention, and so far from finding the obligation resting upon me of adopting the principles and policy there recommended, a reluctant or irksome one, I cheerfully subscribe to both, as in my judgment wise and sound, and most beneficial to the whole state, and all its citizens, and all its great interests taken as a whole.

"If you will permit me, therefore, to refer you to these documents, you will have my answer to your inquiries, and a declaration of the policy in respect to them, which, if elected, I shall feel bound to recommend, as distinctly given as I could give them by repetition.

"I do not find anything in the ground here occupied, and the policy here avowed and advocated, to justify the charge which you say is made against me, of opposition to the completion of the canals of the state, as far and as fast as that can be done without a violation of the public faith, pledged in the great financial act of 1842, and without an enlargement of the present state debt; and if I am charged with opposition to further taxation upon the whole property and people of the state, to meet the interest upon a new debt to be contracted to go on with these works, the charge is just in so far as that I cannot with the opinions I have hitherto entertained, and which yet remain, recommend additional taxation or increased public indebtedness for these objects, any farther than the people of the state, upon a specific reference to them, shall give their assent to the increased burdens upon themselves.

"No apology, certainly, was required from you for addressing to me the inquiries contained in your letter. Nor have I any right, any more than I have a disposition, to place an injunction upon my answer to them. I occupy the position which has called out your letter, as I presume you are aware, under the strongest personal reluctance, but neither you nor any other citizen of the state who has a tax to pay, or a vote to give, is any the less entitled on that account to the full and frank expression of my opinions upon all questions of public interest; and your inquiries relate to questions peculiarly of this character.

"It is a matter of just congratulation that the canal revenues are so strongly improving; and whenever the current revenues of the state shall furnish a surplus, which can be applied towards the completion of the unfinished canals, consistently with the pledges made of these revenues by the law of 1842, I do not suppose there will be two opinions in the Legislature upon the question of re-commencing and completing these works '

CHAPTER VIII.

1844.—Views of Mr. Wright on the Financial Policy of the State well understood—Opposition to Increasing State Debt—Firmness in maintaining his Opinions—Senatorial Conventions—Question of calling a Convention to Revise the Constitution—Constitutional Amendments—November Election—Mr. Wright chosen Governor—Resignation as Senator and Appointment of his Successor—Anti-Rent Disturbances—Efforts to Suppress—Mr. Wright enters on the Duties of his Office—Meeting of the Legislature—Speaker—Governor's Message—Recommendations—Election of Senators—State Officers—President Polk's Cabinet—Discontent—Mr. Wright Declines the Office of Secretary of the Treasury—Defeat of the Constitutional Amendments—Convention Bill—Dissatisfaction—The Canal Bill—Veto—Adjournment—Insurrection in Delaware County—Executive Proclamation—Advice to Landlords and Tenants—Trial of Persons Arrested—Commutation of Punishment—Fall Election—The People in Favor of a Convention—Legislature of 1846—Message—State Printer—War with Mexico—Caucus of Democratic Members of the Legislature—Continued Dissensions—Appointments of the Governor—Tariff Act of 1846—Constitutional Convention—Its Proceedings—Financial Article adopted—Democratic State Convention—Re-nomination of Governor Wright.—1846.

The object of ascertaining the views of Mr. Wright in regard to the completion of the unfinished canals, as avowed in the letter to which his reply, given in the previous chapter, was made, was to decide upon the feasibility of an attempt to procure the passage of a law for their prosecution, because it was thought that any effort would be hopeless, in opposition to his executive recommendations; and his correspondent intimated an intention, on his part, to accept a nomination for the

Assembly, if the prospects were satisfactory. It was also stated, that unfavorable impressions existed in certain localities, more particularly interested in finishing the works, which it was desirable to remove if they were unfounded. The contents of Mr. Wright's letter were not made public previous to the election, and the individual to whom it was addressed did not become a candidate for the Legislature, though his high character and standing, and conceded qualifications for the office, would have secured him the nomination, had even a wish to that effect been expressed. The position of Mr. Wright, however, with respect to the question, was well known, and the fact mentioned by his correspondent, of the existence of unfriendly feelings, clearly shows that this was the case. The substance of the letter, too, it is but fair to presume, was communicated to the prominent members of the party who resided along the line of the Black River canal, and were in favor of its completion. It is creditable to them that its publication was not deemed advisable, if the fear of his defeat prompted the withholding it. But this fact is very strong evidence that his opinions did not concur with their own.

Had it been thought that Mr. Wright in any wise favored the completion of the unfinished works, until there was a surplus applicable to that object, over and above the amount necessary to discharge the liabilities of the state coming due, whether of principal or interest, no small effort would have been made to set him right before the public. His course when filling the office of comptroller was well known; the same principles which then formed the issue between himself and the friends of the original construction of the lateral canals now existed in equal force; though modest and unpretending, he was known to be firm in the advocacy and maintenance of his opinions; and it had never been even hinted that his sentiments were changed. He had always steadily resisted the creation of a debt, without providing means for its payment, in some other mode than from anticipated or imaginary revenues. He was willing to apply an existing surplus, not required for the payment of any liability of the state, wherever it was thought desirable; but further than that he could not, and did not go. He remembered the argument which had constantly been used by those who differed with him in opinion; that the works when finished would supply a revenue sufficient to cancel every obligation. But experience had shown him, that the time for their completion never arrived; that one object seemed to create a desire for another; that the productive works of the state were made to support the unproductive; that new debts were contracted, upon the faith of calculations and estimates based in futurity; that this course was pursued, until the public credit was impaired, the state stocks depreciated in the market, loans denied by the capitalist upon the declared ground that the revenues were insufficient, and it became necessary to stop the expenditures on the unfinished works, and impose a tax upon the people, to meet the current expenses of the government, and pay the interest on the state debt. At the time the original canal debt was created, the most valuable revenues of the state—those, too, that were actual and real—were set apart for its payment. This policy was continued until new works were authorized, which could furnish no revenue, and debts were contracted, relying upon a future income to discharge them. The result was, the disastrous prostration of the state credit. The law of 1842 was enacted to remedy this evil; and a departure from either its letter or spirit could not secure the approbation of Mr. Wright. It is hardly credible that a single elector in the state of New York, in 1844, who cared sufficient about the subject to make an inquiry, remained in ignorance of this fact.

It is not designed by these remarks to impugn the motives of those who afterwards disapproved of Mr. Wright's course upon this question. There was a difference of opinion between them—let it be added, that it was honestly entertained on both sides—but justice to him requires that it should not be said, he received their support for the office of governor in pursuance of any understanding, either express or implied, that he would deviate in the least particular from the line of policy which he had ever advocated; or that there was any substantial ground for misapprehension with regard to his sentiments. The principle that separated them was an important one—to him, of paramount importance—and no consideration, not even the success of the party or of himself, would have induced him to yield or sacrifice it. There could have been no mistake upon this point, for his public acts and conduct formed part of the history of the state; and it was honorable in those who disagreed with him, that they offered him their support, when the opposing candidate entertained opinions more nearly coinciding with their own upon matters of state policy. They might have hoped—and it could have been nothing but a hope—that he would be disposed to surrender a little, a very little, of his opposition to the measures in which they took so deep an interest; but the blame was theirs, not his, of forgetting that there were some things he never compromised.

The members of the convention at which Mr. Wright was nominated indorsed his views to the fullest extent. Had they not done so, his name would never have been placed upon the ticket with his consent. He was prepared promptly to decline the nomination, and communicated his intention to his friends, unless it was tendered under such circumstances. The question of sustaining or disavowing the policy of 1842 was presented more distinctly than ever at this election. The project of calling a convention to revise the constitution had been agitated, for a long time, in some portions of the state, by those who had given up every expectation of accomplishing anything through the Legislature. Six of the eight democratic senatorial conventions presented, in their resolutions, the alternative of the passage of the constitutional amendments, or the call of a convention. In accepting the nomination, Mr. Wright became the representative of the principle imbodied in those amendments, which the great majority of the party approved. As such he was, or should have been, supported—as such he was elected. If any, influenced by a regard for his high character and talents, though differing from him in sentiment, gave him their suffrages, it was a voluntary act so far as they were concerned—not done in ignorance, but understandingly and knowingly; and it ought not to have been supposed that he would ever lose sight of the principles which had constantly guided and controlled him.

The nomination of Mr. Wright infused new courage and animation into the ranks of the democratic party. Where all had been despondency and gloom, everything was now bright and cheering. His name was, in truth, a tower of strength, and its influence carried both the state and the national tickets. For several weeks before the election the opposition were willing to concede that his success was certain, and directed all their exertions in behalf of Mr. Clay. The number of votes polled was immense—amounting to nearly five hundred thousand. Mr. Wright was elected by above ten thousand majority over Millard Fillmore, the whig candidate, and one of their most popular and talented men. The democratic electoral ticket was chosen by a majority of five thousand votes. The difference between the vote for governor and that for electors has been sometimes referred to, for the purpose of establishing a charge of unfairness against the friends of Mr. Wright; but nothing could be more unfounded or unjust. Had he or they uttered a single word or whisper, during the canvass, unfavorable to the success of the electoral ticket, it would have been defeated by an overwhelming vote. If anything, he felt a deeper interest in the election of Mr. Polk than in his own success, inasmuch as all the great national questions which had engrossed his attention for so many years were involved in the contest. There were a number of distinguished men throughout the Union, who devoted their time and talents, in sustaining the democratic candidate; but not one among them all contributed more to the result which followed the combined efforts of the party, than Silas Wright. The true cause of his increased vote was the general confidence in the soundness of his views with regard to the management of the financial concerns of the state. In the city of New York, the great centre of all the commercial and moneyed interests, he received nearly fifteen hundred votes more than the electoral ticket; and yet the feeling in favor of the immediate annexation of Texas was stronger there than in any other quarter of the state.

He did not poll a full vote in those sections interested in the completion of the unfinished canals; but elsewhere he was sustained by the whole party strength, and received the vote of many a tax-payer opposed to him on the national issue.

Shortly after the November election, Mr. Wright repaired to the capital of the state. Having learned that it was the intention of Governor Bouck to supply temporarily the vacancy in the Senate of the United States occasioned by the resignation of Mr. Tallmadge, who had been appointed governor of the territory of Wisconsin by President Tyler, he immediately tendered his own resignation. On the 30th of November, Daniel S. Dickinson, the lieutenant-governor, was selected as the successor of Mr. Tallmadge; and on the same day the vacancy occasioned by the resignation of Mr. Wright was filled, by the appointment of Henry A. Foster, at that time a member of the state Senate. These appointments were only to continue until the meeting of the Legislature, but they were exceedingly unwelcome to that section of the party who had opposed the re-nomination of Governor Bouck, and were calculated to increase rather than allay the ill-feeling which a more moderate policy might have entirely subdued. Both gentlemen were known as decided in their opposition to the financial views of Mr. Wright. Mr. Foster was a member of the House of Representatives, at the time the independent treasury plan was first proposed, and voted with the opponents of that measure on account of his hostility to the specie clause. At first he was classed with the conservatives, but in 1840 he supported Mr. Van Buren. The appointment of a successor not recognized as the firm friend of a measure which it was expected would be soon re-established, and with which Mr. Wright was so thoroughly identified, could not have been agreeable to his feelings. It was regarded by that portion of the party whose sentiments corresponded more nearly with his own, and by those friends who looked forward to the day when he would occupy a more prominent position before the nation, as a movement designed to create an adverse influence at Washington. Whatever impression might have been made on his mind, he uttered no complaint. He might have thought that his own wishes should have been in some degree consulted, considering the evidence just afforded of his popularity among the democratic electors of the state, but the thought did not find utterance. Conscious of the integrity of his own purposes, he was still determined to be the representative of the party, and to regard all with equal favor, unless he was required to make a sacrifice of principle, and then he would do what he conceived to be right.

During the summer and fall of 1844, disturbances were constantly taking place upon the leasehold estates in the third senatorial district. These difficulties were neither new nor of rare occurrence. The first grants of land, within the limits of the present state of New York, were made by the States General of Holland. In 1629 the Charter of liberties and exemptions was granted, by which large tracts were secured to the patroons who made actual settlements within a limited time. Special privileges and immunities were conferred upon the proprietors, and the design was to introduce the manorial and baronial system which prevailed throughout the greater part of Europe. When the colony was transferred to the English they pursued the same policy. The French likewise, in their possessions at the north, adopted a similar plan of conveying seignorial rights. These lands were let by the proprietors upon perpetual leases, with certain reservations customary under the old feudal tenures. Rents were payable in wheat and other products of the soil, and in poultry, or in personal services, which were particularly specified in the leases. All mines and minerals, mill-privileges, the right of way, and other important advantages, were reserved to the landlords; and the tenant could not alienate the farm he occupied without paying a heavy fine. These restrictions operated severely in many cases, and gave rise to frequent difficulties. In 1757 an outbreak occurred on the Livingston manor. The sheriff and his posse were resisted, and several persons killed and wounded in the affray. Similar acts of violence were committed on the Rensselaer manor in 1766, and it was necessary to order out a large military force to enable the sheriff to execute the laws. In the same year the county of Dutchess was the scene of a disturbance, which was quelled by a body of regular soldiers from New York; the leader in the insurrection was executed for treason, and a number of his followers summarily punished.

The aristocratic features of this mode of leasing lands were not regarded with much favor by the whigs of the Revolution, and in 1787 an act was passed by the Legislature entirely abolishing the feudal system. A leasehold system was then devised which seemed to meet with general approbation, for the reason perhaps, that it was something of an improvement upon that which had previously been in existence. Lands were conveyed in fee simple, but subject to covenants running with the same, by which the tenants bound themselves to make payments in produce, and perform personal services, as before. In some cases it was stipulated that a certain quantity of wheat, or a pair of fowls, should be delivered at the manor-house on a particular day, and in others that one or more days service with a horse and carriage should be performed, or a load of wood drawn to the landlord. Reservations of mines and other privileges were made by the landlords; and instead of the fine for alienation, the tenant entered into a covenant that one-quarter, one-fifth, or other specified portion of the consideration money of every transfer or sale, should be paid to the landlord. The conditions of these grants were observed for some years, without exciting much complaint; but wherever attempts were made to collect the quarter sale reservations, especially upon lands which had been improved in value by the labor of the tenants, resistance was offered, either in the shape of verbal protestations, or by obstructing the execution of legal process in favor of the landlords. The disaffection gradually extended, and it was ultimately insisted on behalf of the tenants, that nearly all the covenants in the leases were oppressive in their operation and odious in their character, and that the manorial tenures which they served to uphold and perpetuate, were totally inconsistent with democratic institutions. The subject was frequently discussed in the Legislature, as petitions were presented at almost every session, praying for the passage of a law relieving the tenants from the burdens under which they complained; and in 1812 a commission appointed by that body, consisting of Judges Spencer, Woodworth, and Van Ness, of the supreme court of the state, made a report, in which they expressed their opinion that the quarter sale reservations were void. No definite action was had in the Legislature for the purpose of putting an end to the manorial system. It was generally conceded, that it belonged exclusively to the courts to determine as to the validity of the quarter sale reservations; and that it would be violating the constitution of the United States, to pass any law impairing the obligations voluntarily assumed by the tenants.

Disturbances occasionally took place on the leasehold estates. Threats were made, and violence was offered to officers attempting to execute process in the disaffected districts. But these outbreaks were soon quelled, and as there did not appear to be any organized effort to resist the laws, the individuals concerned in them were usually treated with leniency. One of the largest manors in the state was that of Rensselaerwyck, lying on both sides of the Hudson River, in the counties of Albany and Rensselaer. In 1839, upon the death of Stephen Van Rensselaer, the patroon of the manor, it was found that large arrearages of rent were due, and his heirs attempted to enforce their collection. This was resisted by the tenants; they established armed patrols, and assumed various disguises, to enable them to maintain their opposition to the legal authorities. Eventually, it became necessary to call out a military force, with the aid of which a number of arrests were made, and peace and quiet partially restored. At the session of the Legislature in 1840, commissioners were appointed to mediate a settlement between the landlords and tenants; but they were unable to accomplish any amicable arrangement, and therefore nothing was done to remove the causes of the disaffection. Anti-Rent associations were then formed in all the counties in which the leasehold estates were situated, viz: Albany, Rensselaer, Schoharie, Delaware, Columbia, Greene, Sullivan, Ulster, Otsego,

Montgomery and Schenectady; and a combined effort was made to induce the Legislature of the state to grant them the desired relief. But the character of their claims was such, that they were not favorably considered, and but few members were willing to advocate the enactment of laws designed to abolish well-settled legal principles, and in effect absolutely to annul the covenants of the tenants, and deprive the landlords both of the rents and the lands upon which they were payable.

Soon after the Anti-Rent associations were established, they organized small bands of men, who were armed with deadly weapons, and disguised as Indians. The persons composing these parties were required to hold themselves in readiness, at all times, to resist, by force, the officers of the law, in every attempt to serve process in favor of the landlords. Their expenses were defrayed by assessments upon the occupants of leased lands, the payment of which was rigidly enforced. The inevitable tendency of this systematized plan of resistance was, to produce serious and aggravated violations of law and order. The principal roads leading through the infected districts were obstructed; and one outrage was committed after another, until it was dangerous for any one not known as an Anti-Renter to be found in the vicinity. Peaceable and inoffensive citizens were assaulted on the highway in open day, and forced to join in the cry of "down with the rent," or be subjected to the grossest personal indignities. The example of the Anti-Renters was followed in other sections of the state. The ordinary obligations of tenants under leases executed in pursuance of the Revised Statutes, were pronounced oppressive; and violent opposition was offered if the landlord availed himself of the means provided by law to secure his rights. In some instances the occupants of lands held under contract, or mortgaged for the purchase money, refused to make payments, and when legal proceedings were resorted to, endeavored to maintain themselves on the premises by force.

In the meantime, the influence of the Anti-Renters was exerted at the elections. Candidates put in nomination for the Legislature were selected with the design of securing their votes, and those who were suspected of being unfavorable to their views were sure to encounter their opposition. At length they held regular conventions and nominated their own candidates, either adopting those of one or other of the two principal parties, or making a selection from both tickets; and sometimes they made nominations entirely distinct and separate. In 1844 a number of candidates were supported upon the faith of positive or implied pledges, which were deemed satisfactory to them, and in one or two instances the candidates nominated by the Anti-Rent conventions were elected. The great body of the tenants were probably content to seek a redress of their grievances through the interposition of the Legislature, and disapproved of the acts of violence which were committed; but in many cases the bands of Indians were composed of lawless characters, and as the object of their organization was forcible resistance to the laws, it was not to be expected that they would hesitate in the use of means to render it successful. On the 11th of December, 1844, the sheriff of the county of Columbia was met by a body of men disguised and armed, numbering not far from three hundred, who seized his official papers and committed them to the flames, at the same time declaring that any attempt to distrain for rent, or serve legal process, would be resisted by force, whatever might be the consequences. On the 18th of the same month, a young man present at a meeting of the Anti-Renters, also in Columbia county, but not taking part in their proceedings, was shot dead. The firing of the weapon was said by them to be accidental; but it was the natural consequence of permitting the Indians to carry dangerous weapons; and they rendered no aid to the officers in discovering the perpetrator of the offence. When an attempt was made to arrest those known to have been concerned, either as accessories or principals, in these outrages, the most violent opposition was offered. Several of the ringleaders were apprehended, however, and committed to the jail of the county, in the city of Hudson. The Indians then threatened to rescue their comrades by forcible means. The citizens were immediately enrolled and armed, for the purpose of sustaining the authorities, and application made to the state Executive for assistance. Governor Bouck at once held a consultation with the state officers, at which Mr. Wright, the governor elect, was present, and measures were taken to suppress the disturbances. A large military force was ordered out, and the outbreak finally quelled. About the same time, a murder was committed in the county of Rensselaer, in an altercation growing out of the Anti-Rent difficulties.

These alarming violations of law and order occasioned considerable excitement throughout the state. The public anxiously looked to the Legislature which was soon to assemble at Albany, for the adoption of such measures as would restore tranquillity, and prevent the recurrence of similar disturbances. The appearance of Governor Wright's message was also awaited with intense interest. It was not doubted that the dignity and supremacy of the laws would be maintained, so far as it depended upon himself; still, every one desired to know what were his views upon the subject. There were other important questions too, which it was expected would be brought forward during the session, and an expression of opinion from him was entitled to no little weight.

On the 1st day of January, 1845, Mr. Wright took the oath of office and entered upon the discharge of his duties as governor. The Legislature assembled on the 7th of the month. At the caucus held by the democratic members of the Assembly, on the evening previous to the session, some feeling was manifested by both factions; the contest for the various offices was warm and spirited, and resulted in the nomination, by a small majority, of a candidate for speaker, known to be friendly to the immediate completion of the unfinished canals, who was elected on the following day in the House. An attempt was made to induce the governor to take part in the canvass for the legislative offices; but he determined not to interfere in the dissensions of the party, or do anything to prevent the restoration of that harmony which was so necessary in order to preserve their ascendency in the state. It was his wish to pursue a calm and temperate, but firm and independent course. He was unwilling to exert the influence of his official position to favor any class; though he always reserved the right, as an individual, to speak frankly with any one who sought to know his opinions.

The message was an able, but lengthy document. There were reasons for its being so voluminous, which would not ordinarily have existed. Most of it was prepared before the disturbances took place in the Anti-

Rent district, and these were of too great moment to be dismissed with a brief notice. Besides, he was so reluctant to give cause for offence, that he did not desire to leave an opportunity to have it said, that he had any particular organ among the democratic members of either branch of the Legislature; and his views, therefore, were presented at length, upon all questions which he thought could possibly arise. If he was asked to approve of measures, in opposition to the sentiments contained in his message, no one would have the right to complain because he withheld his sanction.

The condition of the finances was presented in a clear and forcible manner, and the opinions of the executive freely and unreservedly expressed. He stated, that after complying with the conditions of the law of 1842, and applying the amount pledged to the sinking fund, there would still remain a surplus of the canal revenues for the previous fiscal year, of upwards of one hundred and ninety-seven thousand dollars. By the terms of a law passed in 1844, this surplus was required to supply the deficiency in the contributions of former years to the sinking fund; but this fact the governor omitted to mention in his message, although he declared, in express terms, his opposition to its diversion to any other object except the payment of the existing debt. He said:—

"The canal fund, however, as well as the general fund, are burdened with a heavy debt, and it remains to be seen, whether the obligations of this debt, must not as effectually control the discretion of the Legislature, in the application of this surplus money, as any pledge which the law of 1842 could have imposed upon it. The interest of this debt, it is true, is carefully provided for, by that law. Thus, without any provision for the extinction of the principal, may be satisfactory to some, but such is not my view of the rule which binds the faith and honor of the state. I know of no obligation to meet the accruing interest, which does not demand, with equal force, the payment of the principal as it falls due; and so far as the means are possessed, the failure to apply them, to the one case, appears to me to be as much a breach of the faith pledged by the contract, as in the other. Suppose the creditor consent to the postponement of the payment of his principal money. Between individuals acting for themselves as principals, such consent would authorize the diversion of the funds; but if the agent or the debtor were dealing with the creditor in person, would such consent justify the agent, without the sanction of his principal, in the diversion of the funds placed in his hands to pay the debt? And is not this our case? Are we not the mere agents of the people in this matter? They have permitted debts to be contracted upon their credit, and at their risk, to construct the present state canals. The moneys in our hands are the proceeds of the investments thus made, and came from the very source upon which they relied to pay these debts, and save them from oppressive taxation. Have we the right, as faithful agents, without the consent of our principals, even though their creditors should consent, to divert their funds to other objects, and continue the debt upon them? I strongly incline to the opinion that we have not."

But in order that there might be no pretext for appropriating this surplus to other purposes, the governor proceeded to state, that of the whole amount of canal stocks redeemable in the months of July and January following, more than one million of dollars was yet to be provided for. He then added:—"If this be a correct representation of the means and liabilities of the canal fund for the current year, there would seem to be an end to discussion as to the appropriation of these means to any other object than to the payment of the debt, unless the payment is to be postponed. I have already expressed my views in relation to such a diversion: and I am constrained to believe that, whether considered as a question of principle, or one of economy, the policy would be equally unsound."

The general views of the executive upon the whole financial policy of the state, were set forth with extraordinary ability. While congratulating the Legislature upon the favorable prospects for the future, he cautioned them against a departure from that safe and sound rule, the observance of which had elevated the credit of the state and improved the condition of her treasury, and promised so much of prosperity in its continuance.

"Our canal revenues," he said, "are very large, and nothing but the enormous debt charged upon them, keeps the fund so poor as to require the aid of direct taxation to meet its liabilities. Separate from the old debt, more than one million annually of these revenues are consumed in the payment of interest alone. This must be a constant drain upon the fund, and nothing but the payment of the debt can arrest the corroding malady. Postponement can promise no relief, and may bring accumulated dangers.

"A departure from the sound rule of using our means rather than our credit, has brought this debt upon our favorite and favored fund. The only necessarily dangerous stage in our canal policy was passed, when the Erie and Champlain canals were completed and became productive; and a sound and wise financial policy, a faithful administration, and most fortunately located canals, carried us through that stage with safety. Up to that period, borrowing was necessarily the principal resource, and some of the richest revenues of the state were set apart to meet the payments of interest, while the constitution of the state was made to pledge the investments, together with these revenues, for the return of the principal. And even under all these safeguards, loans were made with moderation, and the works were prosecuted in a measured pace. After they were completed, payment of the debt became the object of solicitude, and means were accumulated and the stocks purchased and cancelled, in advance of their falling due, when they could be obtained on reasonable terms.

"In the meantime, other canals were constructed, but the expenditures were kept within the limits of the canal revenues, without losing sight of ample provision for the payment of the existing debts. As an evidence of this, before the policy was changed, the payments made and the moneys accumulated applicable to those payments, had left less than five millions of the canal debt unprovided for. The surplus revenues of the canals were accomplishing much annually towards the construction of new canals, and the enlargement and improvement of the old, and still yielding their annual contributions to a sinking fund, intended to remove the small remaining debt, as the principal should fall due.

"In this state of things, a change of policy came over us, which was based upon a new financial rule of action. The existing revenues were looked upon merely as a fund to meet the interest upon further loans; it being assumed as safe to depend upon anticipated improvements of those revenues for the payment of the principal of the debts. Indeed, it is believed the principle was carried even farther, and that anticipated revenues were depended upon, to meet accumulations of interest, beyond the power of the existing revenues, as well as to cover the payments of principal.

"The reflection does not seem to have occurred to the authors of this new financial policy, that any disappointment in their anticipations of improved revenues, must give their system a shock it could not survive, by imposing a tax upon the people, or disappointment and loss upon the public creditors, either of which alternatives could not fail to arrest the further accumulation of debt upon such a basis. It would seem also to have been overlooked, that the money-lender could draw as accurate a distinction as themselves between their means and their anticipations; and that when the means should have been exhausted, the anticipations might not command the required capital even to test their soundness or their fallacy.

"In any event, loans were obtained in unexampled amounts, until the limit of the existing revenues was reached, when the public credit wholly failed them. Works of internal improvement were prosecuted upon a scale so extensive as to bring the state into competition with itself, and the wages of labor and the cost of subsistence upon one contract were enhanced by the demand for labor and subsistence upon another. An arrest of the means by a failure of the credit of the state, put an end to this strife and to the new public works together, and when a return to the old and safe policy was attempted, it was found that a large proportion of the moneys which had been accumulated to meet the old canal debt, were rendered unavailable by having been loaned to banks which could not pay; that the accruing surplus of the canal revenues, beyond the current annual expenses, was covered by claims for interest; that the general fund must sink under the accumulated and accumulating demands upon it, for interest upon public stocks loaned to railroad companies which had failed, or were in a failing condition; that temporary loans had been made to the amount of more than a million and a half, which were impending over the treasury, without the means of payment; and that contractors and laborers upon the public works were without pay, or with the unmarketable stocks of the state in the place of the money to which their contracts entitled them.

"The issue was therefore present and unavoidable. The people must be taxed, or the public creditors must suffer loss, and the public stocks be dishonored. A resort to the credit of the state was made unavoidable to meet these urgent and instant demands, the accruing interest upon the enlarged debt, and to put the canals in repair for the approaching season of navigation. Public distrust had taken the place of public confidence, and a substitution of the paying for the borrowing policy was made indispensable, before a resort to credit could command a response in capital.

"This was done by the act of 1842. The effect of this measure was almost electric, and was felt not merely throughout the state, but throughout the Union. Under its solemn assurances money was obtained upon loan to relieve the pressing necessities of the public treasury, and to preserve the public faith and honor, by a prompt payment, at the specie value, of the instalments of interest upon the public securities. From this time the credit of the state rose rapidly, and soon attained the par of money; and by the scrupulous adherence to the policy and the pledges of that law which has characterized our subsequent legislation, it has now reached its accustomed honorable elevation."

In regard to the completion of the enlargement, and the prosecution of the work on the unfinished canals, there was no attempt in the message at evasion or circumlocution. A manly directness in the expression of his opinions ever characterized the author, and this trait in his character was most forcibly exemplified in everything he said having reference to the finances of the state. In his letter written previous to the election, he held out no hope that he could be induced to favor increased expenditures, until the most ample means were provided for the payment of the debt; and in his message the same sentiments were urged upon the consideration of the Legislature, as of the highest importance. Not only was this the case; but as if apprehensive that some measure might be proposed which he could not approve, he avowed his opposition in advance, in order that there might be no mistake or misapprehension upon the subject. "I am well aware," he said, "that objects of expenditure, of great and extended public interest, will be pressed upon your attention, and will press themselves upon the minds and feelings of those whose immediate constituencies have a more direct interest in their resumption and completion. The Erie canal enlargement, the Genesee Valley canal, and the Black River canal, are prominent among these objects, and deeply enlist the feelings and interests of large and worthy portions of our fellow-citizens. It would certainly be a more grateful task to recommend a compliance with these earnest wishes, than to feel impelled by a sense of public duty, to point out the necessity of their present disappointment. Yet we must not forget, when acting upon these great questions, that the interests of the citizens of the whole state are committed to our charge, and that a measure which would be wrong towards them as a mass, cannot be right, because portions of the mass would be benefited by it. And it would certainly be wrong to our citizens as a whole, again to depress, or even to hazard, the credit of the state, by a diversion of any portion of the canal revenues required to pay the existing debt, and preserve the public faith. It would be wrong to them to disregard the letter or spirit of the pledges of the law of 1842, and thus incur the risk of a necessity for increased or longer-continued taxation."

The governor expressed his cordial approbation of the constitutional amendments adopted at the session of the Legislature in 1844, and earnestly recommended their incorporation into the constitution. He was very anxious to obviate the necessity of calling a convention, which he plainly intimated would be the only alternative if the amendments failed to receive the required vote of two-thirds. One section of the democratic party was decided in its opposition; but the other section insisted that a convention should be held, if the amendments were not adopted; and nearly all the whigs openly avowed themselves in favor of the project. He believed that if the amendments were sustained, a reasonable hope would be afforded that other desired reforms might be successfully urged in the manner provided by the constitution of 1821, and thus one cause of dissension would be removed, and a great expense avoided, while new safeguards would be provided for the protection of the people. On this point he said: "Our present constitution has remained the fundamental law for nearly a quarter of a century, several amendments having been in that time adopted, in conformity with the provision of that instrument for its own amendment. Hitherto that provision has satisfied the public mind, and led to the amendments demanded by the popular feeling and judgment. I consider it extremely desirable that this should continue to be found practically true, and that such a degree of harmony should at all times prevail between the popular will and the legislative action, in reference to further proposed amendments, as shall supersede demands for constitutional change in any other form. It is a matter of public notoriety, that a portion of our citizens have, for some time thought, and still think, that a call for a convention to revise our constitution, has already become expedient. I have been induced to believe that the desire for amendments upon the very points embraced in those now under discussion, and perhaps upon one or two others in reference to which propositions are also now before you, has excited this feeling and given it its present strength. I know that a further limitation of the power of the Executive over appointments to office, is also a subject upon which many desire an amendment of the constitution. Speaking personally, I hope I may be believed, when I say that any curtailment in that branch of the executive powers and duties, while I am to be honored with the exercise of these high functions, would be most grateful to me; and I am prepared further to say, that I believe many of the officers now appointed upon the nomination of the governor and the consent of the Senate, might be directly elected by the people, or otherwise appointed, with equal safety to the public, and more in accordance with the popular feeling. If the time shall come, however, when the requisite assent of the Legislature shall fail to be obtained, to authorize a submission to the people of such propositions for amendments, as a clear majority of the freemen of the state shall demand and believe to be necessary for the protection of their rights, discontents will be experienced, and other forms of amendment will be proposed, and perhaps successfully urged. Under this conviction, I feel it to be an imperative duty, respectfully but earnestly to request you to give to these, and all other proposed amendments which may come before you, such calm, unprejudiced and thorough consideration, as shall be calculated to satisfy our common constituents with the conclusions to which you shall come."

The various public charities and literary institutions of the state were all referred to in the message in approving terms, and the importance of fostering and encouraging the agricultural interests in the state, by extending the annual appropriations which were about to expire, was urged upon the favorable consideration of the Legislature. The existence of the Anti-Rent disturbances, and the certain tendencies of such infractions of the law and violations of good order, as had recently been witnessed, were depicted in plain but emphatic language. He warned those concerned in the perpetration of such outrages, that they could not hope to escape detection; that they would be certain in the end to meet with condign punishment; and that all the means and the power placed at his disposal, or in his hands, would be employed in enforcing the laws and preserving the public tranquillity. He added, that he felt precluded from discussing the grievances of the tenants, or inquiring how far legislative relief might be extended to them, so long as their violent and unlawful proceedings were continued; "for," said he, "while the question between the proprietors and the tenants was whether the leasehold tenures should be perpetuated, or the rents should be commuted upon fair and reasonable terms, and fee simple titles should be given upon the payment of a capital in money, which invested at a stipulated rate would reproduce the rents to the landlord, the controversy was one in which the feelings and sympathies of our people were deeply enlisted, and strongly inclining in favor of the tenants. Then the question was, not whether rights of property were to be trampled upon, the obligations of contracts violently resisted, the laws of the state set at defiance, the peace of society disturbed, and human life sacrificed; but in what way contracts, onerous in their exactions, and tenures in their nature and character uncongenial with the habits and opinions of our people, could be peaceably, and justly, and constitutionally modified to meet the changed circumstances of the times; and then I might have invited your careful attention to the considerations growing out of these issues."

The governor also recommended the passage of laws to prevent persons from appearing disguised and armed, and conferring additional power and authority upon the executive, to secure the prompt suppression of disturbances. During the session, a law was enacted, declaring it a misdemeanor to appear disguised and armed; also one authorizing the governor, upon the application of the local authorities of any county, to issue his proclamation declaring such county in a state of insurrection, and making it felony to resist the service of process from and after that time, and until the proclamation was revoked. In the month of January, an Anti-Rent state convention was held at Berne in the county of Albany, at which a petition to be presented to the Legislature was adopted, praying for the following measures of relief:—

"For the passage of an act repealing all laws granting special privileges to landlords in the collection of their rents, so that they shall only be permitted to use and enjoy the common right of other creditors, in the collection of their dues, and none other.

"For the passage of an act authorizing tenants, when prosecuted for rents, to set up as a defence against such prosecution, the want of a good and sufficient title to the premises in the landlord or prosecutor; and that such defence be a bar to any recovery against such tenant until the title of the landlord be fully established; to apply in those cases where lands have been leased for a long series of years or in perpetuity.

"For the passage of a law authorizing and directing the assessors of the several towns in this state to estimate and consider the amount of rents charged on leasehold premises, leased for a term of fifteen years and upwards, situated in their respective towns, as the interest of a principal, which principal shall be assessed to the owners of such premises, and the taxes thereon be paid in the towns within which such lands are situated, for their benefit, and in case of default of payment of such taxes, that such leasehold premises be returned in like manner as non-resident lands, and the interest of the landlord sold therefor."

None of these acts were passed by the Legislature of 1845; a majority of the members concurring with Governor Wright in the opinion, that it was unwise and inexpedient to consider the complaints of the tenants, while they were arrayed in hostility to the civil authorities of the state.

In a few days after the commencement of the session, a resolution passed both branches of the Legislature, providing for the election of senators in Congress. In addition to the incumbents appointed by Governor Bouck, there were a number of other candidates proposed by their friends. Both sections of the party exerted themselves to the utmost to procure the election of persons who favored their particular views. Governor Wright was urgently pressed to interfere in the matter; yet he declined taking a part in behalf of any one of the different individuals whose names were mentioned. With the appointment of Mr. Foster he had not been pleased, and he frankly stated his reasons, both to the friends and opponents of that gentleman, and his desire that some other candidate should be selected. When his feelings were made known, it occasioned some unkind remarks among the more violent members of one section of the party; but they ought not, and perhaps did not, expect anything different from him. He could but know that he had most seriously injured his political prospects, in a national point of view, by retiring from the Senate; and that he should entertain, and avow his preference, to be succeeded by some one not suspected of being unfriendly towards himself, was most natural. He may have wronged Mr. Foster by his suspicions; but if so, there are many others who have fallen into the same error. The course of the governor was very mild and moderate, and the more ardent partisans belonging to the faction opposed to the nomination of the incumbents, censured him almost as freely as those upon the other side. The caucus nominated John A. Dix as the successor of Mr. Wright, and Mr. Dickinson was continued in the office to which he had been appointed, and also nominated for the full term of six years. After the nominations were made, overtures were held out by a number of the leading whig members of the Legislature, for a combination with those democrats who had voted against Mr. Dickinson in the caucus, to elect some person in his stead who would be more acceptable to the latter. The interference of the personal friends of the governor, who were understood as expressing his sentiments, prevented any such design from being accomplished, and the candidates of the caucus were fairly and honorably supported by all the members of the party.

The excitement growing out of the senatorial election had scarcely subsided, when the caucus was held for the nomination of state officers. Mr. Flagg received more than two-thirds of the votes, and was nominated for re-appointment to the office of comptroller. The views of Colonel Young in regard to the financial policy of the state, the completion of the unfinished canals, and the appropriation of the public credit for the support and assistance of railroad corporations, and more particularly the open and decisive manner in which he had uttered his sentiments, had caused more bitterness of feeling to be manifested towards himself than to others who agreed with him in opinion. He was defeated in the caucus by one majority. Some of the other votes were equally close, as each faction was anxious to secure as much strength as possible in the canal board. Governor Wright was careful not to connect himself with the active system of electioneering kept up during the contest, though he certainly regretted that Colonel Young and others were defeated, for attempting to uphold the same opinions which he entertained. Efforts were made after this caucus also, to induce a portion of the democratic members to disregard the party nominations, and elect the unsuccessful candidates, with the aid and co-operation of the opposition members. The governor at once interposed his influence, with the consent of Colonel Young, and succeeded in preventing the violent rupture of the party organization which such a movement must have produced.

Mr. Polk was inaugurated President of the United States on the 4th of March 1845. The construction of his cabinet had been a matter of deep solicitude in the state of New York, and when the names of its members were announced, one section of the party as warmly approved, as the other unequivocally condemned. From this time forward the influence of the national administration, if not decidedly opposed to Mr. Wright, was never cordially exerted in his favor, even in the state, whose electors, upon the faith of his indorsement, had elevated Mr. Polk to the presidency. The same influences were brought to bear against him which were employed to undermine the popularity of other distinguished leaders of the democratic party in New York. At one time, George Clinton was looked upon as the most prominent candidate to succeed Mr. Jefferson in the presidential chair. Dissensions and divisions were then fomented and encouraged in his own state, and he was thrust aside to make room for a southern man. Tompkins and the younger Clinton encountered the same species of opposition ; and it was again attempted by the southern and middle states against Mr. Van Buren. The influence and firmness of General Jackson alone prevented the success of the combination. Individually, Mr. Wright could not complain, because the office of Secretary of the Treasury was tendered to him. But it must have been well known at Washington, that he would not accept it. He had been elected governor of the state of New York when, it is not unlikely, any other member of the party would have failed; and he was not disposed to shrink from any responsibility that he had voluntarily incurred. Previous to the election, it was said by his opponents, that if both he and Mr. Polk were elected, a cabinet appointment would be offered to him, and accepted. When these rumors were first circulated, his friends contradicted them, and pledged themselves, that if the people of New York made choice of him as their governor, he would discharge the duties until the last day of his official term. It was a solemn trust which had been committed to his hands, and he would neither surrender it, except to the successor whom the electors should appoint, nor desert his post, for the sake of being relieved from its burdens or its responsibilities. The office of secretary of the treasury was one requiring a high grade of talents. Few men could have filled it as well—none better, than Mr. Wright. In declining it, he was influenced by honorable and praiseworthy motives—such as did not detract from the unselfishness of his conduct, but served to place that noble feature in his character in a yet more attractive light.

The constitutional amendments lingered along for some time in the Legislature, and it was not until a bill providing for a convention was introduced, that they were pressed to a final vote. The democrats had a majority in the Assembly—a bare majority, however, and not sufficient to carry any measure requiring a vote of two-thirds. When the question was taken, the amendments were not sustained by the constitutional majority; consequently, all the efforts of the friends of reform, for the four years during which these amendments were urged, had entirely failed of accomplishing their object. The question then arose, as to what should be done. The utter hopelessness of amending the constitution, in the tedious manner pointed out in that instrument, where there were a respectable minority opposed to such amendment, was clearly demonstrated. A majority of the democratic members of the Legislature elected in 1844, were in favor of a convention, as the only mode that could then be adopted to obtain those reforms which the people desired. But that section of the party who had originally opposed the amendments, insisted that their duty was discharged by voting for their presentation to the people, and they would go no farther. The other side contended, that this was but tampering with the known wishes of their constituents, and that although the former had voted for the amendments when it was certain that they could not pass, yet they were in fact opposed to them. This was denied by the other party, and probably was not strictly true. Their individual opinions, doubtless, were adverse to the adoption of the amendments, but it is not likely that they would have resisted the wishes of their constituents, which had been almost unanimously expressed in their favor.

The whig members of the Legislature, at the commencement of the session, avowed their preferences for a convention. The Native Americans, who had chosen one senator and seventeen members of Assembly, at the election in 1844, were also disposed to favor the project, in the hope of imposing additional restrictions upon the exercise of the right of suffrage by naturalized citizens. The convention bill was discussed for several weeks, and passed the Assembly on the 22nd of April, by a vote of eighty-three to thirty-three. Of the democratic members, thirty-two voted in its favor, and thirty-one against it. Among the latter were one or two members who were friendly to the constitutional amendments, but who still thought that they might be secured without resorting to a convention. All the whig members, except two, voted for the bill. The Native Americans present gave a unanimous vote in its favor. In the Senate, the passage of the bill was resisted with much warmth, and the debate between the speakers belonging to the two sections of the democratic party, was conducted with unusual asperity and bitterness. It was objected by the opponents of the measure, that the bill contemplated the submission of the amendments collectively to the people, for their approval or rejection, and they desired every proposition to be separately presented. It was then amended, by leaving it to the agents of the people, the delegates in the convention, to decide the question of submission; but the opposition to the passage of the bill was still continued. The main argument, aside from the mode of submission, with the opponents of the bill was, that the people had not asked for a convention; but as the bill provided for ascertaining their wishes upon the subject previous to the election of delegates, those who sustained it did not regard this objection as of much force. Besides, more than two-thirds of the members of the Assembly voted for the bill, and unless they misrepresented their constituents, it was evident that a majority of the electors in the state desired its passage.

This question was settled at the November election in 1845, by the popular vote, which was nearly unanimous for a convention.

After a long contest, the convention bill passed the Senate, and the Assembly having concurred in the amendment, it was presented to the governor. The friends of a more liberal system of improvements than had been countenanced by the Legislature of the state since the year 1842, indulged some hopes that the governor would refuse to sign the bill. But he saw that the real cause of the opposition to its passage, with the great majority of those who voted against it, was the fear that the financial amendments would be proposed and adopted in the convention, and he could not gratify their wishes without sacrificing the principles which he had advocated ever since his entrance into public life. He believed that the people desired the convention; he had no fears that an "excess of democracy" would be infused into the constitution; the bill was signed, and the electors of the state approved and ratified the act

Towards the close of the session of 1846, a bill was passed by the votes of the whig members of the Legislature, and of those friendly to the completion of the unfinished canals, appropriating the surplus of one hundred and ninety-seven thousand dollars, to which the governor had alluded in his message, to the prosecution of those works. This surplus, in fact, did not exist, as the law of 1844 required the deficiencies of former years to be made up before there could be a surplus and why such an appropriation should have been made in violation of the law, and in opposition to the recommendations of the Executive, can only be explained upon the supposition, that it was intended to excite feelings of hostility against Governor Wright. If it originated in any other motive, it is hardly possible that there would have been so much feeling upon his returning the bill with his objections. He regretted the necessity that compelled him to interpose his veto, but not to have done so, would have been totally inconsistent with his whole previous course, and the doctrines laid down in his message. It is evident that a number of the democratic members did vote, in the first place, under a mistake or misapprehension; for upon taking the question after the return of the bill, they voted against it: all of them may have been equally deceived, but this is hardly probable, because several of the democratic newspapers published in those localities immediately interested in the passage of the bill, expressed their disapprobation of the veto.

The passage of the convention bill, and the veto of Governor Wright, produced so much additional ill-feeling between the two sections of the democratic party, that they did not hold the customary legislative caucus previous to the adjournment. A majority of them, however, signed and published an address to their constituents, approving of the course of the Executive. He was willing to leave all the questions upon which there had been a difference of opinion, to the decision of their common constituents. If issues had been made, they were not of his seeking. If he had contributed to increase the dissensions in the party, it was done in the discharge of what he conceived to be his duty. He was asked to withhold his signature from a bill which the people of the state demanded, and to ratify another which it was known he could not, and would not approve. Who does not honor Silas Wright, for the manliness and integrity of purpose he displayed, in rising above the trammels of party as the governor of the whole people of the state, and in adhering to his principles at the sacrifice of a temporary popularity?

The enactment of the law to prevent persons from appearing disguised and armed, quieted the disturbances in the Anti-Rent districts for several weeks; but in the month of March they were again renewed in the county of Delaware, and in several cases the execution of process was resisted, though having no connection whatsoever with rent. A number of persons were arrested for appearing disguised and armed, and three of them were convicted and sentenced to imprisonment in the state prison. The principal instigator of the disturbances in the county of Columbia, in December 1844, was also tried in March, but the jury failed to agree He was afterwards tried a second time, found guilty, and sentenced to the state prison. Notwithstanding the firmness of the Executive, and of the courts and juries before whom the offenders were brought, the Indians continued their outrages, merely removing the scene from one section of the state to another. The energetic proceedings of the citizens of Delaware county, restored peace and good order for the time, though disturbances occasionally took place in the adjoining county of Schoharie. In May, one of the deputies of the sheriff of Columbia county was fired at several times, and severely wounded; and in the following month the county of Cattaraugus, in the western part of the state, became the theatre where this insurrectionary spirit was exhibited. But the crowning act of these seditious movements was committed in Delaware county, on the 7th of August. The under sheriff, "while quietly and inoffensively engaged in the discharge of his official duty," in open daylight, was shot dead in the midst of a crowd of spectators, some two hundred and fifty of whom were disguised and armed, and none offering to prevent the commission of the offence, or to apprehend its perpetrator. From twelve to twenty guns were fired, and three balls took effect in the body of the unfortunate officer. This startling murder aroused the indignation of the whole community, and every effort was made by the civil authorities to arrest those who were present at the time of the occurrence in disguise, or were suspected of having participated in the disturbances which resulted in this terrible catastrophe. But the Indians were so numerous, and so determined upon offering violent resistance to the officers of the law, that application was made to Governor Wright to issue his proclamation, declaring the county in a state of insurrection, and to order out a military force for the protection and security of the peaceable citizens of the county, and of the courts before whom the offenders might be arraigned. On the 27th of August, the governor issued his proclamation, in accordance with the provisions of the law passed at the previous session of the Legislature, and at the same time directed a body of troops to be mustered into the service of the state, and ordered on duty in the county of Delaware. The proclamation met with universal favor, except among the Anti-Renters. Its tone and manner were highly appropriate. After reciting the facts and circumstances which had impressed him with the belief that the proclamation was necessary, he thus addresses himself to the citizens of the state, and offers his advice to the parties in the controversy:—

"To the freemen of the state I can make no stronger appeal than is presented in the simple narration of facts I have set forth. These facts show the regular progress to its result in crime and blood, of every attempt to set aside the regularly constituted tribunals of civil society, organized for the protection of personal rights and the redress of personal wrongs, and to make might the measure of right between citizen and citizen. Masks and disguises are never assumed to protect men in the performance of acts towards their neighbors, which the judgment and the conscience approve; and no other acts will promote the peace, order, or prosperity of society, or the happiness, or true interest of him who performs the action. Secret oaths are only administered to add to the protection of the masks, when the conscience proclaims that he who is trusted to look behind the mask may be as dangerous as he who looks upon it; that the danger is in the truth, and is to be apprehended from all who can tell it. When the mind becomes so deluded as to rely upon protections like these, and to act from the promptings which a sense of security of this character, if indulged, will never fail to engender, high crimes are the certain fruit, and the charm of the protection vanishes only when the guilt is incurred. The intelligent freemen of our state will not seek to change their peaceful, and happy, and prosperous institutions, the fruit of the toil and blood of our revolutionary fathers, for a government resting upon such a basis, and producing such fruits. Justice is the emblem of their government, and her light is truth.

"To the tenants who disapprove of this disguised and armed force, and have refused to give their aid or countenance to its organization and action; and they are believed to constitute a numerous and influential body of men; the present presents a peculiarly appropriate occasion to mark more distinctly their separation from proceedings which cannot fail to be fatal to a good cause, and to prejudice good men. If they feel that the tenures by which they hold their farms are onerous; not in accordance with the genius of our institutions, or the spirit of our people; and that they ought to be changed to freeholds; let them see, and feel also, that the natural sympathies of the great body of our freeholders must be with them in these impressions, and that the sure way to avert these sympathies, is to attempt to accomplish a worthy end by worthy means. Let them remember that their present tenures have resulted from voluntary contracts, freely entered into between themselves, or their worthy ancestors, and the landlords from whom they hold; and that the readiest, if not the only way, to make the change they desire, is by a contract equally voluntary, between themselves and those same landlords. Let them be assured that, if they fulfil their contracts hitherto, and offer terms of commutation of their titles, which are just, and which appear to be so to fair and impartial minds, an enlightened public opinion will bring about the acceptance of such terms by the landlords.

"To the proprietors of these leasehold estates, the landlords of these tenants, the present crisis should not be without its lessons of wisdom. Indefensible as have been the attempts to repudiate their solemn contracts, and to wrest from them by force the remedies secured to them by the constitution and the laws for breaches of those contracts, they should not fail to see, at the foundation of these lawless proceedings, a rapidly growing dissatisfaction at the perpetuation of tenures, not in accordance with those by which the great body of the lands of our country are held, and not consonant with the feelings of our people. And, while the power of the state must and will be exerted to enforce the law, protect private rights, preserve the peace and order of society, give security to the life of the citizen, and prevent the prevalence of anarchy and violence, so far as it rests in their power, they should be ready to remove the causes of like troubles for the future, by a prompt and liberal arrangement of arrears of rent, whenever an opportunity shall offer; and, by tendering generous terms to the tenants, upon which they will change the tenures to fee simple titles, put an end forever to this perpetual relation of landlord and tenant—a relation already so fruitful of anything but peace and prosperity to either of the parties. Even if it shall become necessary to employ the military power of the state to enforce the law, as connected with their peculiar interests, they should be prepared, upon all occasions and under all circumstances, to show to the public that it is no part of their object to be benefited in their pecuniary interests, by the misfortunes or the faults of their ill-advised and misguided tenants; but that they are ready to consider, generously, the ability and the means for each tenant to pay, and, even if a coerced sale of his property must be the only rule of settlement, that they are prepared to become liberal purchasers at such sales.

"To the disguised men themselves, and to those less worthy than they, who press them forward into the danger from which they themselves shrink, I have only to say that wrong acts never serve even a good cause; that persistence in crime cannot mitigate the heavy weight upon the mind and conscience of the first crime; and that no disguises are perfect enough to protect the heart from the eye of Him who sees its thoughts and intents.

"For the sake of the character of our state, and of our people, as well as for the peace, and prosperity, and harmony of our society, I earnestly hope that the day may not be distant, when I may be called upon to discharge another and a far more pleasant duty, under a provision of the same law under which I now act, by revoking this proclamation.

"Yet the law must be enforced. Our institutions must be preserved. Anarchy and violence must be prevented. The lives of our citizens must be protected, and murder must be punished. And when that portion of our citizens who, now transported by passion and led away by singular delusions, are ready to strike down the law and its ministers, shall become convinced that a different course is alike the part of wisdom and of duty, and shall again submit themselves to the laws of the state, then, and not before, can I expect to be permitted to perform that more pleasing duty."

The prompt and energetic measures of the local and state authorities to enforce the laws, and provide for the due administration of justice, were attended with the most satisfactory results. The insurrection was quelled, order restored, and the courts and officers left free to exercise their functions, without hindrance or obstruction. The most searching examination was made into the circumstances attending the lamentable issue of these disturbances; and a great number of persons concerned, either as accessories or principals, in the commission of the offence, were arraigned for trial. Several of them plead guilty, and were leniently dealt with. Others were tried and sentenced to the state prison, and two of them were condemned to be hung. From the testimony taken on the trials of the persons convicted of murder, it appeared that neither actually committed the crime, or fired his weapon, though present armed and in disguise. Upon the unanimous recommendation of the jurors by whom the two men were found guilty, Governor Wright commuted their punishment from that of death, to imprisonment in the state prison during their natural lives. Among the arguments offered on the application for a commutation of punishment, it was said that these offences were of a political character, and therefore should be treated with more clemency. In his letter to the sheriff announcing his decision, the governor protested against entertaining such a doctrine, unless it was desired to add the crime of treason to the other offences which had been committed. "I have been urged," he said, "to find a ground for commuting these sentences, in the consideration that the offences are political, and therefore entitled to a different, and more lenient treatment, than ordinary offences of similar grades. To my mind this consideration presents no meliorated aspect of this murder. If I could, in my classification, call this insurrection, commenced and prosecuted to resist the collection of admitted debts, a rebellion, or attempt at revolution of the state government, I should find, I fear, much more room to add the crime of treason to the catalogue already made up, than to discover a ground for indulgence in its political character."

Early in December, it was certified to the governor by the principal civil authorities of the county of Delaware, that, in their belief, the insurrection was effectually quelled; and on the 18th of the month he issued a second proclamation, revoking the previous one, to take effect from and after the 22nd. The firm and decided stand taken by the Executive throughout all these difficulties, called forth expressions of approbation from all parties, both in and out of the state. During the remainder of his administration, there were occasional acts of violence committed, but no disturbances of serious magnitude.

At the annual election in 1845, the people approved the calling of a convention, by a most decisive vote. Of the members of the Legislature chosen at this time, a majority over all parties were in favor of the convention, and of the doctrines laid down in the veto of the governor. The next legislative session commenced on the 6th of January, 1846. The message contained a repetition of the sentiments in regard to the finances of the state, which were so ably presented at the session of 1845, and congratulated the members of the Legislature upon the fact, that much of the business ordinarily coming before them would be referred to the convention that was soon to assemble. He stated that the violent proceedings of the tenants on the leasehold estates appeared to have terminated, and that, in his opinion, it was now proper to afford a redress of their grievances, if within the constitutional power of the Legislature; he therefore recommended the prospective abolition of distress for rent, and the taxation of the reserved rents of landlords. Both suggestions were approved by the Legislature, and bills passed during the session. The message also contained a recommendation in favor of limiting the time for which leases of farming lands should be given, to a short period. The Legislature did not pass a law for that purpose, but an article to that effect was inserted by the convention in the revised constitution, and the reservation of quarter sales and fines for alienation was prohibited. The remaining proposition of the Anti-Renters, to allow them to dispute the titles of their landlords, which, according to well-settled principles of law, were acknowledged by taking leases and attoı ning to them, was not favorably regarded by the Leg islature or the convention.

In 1845 a census of the state had been taken; and the duty of making a re-apportionment devolved upon the Legislature of 1846. The governor advised that a law should be passed at an early day, in order that the members of the convention to be chosen in April, might be elected under the new apportionment. On examining the statistics of the census, it was found, that by re-districting the state, the whigs and the friends of an immediate prosecution of the public works, would probably lose some of the delegates which they could elect under the existing law. They then united their strength, to defeat the passage of a bill applicable to the convention. It was sustained by a majority, however, and became a law in time for the election.

The message of President Polk was likewise referred to by Governor Wright. He expressed his sincere gratification at the prospect of the re-establishment of the independent treasury, under more propitious circumstances than those which attended the enactment of the law in 1840, and avowed his cordial approbation of the views of the President in regard to the modification of the tariff law of 1842.

There were but few democratic members of the Legislature in 1846 opposed to the financial doctrines of the governor, but sufficient to thwart the wishes of the majority in some instances. The question of selecting a new state printer was to be decided at this session. A majority of the democratic members were opposed to the incumbent; and a bill was introduced abolishing the office, in order to defeat the election of the candidate nominated in the caucus of the democratic members. The whigs supported the bill, and it passed both houses. The measure was unquestionably a proper one, though the circumstances under which it was adopted might have been somewhat doubtful. Governor Wright was no factionist, and he cheerfully affixed his signature to the bill. He did not ask whether friends or foes voted for a law that was constitutionally passed, and that the public welfare required, but approved what he thought was just and proper for the reason that it was so.

A short time previous to the adjournment of the Legislature in 1846, the intelligence of the commencement of hostilities between Mexico and the United States reached Albany. Resolutions in favor of sustaining the National Government were passed with great unanimity. A requisition was soon after made upon the state of New York, for troops to aid in prosecuting the war. Governor Wright promptly issued a proclamation, both eloquent in its language, and patriotic in its sentiments, calling for volunteers to enrol themselves without delay; and while he remained in office, he afforded every facility in his power to the authorities of the Union in obtaining the men and means which they required.

The dissensions in the democratic party continued to exist during the session of 1846; but as one faction was largely in the majority, they did not appear of so much moment. Violent personal altercations took place in both Houses, that served to continue the imbittered feelings which had sprung up, and the proceedings of the legislative caucus held prior to the adjournment were not unanimously approved. A few of the members signed another address to their constituents, differing from that adopted by the majority, in its opposition to the course pursued by Governor Wright in regard to the completion of the public works. Other questions were naturally connected with the main cause of division in the democratic party, and in the then state of feeling, the appointments to office attracted greater attention than they otherwise would have done. The governor was not ungrateful to those friends who had aided him in sustaining the principles upon which he placed so much value; neither was the executive patronage bestowed upon them to the entire exclusion of others. Where county conventions of the party were held, he acted in accordance with their recommendations; and in other cases, he endeavored to have the local appointments conform to the wishes of the majority. To satisfy all the applicants was an impossibility; and if he failed in any case to understand the public sentiment aright, the error was unintentional. A very great number of officers appointed by Governor Bouck were re-nominated by him; and this, indeed, was his invariable rule, except where the majority of the democratic party in the particular locality appeared to be opposed.

At the session of Congress which ended in the summer of 1846, a new tariff act was passed, materially changing the provisions of the law of 1842. It was not entirely conformable to the wishes of Mr. Wright, but the actual effect and operation of the law differed but slightly from that which he would have favored. The principle of protection in the restricted sense which he advocated was not abandoned, and the monopoly features of former enactments were removed.

The constitutional convention assembled in June. A majority of the members were democrats; but party questions were not allowed, except very rarely, to interfere with the deliberations of that body. Its proceedings were harmonious, and the constitution, as amended, adopted by a very large vote. The conven-

10

tion decided that it was inexpedient to separate the various articles, but submitted it as a whole. One of the most gratifying results of the convention, to Mr. Wright, was the incorporation into the constitution of those financial doctrines for which he had been contending ever since he first took his seat in the New York Senate. All the essential principles of the act of 1842, and of "the people's resolution," were made a part of the fundamental law of the state. The Legislature was forbidden to create a debt exceeding, at any time, one million of dollars in amount, and prohibited from loaning the public credit to individual associations or corporations. The payment of the state debt was secured out of the revenues annually accruing, and the unfinished works placed in their appropriate position of dependence upon the surplus remaining after supplying the means of discharging the liabilities already incurred. The constitution also provided that no special act of incorporation should be passed; thus preventing for the future such legislation as was witnessed in 1835 and 1836.

During the summer of 1846, the two sections of the democratic party co-operated together more harmoniously than they had done, and it was thought that the divisions would soon be healed. This might have been the case, if personal considerations, and private disappointments, had not continued to operate upon the minds of prominent members of both factions. The influence of the national administration, too, was exerted to secure the election of members of Congress in the state of New York, who were in favor of supporting its measures in relation to the war with Mexico, irrespective of the slavery question connected with the subject. That section of the party with whose views Mr. Wright sympathized, though he never approved the violent and indiscreet denunciations of the heated partisans among them, any more than he participated in the bitter and vindictive manner of the opposing faction, had declared their hostility to any extension of the slave territory; and therefore, the course pursued by the officers of the National Government, and those enjoying its patronage, produced new differences, and new collisions, which prevented the restoration of good feeling or harmony. The democratic state convention was held in October. Governor Wright had been urged to decline a re-nomination; but this would only have resulted in further divisions, and he did not attempt to influence the proceedings of the convention, either one way or the other. If the delegates desired him again to become a candidate, he was disposed to act in accordance with their wishes. He had not sought the office, but it rested with his party friends to say whether he should remain in it, since his original acceptance had been given in pursuance of their emphatic request. Those democratic journals in the state friendly to the unfinished canals, and disposed to advance the projects of the national administration, advised the selection of a new man as a candidate for governor. This movement met with very little favor, and but few scattering votes were given in the convention. Mr. Wright received one hundred and twelve votes out of one hundred and twenty-eight, on the informal ballot. His nomination was then made unanimous, except that a single delegate voted against the motion.

CHAPTER IX.

1846.—Opposition to the New Constitution—Anti-Renters—Integrity and Independence of Governor Wright—The November Election—The Constitution Adopted—Causes of Mr. Wright's Defeat—His Opinions—Adverse Influences at Washington—The National Administration—The Wilmot Proviso—New York Resolutions—The Missouri Compromise—Acquisition of New Territory and Extension of Slavery—Position of Mr. Wright—Retires to Private Life—Contented Disposition—His Name suggested for the Presidency—Letter—River and Harbor Bill—Veto of the President—The Chicago Convention—Letter of Mr. Wright—Popularity in the Northern States—Political Prospects—Mode of Life—Devotes his Time to his Farm—Agricultural Address—General Health—Sudden Illness—His Death—Letter of his Physician—Effect on the Public Mind—Testimonials of Respect—Meeting at Ogdensburgh—Tribute of Mr. Clay—The Merchants in New York—The Pilots—Proceedings of the State Legislature—Remarks of Mr. Spencer—The State Fair—Feeling throughout the Union—Personal Appearance and Habits—Character as a Citizen and a Friend—Style of Oratory—Mental Qualities—Career as a Statesman—His Memory.—1847.

THE decision of the state convention upon the financial questions, out of which had arisen the dissensions in the democratic party, was not entirely satisfactory to the friends of the public works that remained unfinished. The mode pointed out in the constitution for appropriating a portion of the surplus revenues to their completion appeared slow and tedious. Those persons, in particular, whose pecuniary interests were directly affected by the suspension of operations, did not conceal their objections to the article which had been adopted, and their intention to vote against the ratification. They were not pleased with the small sum which, in the most favorable condition of the finances, would probably be set apart for the prosecution of the works, nor with the prohibition against creating a new debt for other objects of the same character. It was suggested soon after the convention adjourned, that an amendment might be proposed to render these restrictions less severe, in case a majority of the people approved the constitution. This announcement contented the greater number of those who desired to see the canals speedily finished ; but the contractors, and others bearing a similar relation to the works, were unwilling to vote in its favor, even with this prospect before them. Experience had shown, that a minority, though few in numbers, might prevent the adoption of an amendment ; and notwithstanding the constitution was modified in that respect, they saw that it would still occupy two or three years to perfect an alteration, where there was any decided opposition manifested.

The changes in the judiciary system made by the amended constitution, were also unpopular in some sections of the state. The election of judges, and of so many other officers who had formerly been selected by the appointing power, by the people themselves, through the ballot boxes, was likewise a new feature that did not meet the approbation of many who felt attached to the old manner of appointment, and were not disposed to regard such innovations with much favor. These objections, however, were principally confined to the eastern part of the state ; but in the middle and western counties the main difficulty was the financial article.

During the session of the Legislature in 1846, efforts were made to induce the governor to pardon the individuals concerned in the disturbances in the counties of Columbia and Delaware, who had been sentenced to the state prison; but he declined any further interference, at that time, on their behalf, alleging as his reason for the refusal, that a proper regard for the dignity of the law, the character of the state, and the security of its citizens, seemed to him to require that they should be kept in confinement, at least until a more healthy tone of sentiment prevailed in the districts where the difficulties had existed. These applications were renewed by the friends of the prisoners, at various intervals, in the course of the summer, and just before the fall election they were pressed with unusual warmth. A large number of the Anti-Renters originally belonged to the democratic party, and they were very anxious that Governor Wright should place himself in such a position as to obtain the votes of themselves and of all who thought with them. Although his official acts had appeared harsh and severe, they were forced to admire the unbending integrity and stern independence which he had displayed. His recommendations to the Legislature, and the prompt action that followed them, had softened, to a great extent, the angry feelings which had occasioned the outbreak, and they were by no means inclined to oppose his re-election. But the release of the prisoners was the object at which they aimed, and that would and must be the consideration for their votes. When they found that he would not yield to their petitions, they attempted to draw from him a promise, or a pledge, that at some future time their request would be granted. His answer was worthy of the man—worthy of the governor. He would give no promises, no pledges, save that his duty should be discharged to the best of his ability. Though unlike the proud and haughty Roman, who could not sympathize with the people, and would have betrayed them to their foes—though unlike Coriolanus in all besides, yet, with him, he despised the vile means which demagogues employed to win the public favor. If he remained in office, none should complain that the executive clemency was withheld when it might be properly bestowed; but he would not sully his reputation with a blot that no honor or dignity could ever have effaced.

When the Anti-Rent convention was held, the selection of Governor Wright, as their candidate for governor, was urged by many of his over-zealous friends; but the majority required something more tangible than mere expectations; they knew his character, and they were fearful that they might look to him in vain. The whig delegates were more positive in their pledges for the nominee of the whig convention, and the Anti-Renters decided to support him at the election, together with the candidate for lieutenant-governor nominated by the democratic party.

At the November election in 1846, there were about four hundred thousand votes cast for the office of governor. In addition to the nominations of the two great parties, both the Abolitionists and the Native Americans had separate tickets, each of which received a considerable number of votes. The majority in favor of the amended constitution, was nearly one hundred and thirty thousand. John Young, the whig candidate for governor, who was also supported by the Anti-Renters, was elected over Mr. Wright, by upwards of eleven thousand majority.

It is as unpleasant a task, as it is ungracious, to attempt to explain away a political overthrow. If the people will not vote for a candidate in sufficient numbers to elect him, he is sure to be defeated. In ordinary cases, that is explanation enough; but there are reasons of more than usual importance, why the causes which prevented the success of Mr. Wright should be made known. It was claimed by his friends, and, perhaps, truly claimed, that notwithstanding his defeat, there was not a more popular man in the state. One thing is certain: there was not another member of the party to which he belonged, who could have obtained anything like the vote he received; and there were very few, if there was one, who would not have been openly opposed at the polls, by great numbers of those professing to entertain the same political sentiments.

Although Mr. Young was elected by the Anti-Rent vote, and would have been defeated if the democrats belonging to that faction had supported Mr. Wright, the latter could have succeeded even against such odds, had he been sustained by the strength of his party, as usually manifested at such an election. The returns plainly indicate, that in those sections of the state where the feeling in regard to the completion of the unfinished canals, was more decided in its character, he failed to receive a cordial or united support. In some counties out of the Anti-Rent districts, the falling off in the democratic votes was out of all proportion with that in other counties, while the whig candidate received a higher number than was given to Mr. Fillmore in 1844. A great many, doubtless, who did not concur in the opinions of Mr. Wright upon questions of state policy, out of regard for his high name and eminent abilities, unhesitatingly gave him their suffrages. But those who were so much dissatisfied with the constitution, in consequence of the financial article contained in it, as to vote against its ratification, were not favorable to his re-election. Other causes may have been alleged for their dissatisfaction with the state ticket; but it is quite evident, that if Mr. Wright had not signed the convention bill, and not vetoed the appropriation of the surplus, he would not have asked for their votes in vain. They were willing to forgive his opposition to the construction of the lateral canals; his recommendation of a state tax in 1832; and his firm and unshrinking course in maintaining the letter and the spirit of the stop and tax law. They might even have overlooked his determination not to countenance an increase of the state debt, for any purpose whatsoever, except an extraordinary emergency should arise; but his approbation of the convention bill was an unpardonable offence. So long as the statute book alone contained the record which they desired occasionally to modify, they might have been satisfied to see him remain in the office of governor; and it is not unlikely that they would have given him their votes. But Mr. Wright had held the power in his hands; it had rested with him to say whether there should be a convention; he had decided in favor of it, because the people desired him to do so; and the result had been the adoption of the financial article. This feature in the constitution was opposed to their interests, and how could they be expected to sustain that man, who, more than all others, had advocated and defended the principles therein imbodied, and had been such a prominent instrument in establishing it so firmly that it could not be easily changed? Some might have done it, who looked to the future rather than to the present; who admired him for his firmness and independence, and honored him for that he would not surrender his convictions of the right for the sake of a transient popularity—but they most certainly did not do this.

Local difficulties and dissensions also reduced Mr. Wright's vote to some extent. The regular nominations in several counties were not regarded by either of the factions. Long-cherished animosities, and continued strife and contention, had produced their legitimate fruits. Ostensibly, there was no division in the party; but, in fact, there was nothing that could be called unity or harmony. The influence of the national administration was not exerted in behalf of Mr. Wright; and this was another cause of his defeat. The new constitution of the state divested him of all patronage, and when the General Government might have essentially aided him, it was busied in attempting to secure members of Congress who were supposed to be free from his control.

But these considerations may be said to have been of little moment. Mr. Wright was defeated. An important question in regard to the finances of the state, had been agitated for more than twenty years; after this long struggle, he, and those who acted with him, had succeeded in incorporating their views into the constitution; it was natural for divisions to spring up, and that he should be one of the first to feel them. It was what he had long anticipated. When he left the Senate of the United States, he knew the time for determining the question, which had been adjourned when he left the office of comptroller, would soon come. He was prepared to meet it. His principles had undergone no change. They were firm and irrevocable; and successful too, though he who upheld them was defeated, at the same election which witnessed their ratification.

Mr. Wright had long entertained the wish to be relieved from the cares and responsibilities of office, and no personal consideration caused him to regret his defeat. In a letter written to a friend within a few months after the election, he referred to the circumstances under which his immediate connection with public affairs had terminated, in a tone very far removed from bitterness or complaint. "You do me but justice," says the letter, "in assuming that the regret I have felt, and yet feel, at my political defeat, last fall, is much more on account of my friends—those who have been friends through good and through evil report, and who have claims upon me which I never could, in any situation, have discharged, than on my own account. Indeed, I had long been sensible that it was time for me to retire, and felt a strong presentiment that, if I did not do it voluntarily, I should find myself compelled to do it without my consent, before much more time could elapse. I was so perfectly convinced, when I consented to be governor, that the termination would be just when and as it has been, that I can scarcely say I have been disappointed. Still, I am now perfectly satisfied that it was my duty to yield upon that occasion, and that my friends did right to urge me to it. Had it not been done, and our state had been lost in 1844, the failure of our party, and our measures and principles in the nation, would have been imputed to us, and to me prominently. That would have placed us in a worse position than we are now in, and the fault would have been said to be, and would have been believed to be, ours; while now we are blameless, and have only shared the fate too often met by honest men, that of a defeat in an attempt to carry out and establish honest principles. Still, there has been something very remarkable in the passage of events. The Independent

Treasury has been established and is in operation. We have succeeded in establishing the most sound and safe financial principles in our new constitution, and yet the party, which alone as a party was favorable to these reforms, was beaten at the very election which adopted them. All this shows that our principles possess a strength with our people which our men do not."

In the same letter, he refers more particularly to the pleasure he had experienced in returning to private life. "Personally," says he, "I am content as a man can be, and not a day passes that I do not find cause for joy, that I am out of the way and clear from the cares and responsibilities of these ever-perplexing public affairs. I have no ambitions to gratify, and no griefs to indulge, and I take a pleasure I cannot express in feeling free to express my opinions as a private citizen."

The adverse influences at Washington which had contributed to Mr. Wright's defeat, and his position with respect to the national administration, were made frequent subjects of comment after the election, and during the winter of 1847. The question as to the annexation of Texas, was disposed of; but the war with Mexico had introduced a new topic for political discussions. Similar questions had often been brought forward, since the original formation of the confederacy, and had always given rise to protracted debates in Congress. At the time of the commencement of hostilities with the Mexican republic, it was supposed that the war would be of short duration, and the terms upon which a peace should be negotiated began to be considered. It was generally understood that the large amount of claims held by citizens of the United States against that Government, and of those in prospective which would be urged on the suspension of difficulties, as an indemnity for expenses, could not be satisfied without yielding up a portion of her territory beyond the original limits of Texas. Slavery did not exist in the northern provinces of Mexico, and it was urged by those members of Congress who were opposed to the extension of that institution, that measures should be taken to prohibit its introduction into any territory that might be acquired. Near the close of the session of Congress, ending in the summer of 1846, President Polk requested that an appropriation of two (afterwards three) millions of dollars should be made, to be employed by him in concluding a peace with Mexico, if an opportunity were presented during the recess. A bill for that purpose was introduced into the House of Representatives; and while the subject was under discussion, Mr. Wilmot, a democratic member from Pennsylvania, moved that a clause be added to the bill, in the following terms:—

"Provided, That there shall be neither slavery nor involuntary servitude in any territory on the continent of America which shall hereafter be acquired by, or annexed to the United States, by virtue of this appropriation, or in any other manner whatsoever, except for crimes, whereof the party shall have been duly convicted. Provided always, That any person escaping into that territory, from whom labor or service is lawfully claimed in any one of the United States, such person may be lawfully reclaimed and carried out of such territory to the person claiming his or her service."

The object of proposing this amendment, now known as "The Wilmot Proviso," was to prohibit the introduction of slavery into that portion of Mexico which might be surrendered to the United States, so long as the territorial character was preserved; and when states were formed and admitted into the Union, the matter would come under their control. The proviso was sustained by a majority in the House of Representatives—the members from New York unanimously voting in its favor—but it was stricken out in the Senate, and the bill failed to become a law.

The views of Mr. Wright upon this question were not then made known, though it was generally understood that he concurred in the vote given by the members of Congress from his own state. The President, and a majority of the cabinet, were favorable to the slaveholding interest; and as there were several candidates for the succession to the presidency among the latter, they were not reluctant to engage in an attempt to weaken his influence and popularity in New York, and in the Union at large. It was said, that he had placed himself in opposition to the administration, which had taken a stand against the proviso, and would countenance no proposition of that character, unless it contemplated the extension of the Missouri compromise line to such new territory as might be acquired from Mexico; and, in the winter of 1847, circumstances transpired which, it was alleged, fully substantiated the charge that had been made. At the second session of the twenty-ninth Congress, Preston King, the representative from the congressional district in which Mr. Wright resided, and his warm personal and political friend, became the mover of the Wilmot Proviso, as an amendment to the appropriation bill, by which the sum asked for in 1846 was placed at the disposal of the President. All the members from New York, except three of the democrats, some or all of whom had opposed the re-nomination of Governor Wright, supported

Mr. King's proposition. While the subject was still pending in Congress, the following resolutions of instruction were adopted in the New York Legislature, by the votes of the whig members and of those who occupied the same ground with Mr. Wright in regard to state politics:—

"Resolved, That if any territory is hereafter acquired by the United States, or annexed thereto, the act by which such territory is acquired or annexed, whatever such act may be, should contain an unalterable, fundamental article or provision, whereby slavery or involuntary servitude, except as a punishment for crime, shall be forever excluded from the territory acquired or annexed.

"Resolved, That the senators in Congress from this state be instructed, and that the representatives in Congress from this state be requested, to use their best efforts to carry into effect the views expressed in the foregoing resolutions."

Mr. Wright was still in Albany at the time these resolutions were before the Legislature, and did not conceal his approbation of the sentiments expressed in them. From this fact, and from the known friendly relations existing between himself and Mr. King, it was inferred that he was in favor of the Wilmot Proviso. Before noticing his position, as subsequently defined by himself, it will not be out of place to refer to a few historical facts connected, in the public mind, with this question, though only indirectly affecting it.

The principle involved in the Wilmot Proviso was very different from any of a similar nature which had been previously discussed, in or out of Congress. In 1784, Thomas Jefferson, as chairman of a committee, a majority of whom were from slaveholding states reported a plan in the old Congress of the Confederation, for the government of the "Western Territory," now composing the states of Ohio, Indiana, Illinois, Michigan, Iowa, and Wisconsin. This plan embraced the condition—that after the year 1800, there should be neither slavery, nor involuntary servitude, in any of the states to be formed out of such territory, otherwise than in punishment of crimes. The ordinance containing this proviso did not receive a vote of two-thirds, and therefore was not adopted. But in 1787 an ordinance was passed, in relation to the North-western territory, which contained an article absolutely prohibiting slavery therein.* Of this article the Wilmot Proviso is almost a literal transcript. In 1789, the first Congress under the federal constitution re-enacted the ordinance of 1787. Mr. Madison was among its most prominent supporters, and Washington approved and signed it. This measure was a concession on the part of the slaveholding interest. The free states yielded nothing —because there was nought to yield. Under the laws then in existence, the territory was slaveholding territory. Virginia, a slave state, had the largest and the strongest claim in it. The slave states made a voluntary surrender to the free states, and agreed that slavery should not continue or be extended north of the Ohio River, in a portion of territory belonging to the Union previous to and at the time of the adoption of the constitution.

Since the organization of the Federal Government, Louisiana and Florida have been acquired by purchase, and Texas, originally forming a part of the former, has been restored, after having once been ceded to Spain. Slavery existed in all these provinces, at the time of

* Article 6.

their acquisition or annexation. Out of the Louisiana purchase three states have been formed—Louisiana, Arkansas, and Missouri. Louisiana was admitted immediately after the purchase. Missouri applied for admission in 1819, and then the question arose which was settled by what has been called the Missouri compromise. Those who desired to make Missouri a free state, insisted that if it had formed part of the Union at the time the ordinance of 1787 was passed, it would have been included within the North-west territory; and not only did they urge that argument, but they demanded that slavery should be prohibited in all new states, not comprised within the original boundaries of the United States, "as a condition of their admission into the Union." On the other hand it was contended, that the territory was slave territory at the time of the purchase, and that the only real point in dispute had been settled by the admission of Louisiana. The principle then maintained by the members of Congress from the northern states went far beyond that of the Wilmot Proviso; but public opinion in that section of the Union was strong and decided in its opposition to the admission of Missouri, if slavery was not prohibited. In 1820, a resolution was unanimously passed in the New York Legislature, of which Martin Van Buren, Roger Skinner, Samuel Young, and other distinguished men, were at that time members, instructing their senators and representatives to oppose the admission of any state, not contained in the original boundaries of the confederacy, without making the prohibition "an indispensable condition." After a long and ardent contest, the slave states again yielded up a portion of their territory, and on the 6th of March, 1820, an act was passed authorizing the admission of Missouri, but forever prohibiting "slavery or involuntary servitude" in the remaining part of the Louisiana purchase lying north of 36 degrees, 30 minutes, north latitude.

Florida was slave territory at the time of its acquisition, and when it applied for admission, no attempt was made to revive the question which had been disposed of in the case of Louisiana. When the project for the annexation of Texas came before Congress, there was a reason for extending the Missouri compromise line to her territory, because it had formed a part of the original Louisiana purchase. No one then thought of extending the compromise to free territory. The South did not ask it—and the North would never have consented.

The subject of contention in the settlement of all these questions—in the passage of the ordinance of 1787; the Louisiana and Florida purchases; the admission of Missouri; and the annexation of Texas—where any contention took place, was either in regard to the acquisition of slave territory, or to the division of slave territory between the free and slave states. The Wilmot Proviso presented a question differing as widely from any before agitated as one pole is separated from the other. It had reference solely to the acquisition of free territory, and to the extension of slavery where it was unknown; and it is for this reason, that no compromise in the adoption of the federal constitution, no compromise which has since been made, has any legitimate connection with it. When the Proviso was first introduced, it was urged that the soil and climate of New Mexico and California, portions of whose territory, if any, were to be acquired, were not congenial to the existence of slavery, and therefore the prohibition was unnecessary, and calculated but to provoke bad feeling and produce divisions and dissensions. But this same argument was worn threadbare at the time of the Louisiana purchase. It was then said, that slavery would never extend to the northern portions of that territory; that there were a few slaves in the settlements along the Mississippi, but it was idle to think of employing them in the interior; and that it would be very unwise to legislate at all upon the subject. What was the result?—Besides Louisiana proper, and Texas, since restored, two slave states, Arkansas and Missouri, were formed; slavery extended as far north as the 41st degree of latitude, and was checked only by the prohibition in the act of 1820. The friends of the Wilmot Proviso thought there was no time like the present to decide so important a question; and that the evil they apprehended should be guarded against at the time of the acquisition of any new territory. In their view, the principle was of too much value to be trifled with—it was not whether slavery should be protected where it had an existence, as was done by the federal constitution—not whether slave territory should be annexed to the Union—not whether an equitable division should be made of such territory between the free and the slave states—but whether the American Government should become the propagandist of slavery, and seek to implant it upon free soil.

It was in this light Mr. Wright regarded it; and hence it was, that he would have felt bound to oppose the administration of Mr. Polk, or any other administration, if it sought to acquire territory for the extension of slavery. His sentiments were freely expressed to his friends, though he endeavored to avoid making them topics of discussion in the public prints. On the 15th of April 1847, he wrote to a gentleman in the city of New York,* in reply to a letter making inquiries as to his opinions, in order to correct what were supposed to be misrepresentations of them, and stated, in definite terms, his position with respect to the principle of the Wilmot Proviso. He said :—

"If the question had been propounded to me, at any period of my public life—'Shall the arms of the Union be employed to conquer, or the money of the Union be used to purchase territory, now constitutionally free, for the purpose of planting slavery upon it'—I should have answered, No ! And this answer to this question is the Wilmot Proviso, as I understand it. I am surprised that any one should suppose me capable of entertaining any other opinion, or giving any other answer, as to such a proposition."

The letter of Mr. Wright in which this passage occurs, was not intended at the time for publication ; but the same letter contained a request, that it should be distinctly announced in the columns of a democratic paper in New York, "that he was opposed in principle to the conquest, or purchase of territory, now free, for the purpose of incorporating slavery upon it ; that he thought it an appropriate time to declare that principle, when an appropriation was asked to purchase the territory ; and that such a declaration, made at such a time, was not in opposition to the administration, unless it was avowed that the administration wished to acquire the territory for the extension of slavery, in which case he would think the administration wrong and the declaration right."

Mr. Wright did regret that Mr. King became the mover of the Proviso, because it was supposed to have been done after a consultation with him, though

* Hon. J. H. Titus.

in fact he was entirely ignorant of that gentleman's intentions; but at no time did he disapprove of his course, or entertain any other sentiment except that of cordial concurrence in the principle of the Wilmot Proviso. The preservation of the federal constitution was as dear—the rights for which his fathers contended, by the side of their southern brethren, at Saratoga and Monmouth, at Camden and Yorktown, were as sacred to him—as if he himself had perilled his life in their defence. On all public occasions, whether in the Senate or before the people, the influence of his example and advice was in favor of the sacred compromises of 1787. At Watertown, with reference to this same question of slavery, he said: "Yet the institution exists among us. It existed in our state when the federal constitution was formed. The convention of '87—the wisest body of men, unquestionably, that ever has assembled for civil purposes within the history of the world—made the compromises which enabled them to form the Union. Without it the Union never would have existed. What were they?—To leave the existence, the measure and management of slavery, exclusively to each state for itself. We, most wisely and gradually abolished it with us.—Other states, whether from choice or compulsion it does not become me to say, have not advanced so rapidly. But there is not one provision in that sacred instrument, which I would less willingly disturb. It is to me as sacred as any of the others—and whilst I live, so far as my voice and action is concerned, the guardianship and disposition of it shall be left to those among whom it exists, without interference from me."

From this declaration Mr. Wright never departed. He was always ready to do everything in his power to secure that protection to the slaveholding interest which was guaranteed by the constitution; but he did not approve of acquiring new territory to extend the institution where it had no existence. He was willing, at any time, to appropriate the means belonging to the General Government, for the purpose of sustaining the national honor and dignity and character; but he did not desire that the blood of the American soldier should fertilize a foreign soil, that it might be cultivated by the slave. He was willing, in a just and righteous cause, that the Stars and Stripes should be planted on the highest peak of the Cordilleras, if they could wave in the sunlight and the breeze, unsullied and spotless, as the signal of freedom, but never to be borne there as the herald of oppression.

Mr. Wright's term of office as governor of the state of New York, expired on the last day of December 1846, and in the month of February following he returned to his residence at Canton. His retirement to private life was to him, personally, a source of great gratification. In one of his letters written in April, he said that he could "scarcely yet realize the sensation," and that he had not known before "what a relief it would be to find himself again a free man." There are few men who, in his situation, would have been so easily contented to lay aside their official honors, and, like Cincinnatus, return again to the noblest of all professions—that of the tillers of the soil. To his happy and cheerful disposition it was no sacrifice—but a pure and welcome joy. Indeed, his only regret was, that he was compelled to remain at home, and prevented from visiting his friends as he wished to do, for fear lest he might be charged with seeking some other and higher honor. "If I were to attempt to tell you," he said, in a letter written to a friend in Maine, excusing himself and Mrs. Wright from paying an anticipated visit, "how happy we make ourselves at our retired home, I fear you would scarcely be able to credit me. I even yet realize every day, and every hour, the relief from public cares and perplexities and responsibilities; and if any thought about temporal affairs could make me more uneasy than another, it would be the serious thought that I was again to take upon myself, in any capacity, that ever pressing load. I am not, however, troubled with any such thought, and am only occasionally a little vexed that I am constantly suspected of cherishing further vain and unreasonable ambitions.

"I cannot make my visit to you this year. I have become a farmer in earnest, though upon a very humble scale, and I find little leisure for recreation. I labor steadily, and enjoy my food and sleep as no politician can. My land is new and hard to work, so that I have not the pleasure of show and appearance, but a call for the more work. Even if my business would permit, I should not dare to travel this year, as I should be suspected of doing it for sinister purposes, which would destroy to me all the pleasures of journeying, and cause me to be received and treated as a moving beggar, not for bread, which might be excused, but for favors I do not ask. After this year I shall be relieved from this embarrassment; and then I hope the time may come when I can visit your state, and yourself and family, and have the pleasure of fishing with you for cod, without the suspicion of being a fisher of men."

The playful tone of this letter indicates anything but the existence of disappointed ambition. The heart of the writer was free as the air he breathed. A load of care and responsibility had been removed from his shoulders. For nearly a quarter of a century—all the best part of his life—he had been in the service of the state or of the nation. He had barely commenced the practice of his profession when he was elected to the state Senate, and from that time, until within a few months previous, he had continued in office. He was frequently mentioned in connection with the presidency in the summer of 1847, and a number of democratic papers in the northern states inserted his name in their columns, as their candidate for the nomination. It has been said, that that high office should "neither be sought, nor refused." Mr. Wright did not seek it, though he might not have refused had it been tendered to him. There was no false delicacy in his reluctance to be considered as an aspirant for the office. He saw that if he was nominated, his opinions on the Wilmot Proviso would become the subject of comment, and the presidential contest might assume a sectional rather than a party character. He was desirous that this should be avoided, and expressed his feelings with entire frankness. In a letter dated in July, he said:—

"I wish you to believe me, when I tell you that I write upon this subject, (the presidency,) wholly free from personal embarrassment. I never have been vain enough to aspire to this high office, and if I had desired it ever so strongly, I am not so blind as not to see that the present period presents no opportunity for a candidate such as I should be. I tell you the truth, however, when I say, elevated as it is, and is justly considered, I do not wish the office.

"My acquaintance with it has long since satisfied me, that no man should aspire to it who has not a stronger hold upon the feeling of the country than I have; and that if obtained, it will give to such a man neither pleasure nor honor. I am not a candidate for the office, and have no feeling about who shall be candidates, beyond my deep feeling for the country and its institutions, and for the democratic party and its principles, upon the success of which I think the country and our institutions must rely for prosperity and success."

During the session of Congress ending in August 1846, the river and harbor bill, making appropriations exceeding thirteen hundred thousand dollars in amount, passed both Houses, but was vetoed by the President, upon the ground that a number of the works specified were not proper objects of expenditure on the part of the General Government, and also, that the money was needed to carry on the war with Mexico. The veto excited astonishment, and was quite unpopular in the northern states, and particularly in the vicinity of the western lakes and rivers, upon which a considerable share of the appropriation was proposed to have been expended. The subject was of vast importance to the inhabitants of that section of the Union, and it was suggested that a convention of the friends of the improvements should be held, to deliberate upon the proper measures to be taken to obtain the desired assistance from the national authorities. The convention met at Chicago, on the 5th of July, 1847. The attendance was large from all parts of the country interested in the completion of the works provided for in the bill vetoed by the President. Almost every prominent man at the North was invited to attend, and address the convention. Several were present, and others sent letters expressive of their views. Among the latter was Mr. Wright. His letter was warmly commended by members of both parties, and was admitted to be the ablest written on the occasion. The following extract from it will long be remembered by those who valued his opinions upon this great question:—

"Were it possible for me to attend the proposed convention, without an unreasonable sacrifice, I should most gladly do so, as my location gives me a strong feeling in reference to the prosperity and safety of the commerce of the lakes.—The subject of the improvement of the lake harbors is one which my service in Congress has rendered somewhat familiar to me in a legislative aspect, while my personal travel upon the two lower lakes has made the necessity for these improvements manifest to my senses.

"I am aware that questions of constitutional power have been raised, in reference to appropriations of money by Congress for the improvement of the lake harbors; and I am well convinced that honest men have sincerely entertained strong scruples upon this point; but all my observation and experience have induced me to believe that these scruples, where the individual admits the power to improve the Atlantic harbors, arises from a want of acquaintance with the lakes and the commerce upon them, and an inability to believe the facts in relation to that commerce, when truly stated. It is not easy for one, familiar with the lakes and the lake commerce, to realize the degree of incredulity, as to the magnitude and importance of both, which is found in the minds of honest and well-informed men, residing in remote portions of the Union, and having no personal acquaintance with either; while I do not recollect an instance of a member of Congress, who has travelled the lakes, and observed the commerce upon them, within the last ten years, requiring any further evidence or argument, to induce him to admit the constitutional power and the propriety of appropriations for the lake harbors, as much as for those of the Atlantic coast.

"I have long been of the opinion, therefore, that to impress the minds of the people of all portions of the Union with a realizing sense of the facts as they are, in relation to these inland seas, and their already vast and rapidly increasing commerce, would be all that is required to secure such appropriations as the state of the national treasury will from time to time permit, for the improvement of the lake harbors. I mean the improvement of such harbors as the body of the lake commerce requires for its convenience and safety, as contra distinguished from the numerous applications for these improvements, which the various competing local interests upon the shores of the lakes may prompt; and I make this distinction, because my own observation has shown that applications for harbor improvements at the public expense are made and passed, within a distance of a very few miles, and at locations where, from the natural position of the lake and coast, a good harbor at either point would secure to the commerce of the lake all the convenience and safety of duplicate improvements. Much of the difficulty of obtaining appropriations grows out of these conflicting applications; and the sternness with which all are passed as necessary to the lake commerce, impairs the confidence of strangers to the local claims and interests in the importance of all.

"It is the duty of those who urge these improvements, for the great objects for which alone they should be made at the expense of the nation, viz: the convenience and safety of the lake commerce, to be honest with Congress, and to urge appropriations only at points where these considerations demand them. The river improvements constitute a much more difficult subject, and the connection of them with the lake harbors, has often, to my knowledge, fatally prejudiced the former. There are applications for the improvement of rivers, about which, as a matter of principle and constitutional power, I have no more doubt than about the harbors upon the lakes, or the Atlantic coast; and there are those which, in my judgment, come neither within the principle nor the constitutional power; but to draw a line between the two classes of cases, I cannot. I have witnessed numerous attempts to do this, but none of them have appeared to my mind to be very sound or very practical. The facts and circumstances are so very variant, between the various applications, that I doubt whether any general rule can be laid down, which will be found just and practical; and I think the course most likely to secure a satisfactory result, with the least danger of a violation of principle, would be for Congress to act separately and independently upon each application.

"There has appeared to me to be one broad distinction between these cases, which has not always been regarded, but which I think always should be. It is between the applications to protect and secure the safety of commerce upon rivers, where it exists, and is regularly carried on in defiance of the obstructions sought to be removed, and in the face of the dangers they place in its way, and those applications which ask for improvement of rivers, that commerce may be extended on them, where it is not. The one class appear to me to ask Congress to regulate and protect commerce upon rivers where commerce in fact exists, and the other, to create it upon rivers where it does not exist. This distinction, if carefully observed, might aid in determining some applications of both classes, but is not a sufficient dividing line for practical legislation, if it is for the settlement of the principle upon which all such applications should rest. I use the term 'commerce' in this definition, as I do in this letter, in its constitutional sense and scope.

"I must ask your pardon, gentlemen, for troubling you with so long and hasty a communication, in reply to your note. It is not made for any public use, but to express to you, very imperfectly, some of my views upon the interesting subjects you bring to my notice, which I shall not have the pleasure of communicating in person, and to satisfy you that I am not indifferent to your request."

The letter of Mr. Wright to the Chicago convention, added a great deal to his popularity, which was now rapidly on the increase in the northern states. When the causes of his defeat at the election in 1846 became known, it prejudiced him but very little—scarcely at all. He had been prostrated, but, like Anteus of old, he had risen again, renewed in vigor and in strength. His course upon the Texas question, and his position with regard to the Wilmot Proviso, in despite of the attempts which had been made, had alienated but few friends from him even at the South; and many of the most influential journals published in that quarter of the country, declared their willingness to overlook their difference with him upon this one point, in view of his great talents and his unquestioned patriotism and integrity. His future prospects at this period, could not have been more encouraging to his ambition

—more cheering to his friends. He was in the prime of life—in the maturity of his powerful intellect; and the star of his fame was just culminating towards its zenith. But that life was destined to be prematurely closed—the fire of that intellect quenched—and the star obscured ere it had reached the meridian.

It was customary with Mr. Wright, while a member of the Senate, to spend a great portion of his time, in the intervals between the sessions of Congress, in cultivating his garden, and a small farm which he owned. He had been taught to labor in his youth, and he did not lose his fondness for it as he grew older. It was a pleasure and a delight to him; and he thought the exercise necessary for the preservation of his health. In 1838, General Macomb, when on a tour of inspection along the northern frontier, made him a visit, the particulars of which were communicated in a letter from which the following is an extract:—

"I had occasion to visit Canton in October, and as soon as I arrived, I inquired for the residence of Mr. Wright. I was directed to a small, neat cottage, whither I made my way; and on approaching it I saw a man with his coat off, wheeling a wheelbarrow along on one of the walks of a very large garden which was attached to the house.—As I came near, I discovered that the laborer was my friend Wright. He received me with great cordiality; said that his garden was cultivated mainly by his own hands, and that he was putting away his winter vegetables, and preparing to depart for Washington towards the last of the coming month. He further said, with the greatest apparent satisfaction, that he had recently purchased a farm, and intended to extend his agricultural operations. He was asked how large the farm was that he had pur chased,—to which he said, 'twenty acres!'—and that either from natural inclination, or the effect of early habits, he was much devoted to the pure and simple pursuits and pleasures of the country."

When he returned from Albany, Mr. Wright resumed the frugal and laborious habits of a plain, unpretending farmer. A short time before his election as governor, he had purchased a farm containing about one hundred acres in addition to what he had previously owned, lying on the outskirts of the village of Canton. A portion of the land had been partially cleared, but the remainder was new and uncultivated. He made some improvements upon it in 1844, though it still required a great deal of labor when he entered upon the duties of his office. After his return, he hired a good and faithful man, who was as fond of labor as himself, and together they commenced ditching, fencing, and clearing up the old timber, in order to fit the land for cultivation. "To the governor," says his physician, in a letter to the author, "it was more a matter of pleasure than of profit thus to employ his time. He labored so hard and so steady, that instead of remaining of his usual full proportions, he became quite spare. His day's work being ended, he would devote the night to reading, and his correspondence, which was always extensive; and which he kept up with, although it required late hours to do so. He was most strictly temperate both in eating and drinking; his food was of the plainest and simplest kind; and he drank no ardent spirits, or wine, except on three or four occasions, during the year. When he was at labor he sweat profusely, and drank a great deal of cold water. He did not avoid the extremes of weather, and was often exposed to the rain and to the night air, without a coat, vest, or cravat; and yet, during the whole time, he was not known to complain of the slightest deviation from perfect health, though he occasionally said that toiling in the hot sun was oppressive to his head."

The deep interest Mr. Wright ever manifested in the cause of agriculture, led to his being selected to deliver the address before the state Agricultural Society, at their annual fair in September. The preparation of it was commenced in July, and occupied his mind for several weeks during the day, and his time during the evening. For nearly ten days previous to the sad termination of his existence, he was very busily engaged in clearing the ditches upon his farm and loading the dirt into a wagon; or in harvesting his grain, and raking and binding it; or in doing other work that required a stooping position of the body. On the 18th and 21st of August, while at work, he experienced sudden attacks of pain in the chest, which did not last foı any great length of time. On sitting down a few moments, they passed off in a profuse sweat, leaving him apparently as well as ever. He mentioned the symptoms of the second attack to others, and stated that he must have injured his health in some way, but did not appear to be alarmed. Yet it is evident that he had a premonition of what was so soon to befall him. On Thursday, the 26th of August, he attended a funeral, and walked with a gentleman, to whom he spoke of the almost instant death of a friend in an apoplectic fit; and there was so much solemnity in his tone and manner, that it made an unusual impression upon the mind of the person whom he addressed. After returning from the funeral, he worked hard until a late hour in the evening, to finish getting in his grain. The day had been warm, and the night was chilly. Before retiring for the night, he revised the address which he had been engaged in preparing, and made a few verbal corrections. This was his last mental effort, and, like everything he said, or wrote, is well worthy to be carefully treasured.

"On Friday, the 27th of August," says the letter of his physician, "he rose in the morning, to all appearance in perfect health. He ate his breakfast as usual, and between seven and eight o'clock went to the post-office, about twenty rods distant from his house, to get his letters and papers. They were handed to him, and he sat down, and commenced reading one of the letters. Before he had read far, he was observed by the clerk to lay the letter down, rise from his chair, and walk across the room. He then complained of a severe pain in his chest. It was at once proposed that I should be sent for; but he observed, that he did not think it would be best; that it would pass off directly; and that he had had two similar attacks before, but he soon got over them. Some peppermint was given to him, however, but as he did not appear to get easier, it was again proposed to send for me. To this he consented. On arriving at the office, I found him sitting in a chair surrounded by his anxious friends, with a pale and haggard countenance, his skin and extremities cold, and his pulse feeble and flickering. But in other respects there was nothing unnatural in his appearance. His consciousness was perfect; he conversed freely; and stated that the pain appeared to be superficial, and confined to the muscles covering his chest, and to his neck and arms, both of which were rendered almost useless."

After taking a simple anodyne, Mr. Wright expressed a wish to return home. The physician and his brother-in-law accompanied him, and offered to support him in walking. But he declined assistance ; his step was free and firm ; and he appeared to walk without difficulty. On reaching his house, he laid down upon the bed, and drafts and other external applications were ordered, to relieve the pain and restore warmth. The physician remained with him nearly half an hour, and made particular inquiries in regard to the symptoms of his attacks, yet he could discover nothing in addition indicating any disease of the brain or of the heart ; there was no exciting cause to produce the attack, as the letter Mr. Wright was reading came from a relative ; and he concluded that they were neuralgic in their character, and had been brought on by severe labor and improper exposure. He then left to visit another patient, but in a few moments was again summoned by the startling announcement, that Silas Wright was dying. He instantly returned, but only to find that all was over. Every effort to restore consciousness proved unavailing. The spirit that animated the mortal frame of the great and good man had fled forever. He is said, by medical men, to have probably died of angina pectoris, or disease of the heart, or blood-vessels immediately connected with it. Shortly after the physician left him, he remarked to his wife, that the drafts were producing too powerful an effect. She took one from his chest to reduce it, and went into an adjoining room. A noise alarmed her, and when she returned to his bedside, it was but to look upon him for the last time in life.

The funeral ceremonies over the remains of Mr. Wright were had on the Sunday following his death. An immense concourse of people assembled from all parts of the county to pay due and appropriate respect to his memory. The attendance was so great that many were unable to witness the services. The discourse was delivered by an old and intimate friend and neighbor, who had been his fellow-student in 1811, and had performed his marriage ceremony. A continued and uninterrupted friendship existed between them from the first period of their acquaintance, and when the speaker referred to the private virtues of the deceased in his early and subsequent life, the audience were most deeply moved. It was the voluntary offering of grateful affection—a eulogy coming from the hearts of those who had known, and revered, and loved him.

The intelligence of the death of Silas Wright produced a powerful effect upon the public mind. It was so sudden—so unexpected—that it thrilled through every heart. When a distinguished public man, who has passed beyond the ordinary limits of mortality, and has apparently fulfilled his destiny upon the earth, is gathered to his fathers, his loss is universally deplored; but when one is cut down in the vigor of manhood, without one note of warning, without any of the premonitory symptoms which usually precede dissolution, the impression is one of deep and awful solemnity. It seems to create a void that cannot be supplied. Like Dewitt Clinton, his predecessor in the chair of state, Silas Wright was removed when a brilliant futurity appeared to smile before him. On the very morning of his death, a paper published in one of the most remote counties in Missouri, hoisted his name as its candidate for the presidency, "subject to the decision of a national convention." Before the sun had set, a Higher Power than that of mere man had decided the question forever. How many hopes were crushed—how many ambitious aspirations blasted—by the death of one, who, it was thought, had so much yet to do, and from whom so much was expected! His loss was mourned without distinction of creed or party, and few there were who did not echo back the exclamation of the poet,*

"Man of the millions, thou art lost too soon!"

The testimonials of regard for the high character of Silas Wright, and the evidences of sorrow for his death, were manifested in all sections of the Union. A public meeting was held of the citizens of Ogdensburgh, in his own county; and among others, the following resolution, presented by one of his most active political opponents, was unanimously adopted:

"Resolved, That having been reared himself under the severe but salutary lessons which labor teaches, his sympathies were keenly awake to the wants and welfare of the toiling million. He was always accessible to their approach, prompt with his counsel to enlighten, and ready to interpose kind offices and attentions where the anguish of disease was to be assuaged, or the pangs of grief alleviated. His life furnishes the invaluable example, that a man may occupy the highest post of honor, and return to private life and severe physical labor, with undiminished dignity."

Mr. Clay was at the White Sulphur Springs in Virginia, when he learned the sad news of Mr. Wright's death. It affected him most sensibly, and he gave utterance to his feelings in a touching and eloquent impromptu to the memory of the deceased. He alluded, in the strongest terms of commendation, to his generous nature, his uncompromising integrity, his

* J. G. Whittier.

accomplished powers in debate, and his eminent public services. What an example was this for politicians—what a reproof to the violent and vindictive partisan! Proud and ambitious though he was, he could forget all their differences of opinion; how earnestly Mr. Wright had combated all his favorite projects; how much he had contributed to his defeat at the presidential election—all these he could forget, at such a time, and be the first to offer a tribute of regard, not more just to the dead, than it was honorable to the living. There are many manly traits in the character of Mr. Clay; he has done many an act of noble disinterestedness—but none more worthy than this of honorable mention.

Some weeks previous to the death of Mr. Wright, a subscription paper was circulated among the merchants in the city of New York, for the purpose of procuring a service of plate to be presented to him in their name. The plate was ordered, bearing the inscription—"Presented to Silas Wright by his mercantile friends of the city of New York, in testimony of their high respect and regard for his public and private character"—and was nearly ready for the presentation. It will now go into the possession of his widow, and be valued, doubtless, as the spontaneous gift of men who sought not official preferment, but who were influenced by their admiration for the talents and attainments of one placed by common consent among the great men of the nation, and who reverenced the virtues which combined to form a character so worthy of respect and esteem.

The common councils of Albany and New York were called together, when the intelligence was received of the sudden decease of Mr. Wright, and took proper measures to express their sympathy. In New York the flags on the public buildings, and of the shipping in the harbor, were displayed at half-mast. Thu pilots of the port also held a meeting, and passed resolutions expressive of their indebtedness to him for "many and signal kindnesses," and of their condolence with Mrs. Wright in her afflicting bereavement. An extra session of the New York Legislature was held on the 8th of September, rendered necessary on account of the recent amendment of the state constitution. On the second day of the session, Governor Young communicated the following message to the two Houses:—

EXECUTIVE CHAMBER,
Albany, Sept. 9, 1847.

"To the Legislature—

SILAS WRIGHT, the late Chief Magistrate of this State, died at his residence in Canton, in the county of St. Lawrence, on the 27th day of August last.

"Although scarcely arrived at the meridian of life, he had not only held the office of Governor of this State, but had discharged, with singular ability, the various duties pertaining to the offices of State Senator, Comptroller, and Senator in the Congress of the United States.

"As a Statesman he occupied a high place among the distinguished public men of the age.

"In private life he enjoyed in an eminent degree, the respect and esteem, of those to whom he was personally known.

"Although his name will go down to posterity without the aid of official records, his eminent public services and great private worth render it proper that I should thus announce to you his death, to the end that such measures may be adopted, as are demanded by the deep feeling that pervades the community.

"JOHN YOUNG."

A joint committee was appointed by the Senate and Assembly, who reported a series of resolutions regretting the loss sustained by the state and country, sympathizing with the kindred and friends, and directing the usual badge of mourning to be worn for thirty days. Eloquent speeches were delivered in the Assembly, by Mr. Perkins of St. Lawrence, and Mr. Hadley, of Rensselaer, before the adoption of the resolutions, and the adjournment which immediately took place. In the Senate, a speech was made by Joshua A. Spencer, who was opposed to Mr. Wright in politics, which was as creditable to himself as it was just and appropriate. He said:—

"Mr. President—Although I have had no opportunity to make the slightest preparation for submitting any remarks, on this melancholy occasion, yet I cannot in justice to my own feelings, permit these resolutions to pass with entire silence. It is indeed, sir, an afflicting dispensation of Providence which has fallen upon our country—not the state only, but the entire country has felt the blow. In truth, a great man, an able statesman, a good citizen, has fallen asleep with his fathers. The statesman whose memory we commemorate, as all well know who are conversant with the history of one of the greatest men in the country, was born in the state of Massachusetts, and was educated in Vermont, where he graduated from one of the highest institutions of learning. He studied his profession in this state, and having obtained a residence in the county of St. Lawrence, he there first commenced his professional and political career. Since that period he has been so well known to the country, and to the world, that I need make no particular allusion to his history.

"Without referring to the local offices which he held, soon after he settled in the county of St. Lawrence, for any other purpose than as furnishing evidence of the just appreciation of his merits as a citizen and a man, and of his ability and talents, I will only remark, that the first office which brought him into general public notice, was that of senator in the Senate of this state. If my memory serves me right, he took his place in the Senate in the year 1824, and from that period I have had the pleasure to know Silas Wright personally, and often, in a legislative capacity, had intercourse with him; and it affords me sincere pleasure to bear my feeble testimony to the great patriotism, integrity, firmness and intellect, which he at all times brought to bear upon every subject—and which distinguished the manner in which he discharged his public duties.

"While holding that office he was transferred to another and larger sphere of action. He was elected to the popular branch of the Congress of the United States in 1826, and again re-elected in 1828. All who know the history of the legislation of the Congress of 1827 and 1828, will remember full well how very soon, indeed that at once, Mr. Wright took and held, and ever maintained a distinguished position in the Congress of the Union. From that station he was transferred to the office of comptroller of this state, which he held for a considerable number of years, and the duties of which office all know to be discharged with singular fidelity. While still holding that position he was again transferred to more enlarged duties. He was elected a senator from the state of New York in the Congress of the United States. And if I am not mistaken in the character and reputation of Silas Wright, it was in that field, more than any other, that he became eminently distinguished as a public man. He was there surrounded by the first talents, not only of his country, but the world. A bright constellation shone there throughout the whole period of his connection with that body; and the most distinguished of his opponents, acknowledged him a foeman worthy of their steel. Courteous in debate, never losing his self-possession, he was ever consistent, clear, logical and convincing.

"From that station, as all know, he was elected governor of this state, which office he held for two years, and had but recently retired from the discharge of those duties, to pursue the quiet walks of agricultural life, on his farm in the county of his early settlement. It is not saying too much to affirm, that there are very few men in this state, or in the nation at large, who have left a more indelible imprint on the records of our country, or whose history will be written in brighter pages than that of Silas Wright. It is not necessary for me to dwell on the public character of this distinguished man: all, even the children of the state, are familiar with it. It may not become me to speak much of Silas Wright in private life, for I had not the pleasure of knowing him intimately in the associations of his neighbors and friends. But there are many others who knew him as such, as well as in the public councils. His great excellence of private worth, in the relations of husband, neighbor, friend and townsman, is universally acknowledged.

"I have but to remark, in conclusion, Mr. President, that this sudden bereavement should admonish us all of the uncertainty of life. No vigor of physical ability, no mental endowments, add to the security of our existence. We have a most melancholy example before us. In the midst of his years, in the day of his greatest usefulness to his country, and with prospects as bright as those of his earliest years, SILAS WRIGHT has been cut down. Let us all be prepared to follow him."

The Agricultural Address written by Mr. Wright, just before his death, was read at the State Fair held in Saratoga on the 16th of September, by his friend John A. Dix, and prefaced with some well-timed and eloquent remarks.* The address was prepared with careful deliberation, and discusses with ability the great questions of political economy connected with agriculture. There is much matter contained in it for earnest thought and serious consideration. Whether its positions be correct, or incorrect, there is not a farmer, not a citizen in the whole land, but will be benefited by its perusal. After it was read, the following resolutions were adopted by the members of the society :—

"Resolved, That the address which has just been read be printed; and that the president be requested to ask the permission of Mrs. Wright to retain the original draft of the address, to be placed in the archives of the society; and to express to her, at the same time, the deep sympathy and regret which is felt by all its members, for the irreparable loss which has so suddenly overwhelmed herself and the state, in a common grief.

"Resolved, That in the death of Silas Wright, late governor of this state, the New York State Agricultural Society have lost a friend and benefactor, an honored and useful member, and the community an illustrious example of republican simplicity in private, as well as inflexible h)nesty and great capacity, in public life.

* See Appendix.

"Resolved, That a committee of this society be appointed by the president thereof, to prepare a brief memoir, illustrative of his character, his virtues, and his eminent public services, for publication, with the address delivered on this occasion, in the transactions for '47—a duty the more gratefully performed, as the last public act of his life, was one of beneficence to the farmers of his country."

But the expressions of sorrow and sympathy, elicited by the death of Mr. Wright, were not confined to his immediate friends and acquaintances; the painful feelings to which it gave rise extended farther and wider: the loss was great, very great to the state he had so long represented in the national councils; but it was equally regretted, equally deplored, throughout the Union. His fame and reputation had extended beyond the limits of New York—they were no longer exclusively her own;—they belonged to the whole country. The powerful intellect which had conferred so much honor upon its possessor, and reflected so much credit upon the land that gave him birth, formed part of that bright galaxy of mind, to which the dweller upon the banks of the Mississippi could point with pride and pleasure, as well as he who resided on the shores of the Atlantic. The painful intelligence, that one so loved, so honored, had passed away forever, in the noontide of life, called forth expressions of regret, at the north and at the south, in the east and in the west. It was not for his own state alone to lament such a calamity—it was for the nation to mourn its bereavement.

In person, Mr. Wright was large and muscular, hale and vigorous. His stature was about five feet and nine or ten inches. His complexion was florid; his hair a light brown; and his eyes of a bluish gray. Constant exercise in early youth had developed his form, and rendered him hearty and robust. He was somewhat inclined to corpulency in later years, but not by any means what could be called gross. He was aware of the plethoric tendency of his constitution, and for that reason, probably, devoted more of his leisure time to manual labor than he otherwise would have done. He dressed quite plainly, and was simple in all his habits. He usually enjoyed excellent health; except in the fall of 1834, he was never known to be seriously ill, until the fatal attack that terminated his existence.

In his domestic relations, he was everything that could be desired—a tender and affectionate husband—a faithful and devoted friend. He had no children. As has been beautifully said of Washington and Jackson—"Providence denied him these, that he might the better serve his country;" or, as he himself expressed it, "that he might be a father to the children of his friends!" His manners were affable, and his address pleasing and agreeable. He never forgot the dignity of his position or of his character; but he always had a kind word and a cheerful smile to greet those who visited him. As a citizen, he was generous and public spirited, and the influence of his example was upon the side of morality and good order. Says one who knew him intimately for many years: "In his social intercourse, I never heard him utter an unchaste word or an immoral sentiment. Whenever he returned from his public positions, to the place of his residence, he returned to the simple, frugal, and industrious habits of a New England farmer, and to the kind and neighborly offices which so eminently distinguished the early rural population of our pilgrim fathers."

In the public schools and seminaries of learning, in his own county, and in the state at large, he took a deep interest. Anything designed to increase the happiness, or promote the prosperity, of his fellow-citizens, was sure to receive his patronage and encouragement. He was not in affluent circumstances, yet he possessed what, to one of his moderate wants, was a competency. Though he had filled many high offices, and occupied situations which afforded him frequent opportunities for the acquisition of wealth, his thoughts were directed to other, and, unless riches are sought in the proper spirit, to what may be called nobler purposes. His punctuality was proverbial. After he became a member of the Senate, his correspondence was extensive, and often proved a great tax to him, in time, if not in money. But he was never forgetful of those who addressed him, and invariably adhered to his rule, not to leave a letter unanswered for a single day, except where the nature of the subject required a lengthy and deliberate reply.

Silas Wright was not an orator—that is, he would not have been termed eloquent, in the common acceptation of the word. There was no attempt at display in his manner, nor rhetorical embellishment in his language; but he was an able and intelligent speaker. He had not the graceful delivery of Clay, or the emphatic earnestness of Calhoun; yet there was a subdued enthusiasm in his style of speaking that was irresistibly captivating; and though his voice was not pleasant, this was almost instantly forgotten in the beauty of his argument. There was nothing declamatory about him. He appealed to no man's passions or prejudices. He was cool and collected, and carefully preserved his own equanimity, while he avoided giving offence, or provoking ill-feeling. He spoke slowly, but distinctly and fluently, and with evident care and deliberation. His hearers were charmed; and listened, but to be charmed again. Every word seemed to issue forth at the proper time, and in the proper place. All was clear, forcible, logical and persuasive.

He was not destitute of ambition; but his was not that low and grovelling passion which seeks its gratification in the present—it was rather that nobler, and purer, and loftier sentiment, which is directed to higher ends and higher aims; which strives for the welfare of one's country and race; and looks to the future, not over-confident, but trustful and hopeful, for a sure reward. He was totally devoid of selfishness. During the administrations of Jackson and Van Buren, he might have commanded some of the most lucrative offices in the gift of the national executive, but he asked for none of them; and when they were tendered to him, he put them aside, not as Cæsar put aside the crown, to have them urged upon him, but because he was content to remain where he was, in the Senate. The sterling qualities of his mind peculiarly fitted him for the sphere in which he moved. It has been said, that "the book of a statesman is the human heart." No one perused it more attentively than he. His foresight and sagacity were remarkable. He was a sound and careful thinker—clear-headed, practical, and discreet. His mind was evenly balanced and well disciplined. Success was not followed by a lack of caution; and danger did not intimidate him. Like the sturdy Alpine hunter, with the mountain-torrent dashing beneath his feet, and the dreaded avalanche thundering in the distance, he was not indifferent to peril, but firmly and calmly prepared to meet it. Politics appeared to him to be a science worthy of the best energies of his mind, and he sought, in his life and conduct, to give it that elevated character which it deserved. He belonged to a higher grade of politicians—he was a statesman.

But was he successful?—for this, after all, unjust as it may sometimes be, is made by many the surest test of ability and sagacity in a public man. In this respect also, his friends and admirers can find nothing to regret. He opposed the establishment of a National Bank—none has been chartered—and there is scarce a prominent politician in the Union who is willing to risk his popularity in advocating such an institution. He sustained the measures of General Jackson's administration; the results of the subsequent elections have shown that the people approved them. He spoke and voted against the Distribution of the Proceeds of the Public Lands—that measure has never yet been carried into effect. He advocated the Independent Treasury system, long and earnestly—the bill was passed—it was repealed, but revived again, and is now the law of the land. He was in favor of a Revenue Tariff discriminating, incidentally, for the purpose of affording protection to the agricultural, commercial, and manufacturing interests of the country,—he lived to see one in force, differing in some of its details from what he would have prescribed, but approximating more nearly to his views than any similar enactment. There were other questions which he regarded as of great importance, though opportunity did not occur to manifest his sentiments as he might have wished, that were still agitated at the time of his death; but let them be decided when they may, and how they may, his influence will be felt in their decision.

It is said, that his friends in the county where he resided are about to erect a monument over his grave. That is both just and appropriate. Such mementoes serve to point the living where the honored dead repose. While they admonish the beholder, of the uncertainty of life, and the certainty of death; they serve to encourage ambition, and enkindle love of virtue, and love of country. Let the memorial be erected, then; and when that silent tomb in St. Lawrence becomes the Mecca of those who shall live after us, the pilgrim may stand beside it, and feel awed in the presence that will hover around that consecrated spot. Yet, there will be a more enduring monument than this—one that will not perish, like the frail handiwork of man. It will be reared in the memories of the American people. The name and the fame of SILAS WRIGHT will live, as long as philanthropy and patriotism continue to animate the hearts of his countrymen.

APPENDIX.

SPEECH,

ON PRESENTING THE RESOLUTIONS OF THE NEW YORK LEGISLATURE, APPROVING OF THE COURSE OF PRESIDENT JACKSON AND OF THE SECRETARY OF THE TREASURY WITH REGARD TO THE REMOVAL OF THE DEPOSITS.

[Delivered in the United States Senate, January 30, 1834.]

I HOLD in my hand, Mr. President, and am about to ask leave to present to the Senate, certain proceedings of the Legislature of my state, in which that body expresses its sentiments in regard to the removal, (as it is called,) of the public moneys from their deposit in the Bank of the United States, made by order of the secretary of the treasury; in regard to the recharter of the Bank of the United States, and in regard to the existing pressure upon the money market in some portions of the country, with its views of the character and causes of that pressure; and in which, also, that Legislature expresses its pleasure as to the course which the representatives of the state, upon this floor, shall pursue, when called to act upon these questions.

In presenting, a few days since, the proceedings of limited portions of the people of their respective states, upon the same subjects, honorable senators took occasion, no doubt properly, to inform the Senate of the number, character and standing, political as well as personal, of those whose sentiments they laid before us; to tell us as well who they were, as who they were not. I beg the indulgence of the Senate, while, following the example set me, I detail some facts in relation to the body whose proceedings it has become my duty to present, tending to show the extent to which the proceedings themselves claim the respectful attention of Congress.

The whole number of members allowed by the constitution of the state of New York to its Legislature, is one hundred and twenty-eight members of Assembly and thirty-two senators. The members of Assembly are appointed to the fifty-five counties of the state according to their respective population, and the whole territory is divided into eight districts for the election of senators, each district having four, and electing one of the four every year. The proceedings which I am about to present, were passed in the House of Assembly by a vote of one hundred and eighteen for, to nine against, and in the Senate by a vote of thirty-three for, to five against them; thus showing the very unusual occurrence, that of the one hundred and sixty members elected by the people to that Legislature, one hundred and fifty-five were present and acting upon these interesting and important questions.

But, sir, if this unexampled strength and unanimity of expression be entitled to weight, and it surely must be, while authentic evidence of public opinion is allowed an influence in our deliberations, that weight is greatly enhanced by the peculiar circumstances attending the expression. All these members of the popular branch of that Legislature, and eight of the thirty-two senators were elected during the first week in November last, one full month after the change of the deposits, while the vote shows that more than thirteen to one of the members of Assembly voted for, while but one of the eight senators, thus elected, voted against the resolutions. Still, the strength of this vote, taken as an expression of public opinion, will be much increased by an examination of its territorial distribution.

It is well known here, and throughout the country, that the extreme western district of the state of New York, has been unhappily, but most severely agitated, in consequence of an outrage, several years since, committed against the liberty, and probably upon the life, of a citizen. The effects of this outrage have been, not only the engendering of the most bitter domestic feuds, but the partial establishment of a geographical line of separation in feeling between that and the other sections of the state. It is, however, a source of high gratification to myself to be able to state, as I trust it will be of pleasure to all liberal minded men to learn, that this unnatural warfare of feeling is most rapidly subsiding; that the deep wounds which have been created by it, in the social relations of that otherwise highly favored section of the state, are healing fast, and that the time is not distant when the evidence of its existence and effects will entirely disappear. In this section of the state, however, not an expression of complaint as to a pecuniary pressure has been heard; and from the best advices, I believe that, at this moment, its business relations of every description are in a more prosperous and easy condition than they have ever before been. Yet to the west and north-west must we look for every vote against the resolutions, and to this section alone for eleven out of the fourteen of these votes. The remaining three are, with one exception, senators not elected at the election of November last, but in previous years, and all are located beyond the reach of the present pressure; in the agricultural, not in the commercial sections. In those portions of the state embracing our great commercial emporium, (and which I think I may, without arrogance or presumption, style the commercial emporium of the United States,) and the extensive cities of Hudson, Albany, Troy, Schenectady and Utica, and an almost endless number of incorporated trading towns and villages, all surrounded by a dense, intelligent and watchful population, amounting together to at least one million eight hundred thousand souls, there was not found a single member of the popular branch of that Legislature absent from his seat, or not with cheerfulness and alacrity recording his name in favor of the resolutions. Of the hundred and twenty-eight members composing this branch of the Legislature, it is worthy of remark, that the city of New York alone elects eleven, and that every representative from that city, in either branch of the state Legislature, responds to the resolutions which I now lay before the Senate.

Of the members of this Legislature, personally, it is not my intention to speak. The situations they hold and their public acts are the legitimate evidence of the capacity and respectability of the individuals. It is as the organ, upon this occasion, of this deliberative body, representing, as they do, two millions of freemen, nearly the one-sixth part of the entire population of the Union; a population, too, as commercial, nay, sir, I may say more commercial, and employing more capital than any other portion of the country, and collecting and paying into the national treasury fully one-third of its whole revenues; a people having as deep a stake, pecuniary and otherwise, in the prosperity of this country, and as firmly and ardently devoted to its welfare as any other equal portion of its citizens; it is as the organ of such a body, representing such a people, that I submit to the Senate this part of their public proceedings—that I ask to place their almost unanimous opinions as to the conduct of the President, of the secretary of the treasury, and of the United States bank, upon your files, by the side of similar expressions from the states of Ohio and New Jersey; also by the side of different expressions from portions of the people from Boston and New Bedford, in Massachusetts; of Salisbury, in North Carolina, and Newark, in New Jersey, and such other expressions of opinions as are, or as may come before the Senate upon the same subjects; and, at this interesting crisis in the affairs of our common country, I respectfully solicit from the Senate that consideration for these proceedings of the Legislature of my state, which a liberal, just, and unprejudiced estimate of the views and feelings of any respectable portion of the citizens of the country may demand, and no more.

Here, sir, I might resume my seat, and I should do so with pleasure, were it not that a part of what I have felt to be an imperative duty upon this occasion remains to be performed.

In presenting the proceedings of a meeting of a portion of the town of Boston, the honorable senator from Massachusetts, (Mr. Webster,) availed himself of the occasion to express his own views as to the existence of a public pressure, of its cause, and of the appropriate mode of relief. He went further, sir, and called upon all, and especially upon those who sustain the administration upon this floor in relation to the change of the deposits, to give their views as to the future as well as the present posture of the pecuniary affairs of the country. As an individual, and as one considering it one of my highest duties to sustain the administration in this measure, I am ready to respond to the senator with entire frankness; but in thus accepting his call, I must not be understood as for one moment entertaining the vain impression that opinions and views pronounced by me here, or elsewhere, will acquire any importance because they are my opinions and my views. I know well, sir, that my name carries not with it authority anywhere; but I also know that so far as I may entertain and shall express opinions which are, or which shall be found, in accordance with the enlightened public opinion of this country, so far they will be sustained, and no farther.

Following then, Mr. President, the example which has been set for me, I shall abstain from a discussion of controverted points, so far as that can be done, and enable me to state unreservedly my opinions, and to make my views intelligible.

First, then, as to the fact of an existing pressure upon the money market, I believe that the recent extensive and sudden curtailment, by the Bank of the United States, in the facilities for credit, which had before been lavished upon the community, has caused very considerable embarrassment to those in our commercial cities, who had extended widely their moneyed operations, and who had made themselves dependent upon these facilities; but, at the same time, I believe that these inconveniences have been in an unimportant degree, either directly or consequentially, extended to other classes of citizens. I therefore believe further, that the extent of the pressure has been greatly exaggerated, and that the motives for that exaggeration are to be found, primarily, in the belief that the present administration may be brought into disfavor with the people, and may be overthrown through the agency of the panic which is attempted to be gotten up, and secondarily, in the hope that the same panic, if successfully produced, may subserve the interests of the institution by which it has been and is to be raised.

Secondly, as to the immediate cause of the pressure, I concur fully with the senator from Massachusetts, that it is an error to attribute it to the mere fact of the change of the deposits. The reasons he has assigned for that opinion are sufficient. They might be amplified and enforced, but it is unnecessary upon the present occasion. Past experience, concurring facts, and the nature of the transaction, all combine to demonstrate that such a change would not, necessarily, draw after it such a result. I concur also with the honorable senator, (Mr. Webster,) in the position, that the evil complained of is to be attributed to the change which has taken place in the positions which the Government, the Bank of the United States, and the state banks have heretofore occupied relatively towards each other, and to the acts which have followed that change. These positions, as at present existing, are pronounced by the honorable senator to be false. That the attitude which the Bank of the United States has chosen to assume towards the Government and the state banks is a false position, I must cheerfully admit; but that there has been anything in the conduct of either the Government or the state banks to justify or even excuse that attitude, I deny, and hope to have an opportunity to attempt to disprove. From the Government directly no loans could be obtained or were expected, and it was well known that the state banks which have been selected as the fiscal agents of the Government, had extended their loans many millions, and to the utmost limit authorized by the public deposits in their vaults. It is neither shown nor pretended that the other state banks have curtailed their loans in consequence of the change of the deposits, except when the curtailments by the Bank of the United States and its branches have compelled them to do so. We have, however, record evidence from itself, that the Bank of the United States has curtailed its loans, since the first day of August last, and up to the first day of December last, to the enormous amount of $9,697,000, and all this curtailment has taken place in the entire absence of any revulsion in trade, of any scarcity in the country, or any other peculiar cause of embarrassment, existing or anticipated. We need not then grope in the field of speculation for the cause of the present pressure. It stands before us recorded in letters and figures which cannot lie, and which leave us without excuse for misunderstanding, or for affecting to misunderstand it.

Thirdly, as to the motives for this conduct on the part of the bank, I have already said, I deny that a justifiable one is to be found either in the conduct of the Government, or of the state banks, towards it; and I repeat the assertion. Whether or not this curtailment of its business has been rendered necessary on the part of the bank, in consequence of former mismanagement, I need not inquire, inasmuch as the bank itself, and all its friends and supporters, here and elsewhere, most strenuously deny that its present condition furnishes any necessity for increased means. I have looked carefully into the instructions originally given by the secretary of the treasury to the state banks, in relation to the course to be pursued by them towards the Bank of the United States, and I find there nothing to warrant an apprehension that any disposition existed on the part of the Government to injure the bank, or to embarrass it in the prosecution of its lawful business. I have examined, with equal care, the instructions given in regard to the transfer drafts, and the circumstances under which they were to be, and were in fact, used. And these acts of the Government, taken in connection with the large amount of money still left in the bank, and which, upon a different supposition, would assuredly have been also withdrawn, I hold to furnish undeniable evidence that no disposition was entertained or manifested on the part of the Government to wrong this institution. The only design evinced was to exercise a legal right, reserved by the charter, to change the deposits, and to continue an uncompromising, to be sure, but constitutional opposition to the renewal of the charter of the bank. That for these constitutional and legal acts, it has pleased the bank to wreak its vengeance upon the community, I neither allege nor believe. That the state banks have made the slightest hostile movements against it, neither is nor can be pretended. What, then, is the motive for this rapid curtailment? I have not the slightest doubt, Mr. President, that, in the language of the resolutions I hold in my hand, it is to be found, and found only, in an attempt of the bank, "at a time of general prosperity, to produce pecuniary distress and alarm, and in exercising its power with a view to extort a renewal of its charter from the fears of the people." So much for the pressure, and the causes of it.

I will now consider the remedy for the evil which the senator proposes. Leaving the discussion of everything constitutional, political and expedient, the senator, with his usual tact, goes directly to the matter in hand; and with the utmost confidence he tells us, that the remedy is not to be found in the restoration of the deposits, but in the recharter of the present bank. Whatever else may be said of this avowal, it must, at least, be admitted, that it does credit to the candor of the senator. For myself, I thank him, and the country will thank him also. It is time, Mr. President, high time, that things should be called by their right names in relation to the depending controversy; that the veil with which it has hitherto been attempted to disguise the subject, should be torn off, and that the people should know what is the question which is, in fact, occupying the attention of Congress. This being done by the declaration of the senator, there is reason to hope that we may hereafter be, if we have not heretofore been, aided by contributions of public sentiment, so far as the Senate may think proper to allow influences of that sort to enter into its deliberations. And, sir, I venture the prediction, that if the expressions now upon our files, or those which shall hereafter be placed there, as evidences of public sentiment, shall be examined, it will appear that the good sense and ingenuity of the senator in devising this remedy, has only placed him upon a level with the common opinion of the whole community, as to the real question in dispute; that every paper favoring the views of the opponents of the administration, has and will, expressly or impliedly, recognize the fact that the question before the public is "bank or no bank," and that the real issue has that direction, not the disposition of the government deposits. A petition for recharter is a mere matter of form which can at any time be brought forward. A few days, or even a few hours, are sufficient for that object, and we ought not to permit ourselves to doubt that such a petition will be forthcoming, or not, according to the decision of this merely incidental ques tion, now made to assume the place and importance of the real issue.

But, Mr. President, while I highly approve of the open and manly ground taken by the senator from Massachusetts, I differ with him *toto cœlo* as to the remedy he proposes. There is no inducement which can prevail on me to vote for the recharter of the Bank of the United States. I would oppose this bank upon the ground of its flagrant violations of the high trusts confided to it; but my objections are of a deeper and graver character. I go against this bank, and against any and every bank to be incorporated by Congress, whether to be located at Philadelphia, or New York, or anywhere else within the twenty-four independent states which compose this confederacy, upon the broad ground which admits not of compromise, that Congress has not the power, by the constitution, to incorporate such a bank.

I may be over-sanguine, Mr. President, but I do most firmly believe that, in addition to the invaluable services already rendered to his country by the President of the United States, he is, under Providence, destined still to render her a greater than all, by being mainly instrumental in restoring the constitution of the country to what it was intended to be by those who formed it, and to what it was understood to be by the people who adopted it; in relieving that sacred instrument from those constructive and implied additions, under which Congress have claimed the right to place beyond the reach of the people, and without responsibility, a moneyed power, not merely dangerous to public liberty, but of a character so formidable as to set itself in open array against, and to attempt to overrule the Government of the country. I believe the high destiny is yet in store for that venerable man, of disproving the exalted compliment long since paid him by the great apostle of republicanism, "that he had already filled the measure of his country's glory," and that he is yet to accomplish, what neither Thomas Jefferson nor his illustrious successors could accomplish, by adding to the proof which he has so largely contributed to afford, that his country is invincible by arms, the consolatory fact that there is, at least, one spot upon earth where written constitutions are rigidly regarded. I know, sir, that this work, which the President has undertaken, and upon the success of which he has, with his usual moral courage, staked the hard-earned fruits of a glorious life, is full of difficulty. I know well that it will put the fortitude and patriotism of his countrymen to the severest test; but I am happy also to know that he has, in this instance, as heretofore, put himself upon the fortitude and patriotism of a people who have never yet failed him, or any man who was himself faithful to his country in the hour of peril.

Of the course which the state which I have the honor in part to represent here, will take in this great contest, it becomes me, forming so humble a part of its voice in the councils of the nation, and known only by the favors I have received at its hands, to speak with great diffidence. In the resolutions I now lay before the Senate, it has spoken for itself upon most of the points involved. As to the others, I feel that my knowledge of the character of its people, and of the known sentiments of whole masses of its public men, will justify me in the confident expression of an opinion, that the state will sustain the executive to the utmost in this controversy; and that I may say to those who are, and long have been, desirous to restore the constitution, in this regard, to its true reading, "now's the day, and now's the hour," for its accomplishment. At all events, I have the right to say, that I will place myself by the side of the President, to the full extent of the views I have given, and that I desire to stand or fall with my constituents, as they shall determine the result.

I have thus responded, and I hope the senator from Massachusetts will allow fully, to so much of his appeal. I will go on, sir, and cover the whole ground. He has asked, if you will neither recharter the present bank nor establish a new one, what will you do? As an individual, sir, and speaking for myself only, I say I will sustain the executive branch of the Government, by all the legal means in my power, in the effort now making to substitute the state banks instead of the Bank of the United States, as the fiscal agent of the Government. I believe they are fully competent to the object. I am wholly unmoved by the alarms which have been sounded, either as to their insecurity, or influence, or any other danger to be apprehended from their employment. I hold the steps so far taken in furtherance of this object, well warranted by the constitution and laws of the land, and I believe that the honor and best interests of the country, imperiously require that they should be fully sustained by the people, and by their representatives here.

That these views are correct, it is not of course my intention, at this time, to attempt to show. In some stage of the debate upon this great subject, I hope to be able, without trespassing upon the superior claims of others, to have that opportunity.

We have been told, and told emphatically, that things cannot remain as they are; that the powers now vested in and exercised by the secretary of the treasury, are too broad, and that legislative aid is required. If I have not misunderstood the import of remarks, it has also been told to us that such aid will be withheld. To this, I, for the present, only answer, that things are now, in this respect, precisely as they were before the incorporation of the present bank; that the same powers which the secretary of the treasury then had, he has still; that by the change of the deposits from the Bank of the United States, the executive department of the Government has been restored to the control over the places for the safe-keeping of the public moneys, which it had by law before these moneys were deposited with that institution; and that all the laws formerly existing upon the subject are now in full force and wholly unaltered, the only effect of the provision in the charter of the bank being to suspend their operation, until the secretary of the treasury should order and direct that the deposits be made elsewhere than in the vaults of that bank. I further state, as my opinion of the law, that by the act of the secretary of the treasury ordering a change of the deposits, and by that act only, the full power of Congress over the whole subject, has been restored.

If, then, the powers of the secretary are too broad, as the law now stands, it is the duty of Congress to restrict them; while, if the powers of the executive branch of the Government are not now fully adequate to the making and executing of all needful orders, rules, and regulations, for the safe-keeping and convenient management of the public moneys, it is equally the duty of Congress to legislate further upon the subject. And whether Congress do or do not legislate in either case, is a matter wholly between its members and their constituents, for which the secretary of the treasury is in no way responsible.

But, Mr. President, while I am prepared to give to this effort of the Government, to make the state banks our fiscal agent for the safe-keeping and convenient disbursement of the public moneys, a full support and a fair experiment, any effort, come from what quarter it may, to return to a hard-money currency, so far as that can be done by the operations of the Federal Government, and consistently with the substantial interests of the country, shall receive from me a cordial and sincere support; and no one would more heartily rejoice than myself, to meet with propositions which would render such an effort in any degree practicable.

Still are we told by the senator from Massachusetts, that things cannot remain as they are; that unless something, which, according to his views of the subject, would afford relief, be done, the pressure, the distress, and the agitation will continue. I have already stated the source from which, and from which alone, in my judgment, the present pressure proceeds. I have stated, also, without reserve, the object which is, in my opinion, intended to be accomplished by it. Of the correctness of my conclusions, the Senate and the country must judge. If they are, as I believe them to be, well-founded, it is undoubtedly in the power of the bank to continue the pressure, and consequently the agitation of the public mind, to some extent, so long as it shall think it to be for its interest, and not incompatible with its safety to do so. It is not for me to speak as with a knowledge of its intentions in this respect, and the senator from Massachusetts disclaims all information upon the point. I can, therefore, only state my opinion; and it is, that the bank has not entered upon this bold measure without the deepest consideration, and that it will not abandon it, the design not being accomplished, but upon the most stern necessity.

Yet, Mr. President, I trust in God that that necessity will soon, very soon, be made manifest, by the attitude which the nation will assume towards this daring and dangerous institution. The glorious American Revolution was but resistance to moneyed power—yes, sir, to the exercise of a moneyed power, without the consent, and beyond the reach, of the people of this country. To this our fathers opposed a stern and uncompromising resistance. Appeals were made to their fears. Distresses in their pecuniary affairs were pictured to them in colors to have deterred any but the pure spirit of patriotism and love of liberty which led them forward. Then the pictures were not imaginary but real; the distresses were not fancy but fact. The country was not then strong, and rich, and prosperous, but weak, and poor, and disheartened: and still their march was onward. They armed themselves upon the side of their country, and stood by their Government; and when their hard and perilous services were paid in paper, worth a fortieth or sixtieth part of its nominal value, the representative of the dollar was the dollar to them, for it gave liberty to the people, and freed them from the rule of avarice. And have we, their immediate descendants, so soon lost their noble spirit? Are we to fold our arms and obey the dictates of a moneyed power, not removed from our soil, and wielded by stronger hands, but taking root among us: a power spoken into existence by our breath, and dependent upon that breath for life and being? Are our fears, our avarice, our selfish and base passions to be appealed to, and to compel us to re-create this power, when we are told that the circulation of the country is in its hands? That the institutions established by all the independent states of the confederacy are subject to its control, and exist only by its clemency? When we see it setting itself up against the Government and vaunting its power? throwing from its doors our representatives placed at its board, and pronouncing them unskilful, ungenteel, or incorrigible? Nay, Mr. President, when it lays upon our tables in this chamber, its annunciation to the public, classing the President of the United States with counterfeiters and felons, and declaring, that as kindred subjects, both should receive like treatment at its hands? I say, sir, are we to be driven by our fears to recharter such an institution, with such evidences of its power, and of its disposition to use that power, lying before us authenticated by the bank itself? Are we to do this after the question has been referred to the people of the country, fully argued before them, and their decision pronounced against the bank, and in favor of the President, by a majority such as has never before in this Government marked the result of a contest at the ballot boxes?

Gentlemen talk of revolutions in progress. When this action shall take place in the American Congress, then indeed will a revolution have been accomplished;—then will your constitution have been yielded up to fear and favor, and your legislation be the *sic volo, sic jubeo*, of a bank. But, Mr. President, I do not distress myself with any such forebodings. I know the crisis will be trying, and I know too, that the spirit and patriotism of the people will be equal to the trial. As I read the indications of public opinion, I see clearly that the true question is understood by the country, and that it is assuming an attitude towards the bank which the occasion calls for. Be assured, sir, whatever nice distinctions may be drawn here as to the share of influence, which expressions of the popular will upon such a subject are entitled to from us, it is possible for that will to assume a constitutional shape which the Senate cannot misunderstand, and understanding, will not unwisely resist. The country, Mr. President, has approved of the course of the executive, in his attempts to relieve us from the corrupt and corrupting power and influence of a national bank, and it will sustain him in the experiment now making to substitute the state institutions for such a fiscal agent. I have the fullest confidence in the ultimate and complete success of the trial; but should it not prove satisfactory to the country, it will then be time enough to resort to the conceded powers of Congress, or to ask from the people what, until every other experiment be fairly and fully tried, they will never grant, the power to establish a National Bank.

SPEECH,

RELATIVE TO THE REMOVAL OF THE DEPOSITS FROM THE BANK OF THE UNITED STATES, THE SPECIAL ORDER BEING THE REPORT OF THE SECRETARY OF THE TREASURY, ASSIGNING HIS REASONS FOR SUCH REMOVAL, AND THE TWO RESOLUTIONS OF MR. CLAY.

[Delivered in the United States Senate, March 26th, 1834.]

MR. PRESIDENT:

I rise with unfeigned reluctance to address the Senate. The debate has been so long protracted, and has been so full and able upon all the points involved in the discussion, that I feel fully conscious I can give no light, and add no interest, to what has been already advanced. I would decline troubling the Senate at all, at this late stage of the debate, were it not that I consider the first resolution as particularly exceptionable, in every sense in which I have been able to view it. I had intended, at an early period of the debate, to offer my views at large upon the whole subject, and I had made some preparations to fulfil that intention; but the progress of the discussion induced me to abandon position after position which it had been my purpose to occupy, in consequence of the full and able views given of them by others, until I have brought myself to the conclusion, to confine my remarks wholly to the first of the resolutions offered by the senator from Kentucky. I came to the conclusion definitely, after the very able argument of my honorable colleague [Mr. Tallmadge], recently made to the Senate, upon all the grounds covered by the second resolution, and generally embracing all the reasons of the secretary of the treasury. I can add nothing more to that argument, and any attempt on my part to do so, would be more likely to weaken the positions which have been so well defended, than to secure the defences, already, in my judgment, sufficiently impregnable. I may also say, that I do not expect to advance anything in relation to the first resolution, which has not before, in the course of the debate, been suggested; but I do hope to offer a more detailed and connected argument upon that single point, than has been offered by those who have preceded me, and who have embraced the whole scope of the special order. I owe it to myself, however, as well as to the Senate, to say that it is my intention to confine myself to a strict legal argument, of the most dry and uninteresting character, and that I can neither expect, nor ask, that attention which I might hope, were the subject less exhausted, and the topics less technical.

The resolution is in the following words:—

"Resolved, That by dismissing the late secretary of the treasury, because he could not, contrary to his sense of his own duty, remove the money of the United States, in deposit with the Bank of the United States and its branches, in conformity with the President's opinion, and by appointing his successor to effect such removal, which has been done, the President has assumed the exercise of a power over the treasury of the United States, not granted by the constitution and laws, and dangerous to the liberties of the people."

This is the resolution, and I consider it, in the broadest sense, judicial, so far as the action of the Senate upon it is concerned. I therefore, preliminarily, lay down the following proposition, which I believe I shall be able to sustain, not only from the language and import of the resolution itself, but from an examination of the grounds upon which its friends seek to justify the action by this body. My proposition is:—

That the resolution contains matter of impeachment, and matter of impeachment only, and therefore that it is unconstitutional for the Senate to act upon it, other than judicially, and upon an impeachment sent up from the House of Representatives.

Art. 1, sec. 2, clause 5, of the Constitution of the United States, reads as follows:—

"The House of Representatives shall choose their speaker, and other officers, *and shall have the sole power of impeachment.*"

Sec. 3, clause 6, of the same article, says:—

"The Senate shall have the sole power to try all impeachments."

Here then, sir, are the constitutional divisions of power, between the two branches of Congress, as to impeachments.

Does the resolution under consideration contain impeachable matter, so as to call upon these powers to enable us properly to act upon it?

It charges that "the President has assumed the exercise of a power over the treasury of the United States, not granted to him by the constitution and laws, and dangerous to the liberties of the people;" and that he has "assumed the exercise of that power, by dismissing the late secretary of the treasury, because he would not, contrary to his sense of his own duty, remove the money of the United States, in deposit with the Bank of the United States, and its branches, in conformity with the President's opinion; and by appointing his successor to effect such removal, which has been done."

The first of these charges, if well made, must be a high crime. An assumption of a power over the public treasury, not granted by the constitution and laws, and dangerous to the liberties of the people, can surely be nothing less.

The second, to wit, the removal of a secretary of the treasury, for an insufficient cause, and under the influence of an improper motive, viz., to acquire a power over the public treasury not granted by the constitution and laws, and dangerous to the liberties of the people, if sustained as charged, cannot be less than a high misdemeanor.

Art. 2, sec 4, of the Constitution, says:—

"The President, Vice President, and all civil officers of the United States, shall be removed from office, on impeachment for, and conviction of, treason, bribery, *or other high crimes and misdemeanors.*"

The advocates for the resolution do not deny that it contains impeachable matter, but they justify the action of the Senate, as they say, "legislatively" upon it.

The honorable senator from Kentucky [Mr. Clay], says, "The Senate ought to act upon the resolution, to protect its legislative powers."

It is not pretended that the *legislative* powers of the Senate have been assailed. The resolution does not assume to recite an act of infringement upon the *legislative* powers of the Senate. It assumes *executive* encroachments, and executive encroachments only, and proceeds at once to pronounce judgment upon them. It proposes no *legislative* act, nor does it assert any *legislative* power. If, then, the Senate has the right to protect its legislative powers, as it no doubt has, the resolution neither asserts the right contended for, nor mentions the violation against which protection is required, nor does it propose any sort of protection. It does not therefore come, in any sense, within this principle of the senator, and the action of the Senate upon it finds no justification in his remark. I pass to the senator's second ground:—

"The Senate may properly act upon the resolution, because the President may perform an unconstitutional act, without the *quo animo*, the intention to violate the constitution."

It is impossible to consider this opinion in connection with the objection to which it is intended to be an answer, without taking it as an admission that the action of the Senate upon the resolution is judicial. The *quo animo* of the President, or of any other officer of the Government, as to any act performed by them, bearing upon their constitutional powers, cannot possibly be material to the Senate in its legislative character. If legislation should be required, growing out of any such act, it would legislate to provide a remedy for the wrong committed, or to prevent a repetition of the act; and in either case, the *quo animo* of the officer performing the act complained of, could not be material. The wrong would not be less, or the remedy different, whether the action should proceed from design or ignorance. If, therefore, the determination of the existence or not of the *quo animo* in the act recited in the resolution, be material to the question whether the Senate can, or cannot, properly act upon it legislatively, that fact proves the resolution to be judicial, until that point shall be judicially decided. And as no object of legislation is either proposed, or to be accomplished by the passage of the resolution, any action of the Senate upon it, going to decide this preliminary question of the *quo animo*, is clearly a judicial action, and therefore an assumption of power, in violation of the constitutional powers of the body.

The position concedes that if the *quo animo* be assumed, the question would be judicial, while the resolution, the *quo animo* being added, would, according to a farther admission by the ground taken, be not only an impeachment, but a judgment of condemnation upon the charges made. It follows then, irresistibly, that the action of the Senate legislatively, would be a judgment of acquittal as to the *quo animo*, and that judgment is as much judicial as a judgment of condemnation could be. Again, therefore, I repeat, that the Senate cannot act upon this resolution constitutionally, in any other than its capacity of the high court for the trial of impeachments. The senator [Mr. Clay] says thirdly:—

"The Senate may act upon the resolution, because the President may not be impeached, even if the act and the *quo animo* are both found against him."

Here we meet a most singular reason for action. The court will condemn the accused, because the grand jury *may* not find a bill against him: the Senate of the United States, will convict the President of the United States, of a flagrant violation of the constitution of the United States, because the House of Representatives, those who hold in their hands the voice of the people of the country, may not impeach him. But again, the fourth reason for action is still more singular.

The action of the Senate is proper, "because a call upon the Senate to act *judicially* in this instance, depends upon a contingency, which no one now expects will happen."

This throws the last proposition into the shade. Here the sentence of condemnation is to be pronounced, because *no one expects* the grand inquest will even indict. The Senate of the United States, are to convict the President of the United States, of a flagrant violation of the constitution, because "no one expects" the House of Representatives will impeach him. Strange causes, indeed, for performing judicial duties, in a legislative character.

The senator [Mr. Clay] has told us of the "bleeding constitution of his country;" and is this the way in which the wounds of that instrument are to be healed? Is an alleged violation of the constitution by the executive, to be cured by a palpable violation of that instrument by the Senate? Will the Senate sanction such reasons for acting upon such a resolution?

But the senator from New Jersey [Mr. Southard], sanctions the same idea by the following language:—

"It is objected to the first resolution, that the Senate ought not to act upon it, because this body may be called upon to act upon the same matter, brought before it in the shape of an impeachment. An impeachment of whom?" says the senator. "An impeachment of Andrew Jackson? An impeachment of Roger B. Taney? Look at the history of the country. Did any one ever hear of the impeachment of those who stand in an overwhelming majority? No, sir, such persons have a shield impenetrable to the Senate."

Here we have the principle fully developed. The Senate is to proceed to judgment of condemnation against the President, because the representatives of the people will not impeach him; because an "overwhelming majority" of the people themselves, whom they represent, are in favor of the President, and approve of his conduct.

If any cause can be more sure than another, to render the Senate odious to the people of the country, it will be attempts here to assume the duties of the immediate representatives of the people; to constitute ourselves the accusers as well as the judges; and, having done this, to resist the known and expressed will of the people, in bringing down upon the head of some too popular servant, the tremendous judicial sentence of this body, without the form of a trial, or even the exhibition of a constitutional accusation.

Do these sentiments come from men who have been raised high in the honors of the republic? Who have themselves been counsellors of a former President? And at a time, too, when a majority of this body, holding this judicial power over their acts, was politically opposed to the administration with which they were thus connected? Sir, I venture the assertion, that they never found that majority attempting thus to condemn them, or their principal, without a trial; and I further venture to say, that that majority, so acting, were sustained by the people.

I assume, in the second place,

That the resolution, if such as the Senate could properly entertain, is irrelevant to the subject before this body, and in relation to which it purports to have been introduced, and therefore, should not be entertained.

The special order before the Senate, is the report of the secretary of the treasury, assigning his reasons for the change of the deposits of the public moneys of the United States, from the Bank of the United States.

It has no reference whatever to the President, the late secretary of the treasury, his appointment or removal, or to the appointment of the present secretary. It relates solely to a single official act of his own, the change of the deposits; and merely assigns, in obedience to an express requirement of law, his reasons for that act. It says nothing of his predecessor in office, of what he would or would not do, or what was or was not his sense of duty. It makes no allusion to him whatever.

Where, then, is the relevancy of this resolution, to this special order?

I next assume that the resolution, if within the constitutional jurisdiction of the Senate; and relevant to the subject of the special order, is erroneous in both of its conclusions, and in the fact assumed, upon which the conclusions depend.

The fact stated is, that the President "assumed the exercise of a power over the treasury of the United States," and the sense in which the charge is made, is learned from the language of the advocates of the resolution. The President is said to have taken possession of the public money; to have opened the public treasury, and taken therefrom its contents; to have united the sword and purse of the country in the same hand; to have robbed the treasury, and taken into his own keeping the money of the people. Now, in this sense, I affirm that the President has exercised no power whatever, over the treasury of the United States. What acts are mentioned as constituting this charge?

The resolution recites that the President removed from office the late secretary of the treasury.

One of the earliest debates in the first Congress, convened under the present constitution of the United States, was upon the question of the power of the President to remove from office, according to the provisions of that constitution. The question was decided by that Congress in favor of the power, as a part of "the executive power" vested in the President by that instrument, and the whole practice of the Government, and of every President, from Washington to the present incumbent of that high office, has been in conformity with that decision. The power was decided to exist, and to be derived from the constitution itself.

It is particularly worthy of remark, that the power to remove the secretary of the treasury, occupied a conspicuous place in the debate, and furnished a very considerable portion of the argument of the speakers on both sides of the question. The decision, therefore, was made, after full argument as to the power to remove this very officer.

The President, then, in the removal of the late secretary of the treasury, did not "assume the exercise of a power not granted to him by the constitution and laws."

But a removal of the secretary of the treasury, does not enable the President to gain access to the treasury of the United States.

There is a treasurer, appointed by the President and Senate, who keeps the keys of the public treasury. Were the President, therefore, to remove the secretary, he would meet the treasurer, and must dispose of him, before he could reach the public treasury.

This officer is removable by the President, but he has not removed him, which fact, of itself, repels the idea that he has attempted to "assume the exercise of a power over the public treasury."

Here might be rested the proof of the falsity of the fact stated in the resolution, that the President "assumed the exercise of a power over the public treasury," but it shall be carried one step further.

It is not even contended that one cent of money was taken from the public treasury, between the time of the removal of the late secretary of the treasury, and the appointment of the present incumbent to that office; nor is it contended that any change of the deposits of money standing to the credit of the treasurer, or any other change or order, affecting the public treasury, was made during that interval.

The advocates for the resolution then admit, that the power exercised over the public treasury, by the President, was not so exercised during the vacancy created in that office, by the removal of the late secretary.

The resolution further recites, that the President appointed the present secretary in the place of the late secretary removed.

The constitution says, "the President shall have power to fill any vacancies that may happen during the recess of the Senate, by granting commissions, which shall expire at the end of the next session."

The President, then, had power to appoint a secretary of the treasury in the place of the late secretary, removed, and in this act he did not "assume the exercise of a power," "not granted to him by the constitution and laws."

When, then, has the President "assumed the exercise of a power over the treasury of the United States not granted to him by the constitution and laws?" It has not been contended that, since the appointment of the new secretary, any money has been drawn from the public treasury, but by his direction. His report before the Senate shows that the deposits were changed by his orders, and gives to Congress his reasons for the act; though it should be borne constantly in mind, that the change of the deposits took not one dollar from the treasury.

It was, if I may be allowed the expression, the mere change of the location of the chest, or the strong box; it was not the use of the treasurer's key; it was not taking any thing from the treasury, or subtracting anything from the amount for which he stood chargeable to the country. The power was exercised over the place for keeping the treasury, not over the money itself.

The foregoing remarks seem to establish conclusively the following propositions :—

That the President "assumed the exercise of a power" over the late secretary of the treasury, by removing him from office, as he had a constitutional right to do.

That he "assumed the exercise of a power" granted to him in terms by the constitution, to appoint, "during the recess of the Senate," the present secretary, to fill the vacancy occasioned by the removal of the late secretary.

That he has not "assumed the exercise of a power over the treasury of the United States," or over the treasurer of the United States, of any description whatever.

That he has not "assumed the exercise" of any power in reference to the subject of the resolution, "not granted to him by the constitution and laws." I might here safely rest my argument upon this first resolution, merely drawing from the foregoing propositions the natural corollary—

That as the President has only "assumed the exercise" of powers expressly granted by the constitution, he has not "assumed the exercise" of any power "dangerous to the liberties of the people," unless the powers granted to him by the constitution of the United States, and exercised by the Presidents of the United States, from the commencement of the Government under the constitution to the present time, are "dangerous to the liberties of the people."

But I feel bound, from a sense of respect to the gentlemen who advocate the resolution, as well as from a disposition to place the whole subject in a clear light before my constituents and the country, to notice the positions taken upon the other side, from which the inference in the resolution is drawn, that the President, in changing his secretary, has "assumed the exercise of a power not granted to him by the constitution and laws."

Neither of the gentlemen [Messrs. Clay and Southard] have been understood as denying the constitutional power of the President to remove a secretary of the treasury, but the attempt seems to be to prove that the removal of the late secretary was made under circumstances to which the power of removal does not extend.

What are the circumstances upon which the gentlemen rely to

take this case out of the general power of removal conferred upon the President? I take their own statements.

There is a law of Congress incorporating the stockholders of the Bank of the United States.

The law directs the deposit of the moneys of the United States with the bank; but gives to the secretary of the treasury the power to change that deposit.

The President thought the late secretary ought to exercise that power, and divert the public moneys from the bank.

The secretary thought he ought not to exercise the power, and refused to do so.

The President considered the execution of the law important to the country, and removed the secretary who refused to execute it.

Here we meet with what has been harshly termed "the act of persecution, usurpation, tyranny, a most flagrant violation of the constitution and the laws of the land, an assumption of the exercise of a power not granted to him" [the President] "by the constitution and laws, and dangerous to the liberties of the people."

I propose to look at this state of facts, at the constitution and the law, and then to test the applicability of these strong denunciations against the President of the United States made in the Senate of the United States.

The positions assumed to justify the conclusions in favor of the resolution and against the President, are

First. That the removal was made because the late secretary refused to do an act "contrary to his sense of his own duty." In other words, it is called "an act of persecution for opinion's sake."

What practical meaning has this position? Was ever an officer removed where the cause of removal did not exist in a difference of opinion between the power of removal and the agent to be removed? where the agent or officer did not refuse to do an act which the removing power thought he ought to do, or insist upon doing an act which the removing power thought he ought not to do?

I answer, there is but one possible case in which a removal from office can take place, without a cause, in one shape or another, growing out of these differences of opinion between the removing and removed officer; and as that case must be utter incompetency, I congratulate the advocates of the resolution upon the fact, that they are not compelled, in reference to the late secretary, whom they so warmly eulogize, and towards whom their sympathies are so kindly extended, to resort to this cause alone for his removal; but are able to show that a difference of opinion between him and the President, furnishes a probable ground for his loss of office. Removal, "for opinion's sake," then, is nothing more or less than a removal growing out of a difference of opinion between the removing power and the officer to be removed.

The power to remove is admitted; but the power to remove on account of a difference of opinion between the removing officer and the officer to be removed, is denied.

What is the practical effect of this construction of the power of removal conferred by the constitution upon the President? It is, that he may remove those who agree with him in opinion; those who are willing and desirous to aid his measures and give efficiency to his administration; those with whom he can live and act in harmony; his political and personal friends: but that he cannot remove those who differ with him in opinion; those who will not carry into effect the measures of his administration; those who are personally and politically hostile to him.

I shall presently examine this power, and see if its proper construction leads to such absurdities.

Secondly. The senator from Kentucky [Mr. Clay] lays down the distinct proposition, that "the secretary of the treasury is not an executive officer, nor is the treasury department an executive department."

A sufficient answer, in legal argument, to this proposition is, that the power of removal, conferred upon the President by the constitution, extends to the removal of the secretary of the treasury, whether he be or be not an executive officer, and whether his department be or be not an executive department; and this the advocates of the resolution admit. The whole proposition, therefore, in its application here, goes merely to question the sufficiency of the cause of the removal, and not to deny the constitutional or legal power. It stands, then, with the proposition just examined, in this respect, and will be further replied to when the power of removal shall be examined.

I cannot, however, be understood as admitting the facts assumed by this proposition, "that the secretary of the treasury is not an executive officer," and that "his department is not an executive department."

I will not, however, enter in detail into the proofs which show that the position, in every sense, is mistaken in fact, as others have already fully done this; but will content myself with taking a very brief view of the position, as compared with the provisions of the constitution alone, wholly without reference to the laws establishing and regulating the department.

The senator from Kentucky [Mr. Clay] read from the President's communication to his cabinet, as follows:—

"Upon him [the President] has been devolved by the constitution and the suffrages of the American people, the duty of superintending the operations of the executive departments of the Government, and seeing that the laws are faithfully executed."

When he said, "This I deny! The constitution does not devolve these duties upon the President.

"The laws organizing the executive departments, except the treasury department, put these departments under the direction of the President; but it is the law, not the constitution, from which he derives his authority."

We will see what the constitution does confer upon the President in relation to the executive departments. It reads as follows:—

"The *executive power* shall be vested in a President of the United States of America."

Now, as I cannot yield to the force of the comment of the learned senator, in another part of his argument, that the provision in the bank charter, "that the business of the institution should be conducted by a board of directors," was not saying "that *all* the business should be so conducted, I must be permitted to believe that the constitution, when it says, "the executive power shall be vested in a President of the United States of America," means that *all* the executive power, not otherwise expressly granted, shall be so vested, and not that a part of it only should pass by that grant, and that the residue should be conferred by Congress, to which body as a Congress, that instrument gives no executive power.

The only grant of executive power, to be found in the constitution, other than that above quoted, is the grant to the Senate in relation to appointments to office; and as this last grant is defined and specific, it certainly cannot extend to an executive supervision over the executive departments.

If, then, the treasury department be an *executive* department, the constitution has devolved upon the President the duty of superintending its operations, as it has "vested" in him all the "executive power" of the Government, except the specific grant to the Senate, relating to appointments.

Is the treasury department an executive department? The duties of it are executive. The head of it is appointed as the executive officers are; is made one of the constitutional advisers of the executive; a member of his confidential cabinet; and is bound to give his opinion, when called for, in any matter relating to the executive Government—the characteristics of the department, therefore, are purely executive. But, if not executive, to which of the other great departments does it belong? The constitution has created another, called the legislative department. The following is the provision:—

"All legislative powers herein granted, shall be vested in a Congress of the United States, which shall consist of a Senate and House of Representatives."

Surely, the treasury department can find no place under this grant. Its duties are in no respect legislative. The secretary does not receive his appointment from the people, the states, or the legislature, and he is removable at the pleasure of the President, but not otherwise, except upon an impeachment by the House of Representatives, and a judgment of condemnation by the Senate. The legislature cannot remove him.

The constitution has created a third great department of the Government, called the judicial department. The following is the provision:—

"The judicial power of the United States shall be vested in one supreme court, and in such inferior courts as the Congress may from time to time ordain and establish."

The treasury department certainly is, in no judicial sense, a court, and cannot, therefore, be a judicial department.

From the constitution itself, then, it appears, that the treasury department is an executive department, and cannot belong to either of the other great departments into which that instrument has divided all the powers of the Government of the United States.

That Congress has not the power, by the constitution, to establish a similar department, and divest it of the executive character given to all those departments by the constitutional disposition of the governmental powers.

That the constitution has vested in the President of the United

States "the executive power," and by virtue of that grant of power, has devolved upon him "the duty of superintending the operations of the executive departments of the Government."

I am discharged, therefore, from all necessity of an examination of the laws relative to this department, as they surely will be so construed as to make them conform to the constitution, unless provisions shall be found wholly irreconcilable to it, and no such provisions have been pointed out.

What then is this supervisory power of the President over the executive departments?

The constitution answers in the following language:—

"He [the President] shall take care that the laws be faithfully executed."

In what manner is he to do this? The senator from Kentucky [Mr. Clay] contends, that this clause of the constitution only means "that if resistance to the law be made, the President shall see that such resistance be overcome." The senator considers the power as intimately connected with the power to call out the militia to enforce the laws, and as going no farther than to oppose and to overcome resistance against the execution of a law. This would confound this most important duty of the President with his powers and duties arising under the various laws which have been passed "to provide for calling forth the militia to execute the laws of the Union, suppress insurrections, and repel invasions;" powers and duties strictly military, and derived by the President, not from the constitution, but from laws of Congress passed in pursuance of the power given to that body by the provision of the constitution above recited.

With proper submission to the views of the honorable senator, I think it most clear that the power in question is wholly of a civil character, and that the duty imposed pertains exclusively to the executive power of the President. It enjoins upon him constant vigilance over all the civil affairs of the Government. "He shall *take care* that the laws be faithfully executed." It may be inquired, "Suppose he meets with a refusal on the part of the officer to do his duty and to execute the laws, how is he to enforce obedience?" I answer—not by calling out the militia upon the officer, but by promptly removing him from his office, where that power is in his hands, and, where it is not, by laying the facts before the House of Representatives, to the end that an impeachment may remove him.

It is unquestionably for this purpose that the wisdom of the convention vested "the executive power" in the President; and this apparent necessity which induced the decision by the first Congress under the constitution, that the power of removal from office was a part of the executive power, and was in the hands of the executive.

The senator from New Jersey [Mr. Southard] was understood to contend, that the cause of the removal, operating upon the mind of the President to induce the act, was material to the constitutionality or unconstitutionality, legality or illegality, of the act of removal. Indeed, I am unable to discover the force of this argument, as made by the senator, and as applicable to the resolution, unless he intended to give it this direction. The resolution charges, that the President has "assumed the exercise of a power" "not granted to him by the constitution and laws;" and the senator expressly admitted the power, in some cases, to remove, and denied it in the case recited in the resolution, upon the ground that the cause of the removal was insufficient to justify the act.

This brings me to an examination of this power of removal. Its existence in the President has not only been before shown, but is admitted to some extent, by all the advocates of the resolution. What, then, is the extent of this power?

The power itself was decided, by the first Congress convened under the constitution, to exist in, and to be derived from, that instrument, as a necessary part of "the executive power" vested in the President. As such it has been exercised by every executive under the constitution.

This instrument imposes no limitation whatever upon the power, other than the liability to impeachment for any abuse of that, as well as of any other power conferred upon the executive, which shall amount to a high crime or misdemeanor. The cause of the act of removal, therefore, as the motive which, in the mind of the executive, induced it, is not a constitutional limit upon the exercise of the power, but a mere test of the liability incurred in its exercise in any given case.

It follows, then, that if the President, so far as the constitution is concerned, has power to remove the officer for good cause, a removal of him for an insufficient cause, or from a bad motive, does not make the act unconstitutional; the cause and the motive having relation only to the liability of the executive to an impeachment, and not to the validity of the act of removal.

It remains to inquire, whether any law of Congress has restricted this power, or connected its exercise with the cause or motive which leads to it. The very remark shows what the answer must be, as the power, being derived solely from the constitution, and being unlimited by that instrument, any law which should impose limits would be unconstitutional. But without resting upon this answer, my research has not enabled me to find any such law; the advocates of the resolution have referred to no such law; and I believe I am safe in saying that no law has ever been passed, assuming to impose restrictions or limitations upon the executive power of removal from office of the secretary of the treasury. Any removal of that officer by the President, therefore, whether made in consequence of a difference of opinion between the officers, or from whatever cause—whether he be denominated an executive officer, or be not—cannot either be unconstitutional or illegal.

As to this first resolution, then, I now come to the following conclusive and simple propositions:—

The resolution charges the President with having "assumed the exercise of a power over the treasury of the United States, not granted to him by the constitution and laws, and dangerous to the liberties of the people."

The charge is based upon the assumed facts, that the late secretary was removed from office, "because he would not, contrary to his sense of his own duty, remove the money of the United States, in deposit with the Bank of the United States and its branches, in conformity with the President's opinion;" and that his successor, the present secretary, was appointed to "effect such removal, which has been done."

The conclusions are:—

That the President has, by the constitution, the power of removal of a secretary of the treasury, wholly without limitation, he being liable to an impeachment for a criminal exercise of the power.

That he has, by the constitution, the unlimited power to appoint, "during the recess of the Senate," a secretary of the treasury, whenever that office shall be vacant, he being also liable to impeachment for a criminal exercise of this power.

That neither the removal from office of a secretary of the treasury, nor the appointment of a successor to fill the vacancy, is an assumption of "the exercise of a power over the treasury of the United States;" or, if it is,

That it is "the exercise of a power over the treasury of the United States," vested in the President by the constitution, as necessarily growing out of his unrestrained power of removal, and his equally unrestrained power "to fill any vacancies that may happen during the recess of the Senate."

Here I leave this first resolution, repeating, that any action of the Senate upon it, other than in its judicial capacity, will be a flagrant violation of the constitution; that considered legislatively, it is wholly irrelevant to the subject before the Senate; that it is entirely erroneous in its assumptions of fact and conclusions of law; and that any acts of the President to which it alludes, wholly fail to justify the harsh terms which have been applied to them by the advocates of the resolution.

But we are still called upon to vote for this resolution; and who, Mr. President, is it upon whom the sentence of the Senate is thus to be passed without a trial? The officer, sir, is none other than the chief executive officer of the Government—the President of the United States; he whom the people elected to that high station, by their free suffrages, against the popularity and power of a competitor holding the office, and wielding its patronage—a patronage now represented to be so immense and irresistible and dangerous;—and wielding it too with the aid of skilful and experienced advisers. It is no other than that President, who after four years of official trial before the people, was re-elected against another competitor, selected from among the distinguished of his countrymen, for his superior hold upon the popular feeling of the country, and re-elected, too, by a vote more decisive than any which had ever before marked the result of a long and severe political contest. Such, Mr. President, is the officer—I had like to have said,—upon his trial. No, sir, it is not so—who is not to be allowed a trial; but who is about to receive the condemnatory sentence of the Senate unheard.

Who, sir, is the man, the citizen of our republic, upon whom we are about to pronounce our high censures? Is it Andrew Jackson? Is it that Andrew Jackson, who, in his boyhood, was found in the blood-stained fields of the Revolution? Who came out from that struggle the last living member of his family? Who, when the sound to arms again called our citizens around the flag of our country, posted himself upon the defenceless frontiers of the South and West, and bared his own bosom to the tomahawks and scalping-knives, sharpened for the blood of unprotected women and children?

Who turned back from the city of the West, the confident advance of a ruthless, and until then, unsubdued enemy, and closed the second war against American liberty in a blaze of glory, which time will not extinguish? Who, when peace was restored to his beloved country, turned his spear into a pruning hook, and retired to his Hermitage, until the spontaneous voice of his fellow-citizens called him forth to receive their highest honors, and to become the guardian of their most sacred trust? Is this the man who is to be condemned without a trial? Who is not entitled to the privilege allowed him by the constitution of his country? Sir, this surely should not be so. For the very act which saved a city from pillage and destruction, and the soil of his country from the tread of an invading enemy, this individual was accused of a violation of the constitution and laws of his country. For the very act which entitled him to the proud appellation of "the greatest captain of the age," he was convicted and condemned as a criminal. But, Mr. President, he was not then denied a trial. Then he was permitted to face his accusers, to hear the charges preferred against him, to offer his defence, and to be present at his sentence. In gratitude for these privileges of a freeman, he stayed back with his own arm the advancing wave of popular indignation, while he bowed his whitened locks to the sentence of the law, and paid the penalty imposed upon him for having saved and honored his country.

Grant to him, I beseech you, Mr. President; I beseech the Senate, grant to that old man the privilege of a trial now. Condemn him not unheard, and without the pretence of a constitutional accusation. His rivalships are ended. He asks no more of worldly honors. "He has done the state some service." Age has crept upon him now, and he approaches the grave. Let him enjoy, during the short remainder of his stay upon earth, the right secured to him by the constitution he has so often and so gallantly defended, and, if indeed, he be criminal, let his conviction precede his sentence.

SPEECH ON THE TARIFF.

[Delivered in the United States Senate, April 19th and 23rd, 1844.]

[Mr. McDuffie, of South Carolina, introduced in the Senate a bill proposing to reduce all duties, under the present tariff law, which are above the rate of 20 per cent., to that rate, by gradual reductions. That bill was referred to the Committee on Finance, and the committee reported the bill back to the Senate, without amendment, with a resolution recommending its indefinite postponement, upon the ground that the constitution requires that all such bills shall originate in the House of Representatives.

The question being upon this resolution, reported by the Committee on Finance, Mr. Bagby, of Alabama, was entitled to the floor, and he yielded it to Mr. Wright.]

Mr. President: My honorable friend from Alabama is entitled to my thanks for thus generously yielding to me the privilege to address the Senate at this time, and I sincerely tender them to him.

The question in form, is the bill introduced by the honorable senator from South Carolina, [Mr. McDuffie,] and the resolution of the committee proposing its indefinite postponement; but the question in fact, and to which the discussion has been principally directed, is the modification, in any form, and to any extent, of the present tariff law. The latter is the question it is my exclusive object and purpose to discuss.

In reference to the bill referred to, and the resolution of the committee proposing a final disposition of it, I will merely remark, that the difficulties which have been suggested against originating such bills in the Senate, under the provision of the constitution, that "all bills for raising revenue shall originate in the House of Representatives," have not been obviated in my mind, and I cannot vote for the bill of the honorable senator in the shape in which he has presented it.

The question whether any, and what, modifications ought to be made to the present tariff law, is one of great importance, of which I am not insensible. I believe I feel as deeply as I am capable of feeling, its magnitude and delicacy. I have not forgotten that it is a question affecting all the great interests of the country, and, to a greater or less extent, the private interests of almost every citizen. I am not insensible that it intermixes itself with the political feelings, as well as interests, of parties and individuals; and that, at a time like the present, pending a heated political canvass, it cannot be kept separated from the prejudices and passions which such a canvass is too liable to excite. Still, I feel it to be my duty to discuss the question fairly, and candidly, and fully, and that duty I intend to discharge. I shall endeavor to regard all the interests and all the feelings to be affected by the discussion; and to express my opinions without reserve, upon all the points I shall raise. That I shall avoid errors I dare not to hope; but that I shall be able to express myself in a manner not to give just offence to any individual, or to any interest, and much less to any member of the Senate, I do earnestly hope.

The manner of the passage of the present tariff law, and the circumstances which attended its passage through both Houses of Congress, and especially through the Senate, gave the fullest assurance to the country that some, at least, who voted for it, did not expect it would produce content and quiet in the public mind, or that it could be permanent. I was one of those who entertained these anticipations in regard to that law, at the time of its passage, and I gave expression to them upon that occasion. After I found my efforts, and those of all others, to remedy its manifest defects, must be ineffectual, and that the law must pass as it was, or not at all, my conclusion to vote for it was one of the most reluctant I had ever formed as to the discharge of a public duty; and I could not consent to give that vote, without placing upon record the reasons for it, and an assurance of my future readiness, whenever the opportunity should present, to correct the errors which I felt convinced were prevalent in the provisions of the act. That assurance was distinctly given in the remarks to which I refer. It has never been forgotten by me, nor have I been permitted to forget it; for my friends, and especially the honorable senator from New Hampshire, [Mr. Woodbury,] have been careful to remind me of it in the course of this debate, for which I thank them.

Among the reasons then given for my vote, I beg to bring the recollection of the Senate to that of a suspension of the distribution of the proceeds of the public lands. That reason alone was most powerful with me, and most especially so as connected with the legislation of Congress of this character. I considered that a measure directly calculated, if not intended, to produce the necessity for high duties; and its continuance, even for a few years, appeared to me strongly to threaten to make that necessity perpetual, by making the repeal or suspension of that law impossible. I should, therefore, have voted for an otherwise very bad law, to accomplish that great good. My other reasons were connected with the then state of the treasury, the condition of the public credit, and our rapidly accumulating national debt; and I will content myself with a simple reference to them, as then given.

In proceeding with this discussion, I am not at liberty to forget the character and extent of the various interests it is my duty to represent, in legislating upon this subject. The mechanical and manufacturing interests of the state of New York are second to those in few of the states of the Union. They exist to a large extent, and in almost all their varieties, in that state, and are rapidly increasing and very important interests.

The commercial interest of the state is very far greater than the same interest in any other of the states, and the enterprise and energy engaged in it are certainly second to none. Its health and prosperity are highly essential to the well being of all the other great interests of the state and country, and they should not fail to command the careful attention of every representative from the state in Congress.

The agricultural interest of the state is the basis of all the others, and is paramount to all in extent and importance. Represent what else he may, every representative from the state, out of her principal city, represents an agricultural interest greater than any and all others, and of which not one of them can, or will, be unmindful. The agricultural interest of New York is a less exclusive interest than in some of the other states; but it is second in extent of capital, and in importance, to the same interest in few, if any, of the states.

The great interest of labor, as an independent interest, distinct and separate from capital, exists as much more extensively in this state than any other, as the population of the state exceeds that of any other. This interest exists in all the others, pervades them all equally, and is equally indispensable to them all. So far, therefore, as it is to be affected by this legislation, it is paramount to them all, and presents an equal claim to the watchful care of every representative, come from what state, or from what part of any state, he may.

Such is a brief view of the great interests addressing themselves to me when called upon to act upon the subject of the tariff. Such are the interests to which I acknowledge direct responsibility for my action here; and to assume that I do, or can feel, hostility towards any one of them, would be to assume, that I do and can entertain most unnatural feelings, without the slightest possible foundation for them. In proportion to the existence of these great interests in the state, I am, so far as I know, equally indebted to all. My personal relations towards all have ever been equally amicable; my personal interests are intimately connected with the prosperity and success of all; and if my personal feelings are partial to any one, to the prejudice of any other of them, I am entirely unconscious of the fact. So far as I know myself, I am equally disposed to do justice to every one of these interests, and if the opinions I shall express, and the policy I shall recommend, shall prove me mistaken in fact, I certainly am not in the intention. There may be points of conflict between these great interests, touching our legislation of this character; but I lay it down as a rule which cannot be mistaken, that the law affecting all, which is best for all collectively, is the best and wisest law for each interest separately considered; for it is impossible that either can derive permanent benefit from that measure which shall inflict permanent injury upon any other. Intending to preserve the strictest observance of this rule, I will proceed to the discussion.

And I will premise, that it is the settled and determined policy of the Government and people of this country to raise, by duties upon imports, so much revenue as the public treasury shall require, and the wants of the Government, economically administered, shall demand, beyond the permanent receipts from the public lands. This, I believe, is a position assented to by all, practically speaking. There may be individuals who believe it would be more equal, and more economical, to raise this revenue by direct taxation upon the property of the country, as a theoretical proposition; but I do not suppose that a single individual in the whole country contemplates a change from this indirect, to a system of direct, taxation, to raise the revenues necessary for the support of this Government, in a time of peace. I certainly contemplate no such change; and I should consider any proposition to effect it unwise, inexpedient, and wholly inadmissible.

Assuming, therefore, that this portion of our necessary revenues are to be raised by imposts, as a permanent and settled system, I will first lay down the rules by which I think those imposts should be graduated, and by which I consider the right and the claim to protection, on the part of any interest to be limited, before I examine the present tariff law with reference to modifications.

First, then, every duty upon a protected article is necessarily protective to some extent. It serves to give an advantage to the producer of the article in this country over the foreign producer, in the markets of this country; because the foreign article must pay the duty, and the domestic article does not. In this respect, it is immaterial whether the producer of the article in the foreign country, or the consumer of it in this, pay the duty. If the former pay it, he sells his article at a less profit, or at a loss, in consequence; while, if the domestic consumer pay the duty, it is because it adds to the market value of the article in this country; and in either case, the domestic producer reaps the advantage.

Second. Every duty is necessarily prohibitory to some extent. Any branch of trade wholly free from taxation will necessarily be entered into more readily, and carried on more extensively than when taxed; though light duties will exert a much less proportionate prohibitory influence than heavy ones. The capital required will be increased in about the proportion of the duties assessed, because the importer must pay the duties before he can offer his goods in the market; and when the duties are made heavy, the hazards of the trade are greatly increased, from the increased outlay of capital, and the increased risk of finding consumers at greatly enhanced prices. Hence the greater proportionate prohibitory action of high duties.

Third. Every duty is a revenue, as contradistinguished from a protective duty, so long as its revenue are paramount to its prohibitory powers. That rate of duty, upon any given article of import, which will yield the largest amount of revenue, is the highest revenue duty which that article will bear, and affords the highest protection which can be given to the article, when of domestic production, consistently with the object of raising revenue. Any less rate of duty upon the same article is, of course, within the revenue range, and is a revenue duty, though not the highest which may be imposed to raise revenue. Up to that highest rate, the only way to increase the amount of revenue to be derived from the importation of the article is to increase the rate of the duty. Within this range, the protection afforded is incidental to the revenue power of the duty; and if the revenue be required, the protection is a necessary and unavoidable incident, and cannot afford just ground of complaint to any interest. This I consider the true limit of the right and claim to protection.

Fourth. Every duty is a protective, as contradistinguished from a revenue duty, when its prohibitory become paramount to its revenue powers. Raise the duty upon the given article above the highest revenue rate assumed under the last head, and the importations of the article will be either wholly prohibited, or so greatly diminished, that the amount of revenue derived will be less, though the rate of duty paid is greater. If the prohibition be perfect, there will be no revenue. In either of these cases, the protection to the domestic article is greater than before supposed; but it is obtained at the sacrifice of revenue, not as incidental to it. The prohibitory have become paramount to the revenue powers of the duty. The positions are reversed; and the revenue derived, if any, has become a mere incident to the protection afforded. This is making protection the principal, and revenue the incident. It is exercising the power which the constitution has given to Congress, "to lay and collect taxes, duties, imposts, and excises," not to put money in the public treasury, but to prohibit imports, and diminish the revenue for the sake of the protection afforded. I am compelled to consider it a very questionable exercise, both in principle and expediency, of these taxing powers.

It follows, from these positions, that free trade is the absence of duties, and prohibition the destruction of revenue, either of which will equally destroy our system of revenue from imposts, and force a resort to direct taxation; that a fairly arranged system of revenue duties is the medium between these extremes; and that such a system will necessarily extend to our domestic interests an amount of incidental protection equal to the whole amount of the revenue required from this source, and still leave a healthful and stable foreign trade.

I hope I shall be understood, and that I have been able to express the opinions I entertain upon these points. If so, it will be seen that the articles upon which the requisite amount of revenue should be assessed and collected, and the rates of duty to be imposed upon each, within the revenue range, are, in my opinion, entirely within the discretion of the Legislature, as a question of principle. Congress has always allowed the importation of some articles free of duty, and its right to do so has never been questioned. Can there be any more question of its right to impose one rate of duty upon one article, and a different rate upon another, keeping within the revenue limit in all cases? I think not. The imposition of duties to prohibit trade, and defeat revenue, appear to me to be the ground of complaint and question; not the imposition of duties to raise and collect revenue, although more heavy upon one article than another.

The power to discriminate, then, as to the articles to be taxed, and as to the rate of tax to be imposed upon each, within the range of revenue duties, I consider perfect and unquestionable; and whether it should be exercised to favor necessaries at the expense of luxuries, the poor at the expense of the rich, to extend incidental protection to a domestic interest against the too strong competition of a foreign competing interest, or for any similar object, appear to me to be questions purely of legislative discretion, and not at all of constitutional power. I think this point has been obscured by confounding the limit of the power with the object of its exercise. I do not admit the rightful exercise of the power, beyond the revenue limit, for any object; and within that limit, I admit it for all objects, within the reach of legislative discretion. In this way the argument is disembarrassed from all the difficulties which have been thrown out, about recommending discrimination for one object, and denying the power to exert it for another. It is a power which, thus limited, may be greatly abused. It may be exercised against necessaries to favor luxuries; against the poor to favor the rich; against the protection of domestic interests to favor foreign producers; or in any other perverted manner; but such liability to abuse does not disprove the existence of the power.

A single remark further will bring me to an examination of the practical operations of the present law upon the trade and business of the country. It is, that, because the rule laid down recognizes the highest rates of duty consistent with revenue to be the proper limit of legislative discretion in arranging and imposing duties, it does not follow that this limit is always to be reached in fixing the rates of duty. The state of the public treasury and the wants of the Government for proper expenditure, are to control that discretion within this limit. No more revenue should be drawn from the pockets of the people than the economical administration of this Government renders indispensable. While the revenue limit can never be exceeded to obtain revenue, because duties above that line prohibit importations so as to diminish revenue, so duties should never be imposed, within that line, for the mere sake of the incidental protection, when the money to be realized from the tax is not required for the public service.

With these limitations kept constantly in view, I am now prepared to enter upon an examination of the present tariff law, in its practical action upon the foreign commerce of the country, as shown by the custom-house returns made to the treasury department, and the tables of commerce and navigation for some few years past. In the statements I propose to make, and the results I have arrived at, I depend mainly upon the documents I find appended to a report of the committee of ways and means of the House of Representatives, made to the House on the 11th of March last. This report has been laid upon the tables of the members of the Senate, and is therefore within the reach of every senator. I first refer them to "Appendix A," which shows that the whole amount of the importations, for the year commencing on the first of October, 1842, and ending on the 30th September,

1843, was - - - - - - - -	$89,260,895
That of these imports, the free articles amounted to	40,470,961
Leaving the amount of articles paying duty at -	48,789,934
Of these dutiable goods, those re-exported, with a drawback of the duty, were - - - - -	4,363,440
Thus leaving, for the consumption of the country, and to pay duty, in fact, but - - - - -	44,426,494

The present tariff law was approved by the President on the 30th August, 1842; so that the year above given is the first and only one in which its practical operation upon the trade of the country can be tested by the returns.

A comparison of this year's business with the total and dutiable importations of the six previous years will give a general view of the diminution of our trade under this law. The importations of those six years were as follows :—

Years.	Free of duty.	Paying duty.	Total importations.
1837	$69,250,031	$71,739,186	$140,989,217
1838	60,860,005	52,857,399	113,717,404
1839	76,401,792	85,690,340	162,092,132
1840	57,196,204	49,945,315	107,141,519
1841	66,019,731	61,926,446	127,946,177
1842	30,627,486	69,534,601	100,162,087

An examination of these figures will show that the entire importations of the single year, under the present law, are nearly eleven milions less than the importations of 1842, which was very much the lowest of the six years; and almost seventy-three millions below the importations of 1839, the highest of those years. The changes in the character of the importations will still more clearly exhibit the influence of this law upon the trade. Under the compromise act, the class of free articles was very large, and during the whole period of the operation of that law, about one-half of the entire importations, as an average, were free of duty. That will be remarked as to five of the six years, by a reference to the figures given above—the advantage being about seven millions on the side of the free goods.

On the 11th of September, 1841, an act was passed "relating to duties and drawbacks," which imposed a duty of 20 per cent. upon all free articles, and all articles then paying a less duty, with certain enumerated exceptions, the principal of which are tea and coffee, raw and undressed hides and skins, coarse wool, gold and silver coins and bullion, and the list of articles used in manufacturing. This act was in force as to all the importations of 1842, except so far as those importations may have been reached by the present law; and the consequence was, that the amount of free articles fell down, from more than an average of 60, to 30 millions; and the dutiable articles rose up to 69 millions; being more than the average for the five previous years, although the importations of the year were much less than in any one of the five, and very far below their average. In this single year the dutiable articles much more than doubled the free. Under the present law the free and dutiable articles are very much the same as under the law of 1841, except that the coarse wool, and raw and undressed hides and skins, are added to the dutiable side, at the low rate of 5 per cent.; and yet the dutiable importations, in the first year of its operation, are nearly 21,000,000 less than under the act of 1841, which was in force but one year; and the free importations have gone up again almost 10,000,000 above what they were under the last-named act, and to very nearly the one-half of the entire importations of the year. This, too, has taken place after the change from the free to the dutiable side of full 3,000,000 in the articles of wool and skins. When to this astonishing change in the character of the imports, in a single year, is added the fact that, of the 40,000,000 of free imports, in 1843, about 24,000,000 consisted of gold and silver coins and bullion alone, the influence of the law upon the trade of the country cannot fail to be seen. The exchanges of commerce have been crippled to an unexampled extent, and our produce sent abroad for a market must be sold for what it will bring in coin, as the merchant dare not exchange it for merchandise, and encounter our duties.

This is a general view of the whole imports; of the whole foreign trade of the country. It affords the ground for a very imperfect judgment as to the effect of the law in detail. The rates of duty are very various, and upon some articles of importance they are moderate, and upon some very low. Upon other large classes of articles, again, they are very high and extensively prohibitory. A detailed examination, therefore, is necessary to present the action of the law in its true light; and to enable me to make that examination I have referred to other tables appended to the same report. "Appendix B" is a comparative statement of dutiable imports, for the six years which have been mentioned, and for the first three-quarters of the one year under the present law; exhibiting the articles as named in the present law, and the amount of importations of each article, so far as that can be ascertained from the different forms in which the import tables have been kept, under the different tariff laws. The first column shows the average importations for the three years, 1837, 1838, 1839; the second, the same average for the three years, 1840, 1841, 1842; and the third, the actual imports for the three-quarters of a year, commencing on the 1st of October, 1842, and ending on the 30th of June, 1843. "Appendix D, No. 2," exhibits the actual importations, for the same three-quarters, of each article paying *ad valorem* duties under the present law, the amount of duties actually paid upon each article so imported, and the rate per cent. of the duty fixed in the law, where there is no *minimum*, and the rate per cent. to which the duty paid amounts, where there is a *minimum*. "Appendix D, No. 3," gives the same information, for the same period, as to all the articles imported, paying specific duties under the present law. In this table the rates per cent. of the duty are calculated at the treasury, from the value of importations of each article, and the amounts actually paid in duties; and both these documents are authenticated by the official signature of the register of the treasury. To these three tables reference is to be had for the data upon which the following particular statements are based.

From the 1st of October, 1842, to the 30th of June, 1843, being the first three-quarters of one year of the operation of the present tariff law, the importations of wool, costing more than seven cents per pound, were valued at $54,695; and the amount of duties paid upon that sum was $21,941 88, being at the rate of 40.11 per cent. The average value of the importations of this same description of wool, for the three years, 1837, 1838, and 1839, was $801,087; and for the three years, 1840, 1841, and 1842, $1,004,312. This is equal to an average, for the six years, of $902,699 per year; while the $54,695, for three-quarters of the year, under the present law, is only equal to the rate of $72,927 per year; showing a falling off of the importations, compared with the average of the six previous years, of more than 91 per cent.

The value of the imports of cloths, cassimeres, and other woollen goods paying a duty of 40 per cent., for the same three-quarters of a year, was $1,472,381, upon which there was paid in duties the sum of $588,952 40. The average value of the importations of these same goods, for the six years before named, was $5,613,920 per year. The average importations for one year, under the present law, at the rate of the three-quarters given, was $1,963,175, showing a falling off in this importation, as compared with the six years, of 65 per cent.

The whole importations of the manufactures of cotton, for the same three-quarters of a year, were valued at $2,958,796. The nominal duty, in the law, upon all these goods, is 30 per cent.; but the *minimums*, or artificial valuations, which the law fixes upon various portions of them, makes the actual duties paid vary from 30 to 70 per cent., and raises the average upon the whole to more than 38 per cent. Still the tables of importation, if carefully examined will prove beyond question that large classes of the cheaper cottons are entirely prohibited by the operation of these *minimums*. Thus, every yard of printed or colored cotton cloth, cost what it may, is to be valued at 30 cents per square yard, provided it cost less than that sum, and is to pay the duty of 30 per cent. upon that valuation; while all know that it is almost difficult, at this day, to find, in a country store, a yard of cotton calico of so high a price as 30 cents, while much is retailed for 10 and 12 and 15 cents. I will refer senators to pages 72, 73, 74, of this report of the committee of ways and means of the House, for a statement of the rates of duty upon the whole range of cotton manufactures, calculated upon the English prices, where they will find, if the importations could be made, that the duties would range from 30 to 162 per cent. The average importations of the manufactures of cotton, for the six years named, was in value $10,047,099 per year; and the average per year, under the present law, calculated from the three-quarters above given, is but $3,945,061—being 60 per cent. less than the rate of importations for the six years.

Worsted stuff goods, worsted yarns, mits, gloves, and the like, were free of duty under the compromise act; and a duty of 20 per cent. was imposed by the act of 1841. By the present law, that duty is raised to 30 per cent. This is a class of goods manufactured to a very limited extent in this country; and the duty, upon every principle, should be a revenue duty only. The average importations, for the six years, were valued at $4,581,587. The average per year, under the present law, calculated from the three-quarters, is $608,068—showing a falling off, in comparison with the six years, of 83 per cent.

Silks were free under the compromise act, and paid a duty of 20 per cent. under the act of 1841. By the present law, the duties are mostly specific, and levied upon the pound weight, but differing somewhat upon different descriptions of goods. These duties, calculated *ad valorem*, range from 16 to 65 per cent.; while the *ad valorem* duties imposed by the law vary from 20 to 40 per cent. The actual average duties paid upon the importations of the three-quarters, of silks paying specific duties, was 32 per cent.; and of silks paying *ad valorem* duties, 26 per cent. The average value of the importations of all silks, for the six years, was $15,247,330 per year, and the average per year of the same importations, under the present law, calculated from the three-quarters, is $3,622,347—

being 76 per cent. less than the rate for the six years. Upon these goods, too, the specific duties have the effect to impose the highest tax upon the cheapest and most common article. A plain, firm, black silk, such as is most usually worn by those who wear silks in the country, will weigh much more than a fine, rich, figured French silk, such as is worn by the more wealthy in the cities; the cost of the former will be about half that of the latter; and yet the pound weight of each pay the same duty, making the rate, upon the common article, from 40 to 50 per cent., and upon the rich article from 20 to 25 per cent.—just about half. Here, too, there is no manufacture to protect, and no apology for any other than revenue duties.

Upon carpets, the duty is also specific, being levied upon the square yard; and the rates *ad valorem*, calculated upon the actual importations, range from 28 to 87 per cent. Although the amount of duty varies upon various descriptions of carpeting, yet the heavy rates fall upon the common and cheap goods, and are almost entirely prohibitory of them. The whole importations, for the three quarters, were valued at but $181,810, and of this amount $150,948 was Brussels carpeting, a description much more expensive than that in most common and extensive use. Of the remaining $30,000, $17,099 was an importation of 7,372 yards of Wilton carpeting, the foreign cost being about $2 50 per yard, and the rate of duty but 28 per cent.; while upon the Brussels, it was 42; and upon the treble ingrained, a much more common article, 87 per cent. The rate of diminution in the importations of carpeting, during the one year, under the present law, compared with the six previous years, is 41 per cent.

Cotton bagging is another article upon which heavy specific duties are imposed, averaging about 53 per cent. *ad valorem*. The average value of the imports, for the six years, was $379,718; and for the one year, under the present law, calculated from the actual imports of the three-quarters, $141,755—being a falling off of 62 per cent.

The duties upon glass ware, and window glass, are also specific; the former upon the pound weight, and the latter upon the superficial measure. The rates *ad valorem*, upon the actual importations of glass ware, ranged from 29 to 186 per cent.; upon window glass, from 62 to 243 per cent.; and upon vials and bottles from 11 to 165 per cent. The value of the whole importation of crown window glass was but $310; and upon that were actually paid $688 75 of duties—being 222 per cent. upon the whole. The total value of the importations of glass paying specific duties, for the three quarters of the year, was but $55,214, while the value of the imports of large glass plates, plates silvered, painted glass, &c., paying *ad valorem* duties averaging but 32 per cent., were $61,591. The falling off in the importation of glass of all descriptions, comparing the one year with the six, is 77 per cent.

The average importations of sugar and sirup of sugar, for the six years, was $7,600,449; and for the one year, under the present law, calculated from the actual importations of the three quarters, $3,376,824—exhibiting a falling off in the importations of this article of 55 per cent. The duties upon sugars, calculated *ad valorem* upon the actual importations, range from 67 to 101 per cent., the highest rate being upon loaf and other refined sugars. The rate upon sirup of sugar is 161 per cent.; and the provision of the law shows that it was intended to be prohibited. The importation is merely nominal—but $57 in value in the three quarters of a year. The rate *ad valorem* of the duty upon molasses is 51 per cent.; and the importations had fallen off 52 per cent., comparing the one year with the six. The average value of the importations, for the six years, was $3,192,683; and for the one year, under the present law, calculated from the actual imports of the three quarters, $1,513,693.

The importations of hemp, cordage, and sail duck, together, for the three quarters, amounted to only $695,571, being at the rate of $927,428 per year; while the average importation, per year, of the same articles, for the six years, was $1,408,525—showing a diminution of the imports of these articles, under the present law, at the rate of 34 per cent. The rates *ad valorem* of the duties upon hemp are less than 32 per cent., and upon duck less than 23 per cent. Upon some articles of cordage the rates are enormous. Of untarred cordage, the value imported, in the three quarters, was $5,798, and the duties actually paid amounted to $10,103 71, equal to the *ad valorem* rate of 174 per cent. So, of untarred yarns the value imported was $1,028, and the duties actually paid $2,046 96, equal to 199 per cent. Here the prohibition upon these manufactures rests most heavily.

The actual importations of paper, for the three quarters, were very trifling, the whole value only amounting to $32,180, being at the rate of $42,907 for a whole year. $17,752 of this amount was paper hangings, paying an *ad valorem* duty of 35 per cent.; and the residue, $14,428, paid specific duties, ranging from 16 to 97 per cent. The duties are specific upon almost all articles of paper, and are entirely prohibitory upon a very large proportion of them, there being no importations. The average imports of paper of all kinds, for the six years, was $150,685—showing a falling off, as compared with the one year, under the present law, of 71 per cent.

The duties upon leather under the present law are mostly specific, and upon the actual importations of the three quarters ranged from 13 to 60 per cent.; but the whole importations only amounted to $237,217, being at the rate of $316,289 per year. The average value of the importations for the six years was $805,349; those for the one year, under the present law, being 60 per cent. less than that rate. Here, again, a large share of the duties are entire prohibitions.

Raw and undressed hides and skins were free of duty previous to the passage of the present law. The average importations for the six years were $3,130,435 per year, and for the one year under the present law, which imposes a duty of 5 per cent., $3,104,095, being a falling off of less than 1 per cent., as compared with the six years. This may serve to illustrate the trifling prohibitory power of so low a duty.

I will only weary the patience of the Senate by the examination of a single other article—iron; but its various descriptions, and the great variety of its manufactures, will make that examination somewhat tedious.

The rate of duty actually paid upon the importations for the three quarters of bar-iron, manufactured by rolling, is 77 per cent.; and the value of the importations is $511,282; being at the rate of $681,709 per year. Upon hammered bar-iron the rate of duty is 32 per cent., and the value of the imports is $327,550; being at the rate of $436,733 per year. Iron in pigs pays duty at the rate of 72 per cent., and the importations are valued at $48,251; being at the rate per year of $64,335. The average value per year for the six years, of the importations of the rolled bar-iron, was $2,252,174; of the hammered bar-iron, $1,597,249; and of the pig-iron $276,743; thus exhibiting a diminution of the trade, upon a comparison of the six years with the one, of 69 per cent. in the first, 72 per cent. in the second, and 76 per cent. in the third article.

Of the various manufactures of iron paying specific duties, which, calculated *ad valorem*, range from 11 to 137 per cent., the value of the whole imports for the three quarters was $282,038; equal to a rate per year of $376,050. The importations of the various manufactures of iron paying *ad valorem* rates of duty ranging from 20 to 30 per cent., were valued at $773,479; both classes of these imports amounting to $1,055,517; being a rate per year of $1,407,356. The average importations per year for the six years of all these manufactures of iron, was $1,498,830—showing a diminution of the trade in these articles of but 6 per cent.

I am well aware that these comparisons do not form a perfect standard by which to judge of the influence of this law upon the foreign trade of the country. The imports of the fourth quarter of the last year may have been larger, in proportion, than were those of the three first quarters, upon which my calculations have been based; and to that extent the results will vary from the fact. I believe the importations of the last quarter of that year were beyond the average; but I have them not, specifying the values of imports of each article, so that I can use the information. Then the period I have taken for the comparison, was one of great unsteadiness in trade, as the aggregate importations for the several years clearly shows. The first of these years, 1837, was that in the early part of which the great crash came upon the bloated credit system of the country, when all the banks suspended specie payment, and general disorder prevailed throughout all branches of business. Regularity and steadiness are not yet perfectly restored, since those extreme revulsions, and it is far beyond my power to tell what influence predominated over the trade of the country, for any single one of those years.

Still I think these results might be safely relied upon, as approximations towards accuracy, and as establishing, beyond the power of question, the prohibitory character of this law. As an additional mode, however, of testing the same point, I have made a tabular comparison between the importations of 1842 and of 1843, taking the averages before used, calculated from the three first quarters, as the true importations of the latter year. I prefer to make this comparison, because I am not aware of any other visible cause, than the legislation of Congress, materially to affect our trade in the latter year, which did not exist to the same degree, and in equal force, in the former. Both were years of serious depression in business and stagnation of trade; but I am not aware that, independent of the influence of legislation, the latter was more so than the former. At the commencement of the first year, the duties, upon all the articles I have examined, except raw and undressed hides and skins, were 20 per cent. *ad valorem*, by the provisions of the act of 1841; or near to, and approaching that point, under the operations of the compromise act; and at the commencement of the second, the present law took effect practically. My table includes the articles I have examined above, and no others, and is as follows:

Name of Articles.	Importations of 1842.	Importations of 1843.	Diminution.	Rate per cent.
Wool, costing more than 7 cents per lb. - - -	$95,655	$72,927	$22,728	23
Cloths, &c., paying 40 per cent. duty - - -	4,517,864	1,963,175	2,554,689	56
All cotton manufactures -	9,578,515	3,945,061	5,633,454	58
Worsteds - - - - -	2,957,977	770,779	2,187,198	73
Silks - - - - - -	9,480,331	3,622,347	5,857,984	61
Carpetings - - -	292,309	242,413	49,896	17
Cotton bagging - - -	421,824	141,755	280,069	66
Glass - - - - - -	558,509	155,740	402,769	72
Sugars - - - - -	6,503,563	3,376,824	3,126,739	48
Molasses - - - - -	1,942,575	1,513,093	429,482	22
Hemp, cordage, and sail duck	949,808	927,428	22,380	2
Paper - - - - -	48,067	42,907	5,160	10
Leather - - - - -	912,585	316,289	599,296	65
Raw and undressed hides and skins - - - - -	4,067,816	3,104,095	953,721	23
Iron—				
Bars, &c., rolled - -	2,053,453	681,709	1,371,744	66
" not rolled - -	1,041,410	436,733	604,677	58
In pigs - - - -	295,284	64,335	230,913	78
All other manufactures of	3,552,642	1,407,356	2,145,286	60

Here is the comparison, at one view, between the importations for 1842 and 1843, of the articles named, and the names of the articles; and the sums will show that they constitute a heavy proportion of all the dutiable imports, and the heaviest of what are denominated the protected articles. I have incorporated with these articles worsteds, silks, and raw and undressed hides and skins, for a double purpose; the first two to show the prohibitory action of the bill upon articles not of the protected class, and the last to show

how much better the importations kept up when the duty was very light, and still what an effect was produced upon cheap heavy articles by a very light duty. These articles, compared with some of the others, will also show how much more severely heavy duties affected the trade in some articles than in others. Take the worsteds. The duty under the act of 1841 was 20 per cent., and the present law has raised it to 30 per cent. The trade has fallen off, in the single year, 73 per cent. Take the silks. They were at 20 per cent. under the act of 1841, and range from 16 to 65 per cent.; but average, upon the actual importations of the three quarters of 1843, only 32 per cent. Yet the trade has fallen off 61 per cent. The duties upon woollens, cottons, iron, sugar, and other of the protected articles, are much higher—some of them more than double these rates—and yet the trade has fallen off less.

Still, the rate of diminution of the trade, upon the most of the articles named, whether the comparison with the one or the six years be taken, is most marked and severe, and cannot fail to be alarming to the commercial interest.

These comparisons show the futility, as a standard of judgment, in reference to the influence of any tariff law, of general averages of the duties upon all the dutiable imports, and much more of such an average upon all the imports, free and dutiable. Such comparisons are made to assume that the more favorable appearance, the more prohibitory shall be the operation of the law under which they are made. Duties so high as to be entirely prohibitory are not comprehended at all in such calculations. To illustrate, by a strong example, suppose every duty imposed were raised to a rate of perfect prohibition, so that no dutiable article could be imported, and that all our foreign imports were free of duty: then such a comparison would show that our commerce was not taxed at all by duties, and yet the richest part of it would be destroyed by a prohibitory tariff. So take, of the articles above named, paper and undressed hides, and make an average of them, and it will show a very low rate of tax upon the combined importations, because the hides pay but 5 per cent. duty, and the import amounts to millions, while paper is almost wholly prohibited—the whole imports being less than $50,000 per year; and this, although paying duties varying from 16 to 97 per cent., consists of the articles of paper paying the lightest rates, and which can, therefore, come in.

Take the actual importations of the three first quarters of 1843, further to illustrate the fallacy of this standard of averages. "Appendix D, No. 2," before referred to, is a table of these imports, paying *ad valorem* duties under the present law. At the foot, the amount of imports will be found to be $16,684,875, the amount of duties paid, $4,153,686 13, equal to the average rate of 24.89 per cent.; not a very high rate of duty for many articles. The rate of these duties fixed by the law upon the articles named in this table, will be found to range from 1 to 50 per cent., these rates being the extremes of the *ad valorem* duties imposed by the law. Yet the articles before examined, which pay *ad valorem* duties, hides and skins excepted, comprise $2,277,368 less than half this amount of importations, and pay $113,850 51 more than half of the whole amount of these duties, averaging the rate of 36.11 per cent. This shows that an average of the *ad valorem* duties, by themselves, furnishes no standard by which to judge of the weight of the tax upon a large portion of the imports embraced in the calculation.

Take then "Appendix D, No. 3," which is a table of the actual importations, paying specific duties; and the amount of importations of this character will be found to be $12,494,340, the duties actually paid upon them $6,300,449 12, and the rate, calculated *ad valorem*, to equal 51.15 per cent. upon the whole. Here is an entire class of importations of more than $12,000,000, paying duties to more than one half their entire value in our markets, at the time the duty is imposed. Yet average all these dutiable imports together, those which pay *ad valorem*, and those which pay specific duties, and what will be the result? The entire amount is $29,179,215, and the entire amount of duties paid is $10,544,138 25, being only equal to 36.13 per cent., almost exactly the average before given for almost one half of the *ad valorem* importations. This is an exhibition of the average argument upon dutiable importations.

A single example of its application to the whole importations, free as well as dutiable, and I will leave this topic. The dutiable importations of the three quarters, as just stated above, amount to $29,179,215. The free importations, for the same period, amount to $35,574,584, as see "Appendix D, No. 1." These sums, together, make the whole importations of the three quarters, amount to $64,753,799; and the whole amount of duties paid upon these importations was $10,544,135 25; only equal to the rate *ad valorem* of 16.28 per cent. Here, then, will the gentlemen say, who rely upon these averages as a standard of judgment—here, is all the tax upon our trade, 16 per cent.; and can any reasonable man complain of that? And yet it is shown, upon the face of the very papers from which this average calculation is drawn, that one entire class of importations pay duties to more than half their value, that the whole dutiable importations pay an average rate of more than 36 per cent.; and that the trade, in large and important classes of articles, has fallen off 50, 60, 70, and more, per cent. in the first year's operation of the law; thus exhibiting a prohibitory power much more startling than the high rates of duties paid.

These comparisons must show, to the satisfaction of every mind, that general averages are most deceptive guides, and that averages of the rate of duty, even upon any two articles of import, much more upon selected classes, may be made to convey the most erroneous impressions; and they must lead to the conclusion, which it is my object to establish, that the only useful or truthful comparisons are those which compare the duties paid upon each important article of import with the value of the importations of that article.

I have already alluded to my comparative examinations to show that different articles of import will bear very different rates of duty, with the same proportionate effect upon trade, and that the same rate, applied to all articles of import, will exhibit very different prohibitory effects, as between the different articles. I recall this allusion now, for the mere purpose of deducing from it the position that discrimination, as to the rates of duty, within the revenue principle, and revenue range of duties, as I have defined them, will be found not merely admissible, but absolutely necessary, both for the accumulation of revenue, and for the benefit of trade, even if no other considerations in favor of discrimination shall be considered.

I have also alluded to these comparative examinations to show that the specific duties of the present law, as a general remark, and any system of specific duties so arranged, as well as the principle of *minimums*, must make the tax unequal and unjust; must bear the most heavily upon the most common and cheap article falling under a given duty, and therefore most heavily upon the poor and laboring classes. I am not prepared to say that, with perfect and minute information in all the manufacturing branches, a system of specific duties could not be arranged, which would be just and equal in this sense; but I am prepared to say that, with the information at present possessed by myself, and, I believe, by Congress, as a body, or by any one of its committees, such a system cannot be proposed as will avoid this radical and fatal defect. I say fatal defect; for I hold that to be so, in any legislation upon this subject, which taxes labor to the relief of capital, and imposes double the rate of duty upon poverty which is exacted from wealth. That is the effect of our specific duties. Take the cotton cloths. He who can purchase and wear qualities worth more than 20 or 30 cents by the square yard, pays a duty of 30 per cent., while he who must purchase and wear such qualities as can be purchased from 6 to 10 cents, must pay three times that duty. I cannot better illustrate the practical operation of this description of tax, upon the laboring classes, than to borrow the illustration of a witness examined before a committee of the British Parliament, I believe, in the year 1842. The witness said, if the coat of the man of capital was taxed too high, he had only to take a coat of an inferior quality, and procure it for the same money he had been accustomed to pay for his coat, though he would not have one quite so fine, if just as warm. Not so with the laborer. He wears the cheapest he can get, under any state of the taxation; and that coat he must have, be the tax what it may, because he cannot fall back upon an article of inferior quality, or less heavily taxed. This will not apply to our woollens, because, though taxed heavily, they are taxed equally, by a uniform *ad valorem* duty; but it does apply to the coarse cottons, and especially to the whole class of fustians, which are the peculiar clothing of the laboring classes of the cities and manufacturing districts.

I will now proceed to examine the influence of these high and prohibitory duties upon the great branches of industry of the country; and

First. Upon manufactures. The manufacturers themselves pray for stability in our legislation upon this subject. They say that their interests are best promoted by regularity and permanency, and that the fluctuations consequent upon changing legislation, are, almost, more injurious, than the protection they receive is beneficial, to their employments. This is to say, they want a moderate and reasonable system, not a prohibitory one; for they cannot but know that extremes in our rates of duty, be they too high, or too low, must themselves compel change. If too high, our commerce must be destroyed, and discontents thus engendered, or a surplus of revenue must be thrown into the public treasury, and a reduction of duties thus compelled; while, if too low, the necessities of that treasury will speedily force a change in an upward direction. It is the moderate, reasonable, revenue system alone, which can be stable. Based upon the wants of the treasury, and wisely and justly arranged, with reference to all the great interests of the country, there is no reason why, in times of peace, such a system should not be stable; because the wants of that treasury are not subject, at such periods, to material changes. The incidental protection afforded, by such a system, to one interest, and the incidental burden thrown upon another, would form no just subject of complaint to either. The tax would be necessary for the support of the Government, and all would concede to the justice and wisdom of so distributing the taxation, as to make it the least burdensome to all, as one entire whole. Not so when the tax is imposed for protection, and not for revenue. Then it is a burden imposed upon one interest, solely for the benefit of another; the supply of the common treasury ceasing to be the regulator of the tax. Under such a system, contentment cannot be expected, or even hoped for; and, under a Government resting upon the popular will, constant changes, and extreme fluctuations, must and will, be its fruit.

To the manufacturing interest, then, if stability be the most important element in its protection, the revenue arrangement of duties presents the most important and desirable system. It alone presents a national, instead of a sectional, basis for the arrangement of our duties upon imports; it alone presents an object—the supply of the national treasury—equally interesting to all, and equally controlling with all; it alone appeals to the whole public mind for approbation, and alone, therefore, can assure the promise of contentment and stability. It offers to this interest that degree of protection which the collection of revenue, for the support of the common Government, will afford, and leaves the discriminations, within that limit, to the common Legislature, but rejects prohibitions, destructive to itself, to favor any interest. Is this right? Is it best for all? If so, is it not the best system for the manufacturing interest itself?

I have, in the preceding remarks, treated the duty upon imports as a tax, and I have intended by the term, a tax upon the consumer, in this country, of the article of import upon which the duty is imposed. I have not been unaware that this raises the question, who must pay this duty? This question I do not intend to avoid, nor do I intend to discuss it. I have heard too many discussions, upon legislation of this sort, not to know that this point presents an interminable field for argument. That broad field I have not the qualifications, even if I had the disposition, to enter; and my object, therefore, is rather to make one or two inquiries, to elicit information, than to controvert any position which has been, or which may be, taken in the course of the debate.

I will merely premise that it is claimed, in favor of the protection to the manufacturing interests of this country, which it is supposed to be the duty of Congress to extend, that the foreign producer, and not the domestic consumer, will be the real payer of our duty. That position I will assume to be the true one, and will illustrate my inquiry by taking a supposed case, based upon it.

I will suppose, for the sake of the illustration, that our trade, for the year 1842, was perfectly free of all duties upon imports; that A. B., a merchant of the city of New York, imported, during that year, 50,000 yards of woollen cloths, which cost him, delivered at the custom-house in New York, $100,000. He sold these cloths in that market, during that year. In consequence of his low sales, the manufacturers of woollens of this country came to Congress, and prayed a duty upon woollen cloths, to protect their interests; and Congress, considering their prayer reasonable and proper, and requiring a revenue from this importation, imposed a duty upon the importation of woollen cloths, of the year 1843, of 25 per cent. The same merchant goes to Liverpool, in the year 1843, and tells his English manufacturer, "I want the same quantity of cloth which I purchased of you last year; but I cannot pay you the same price for it, because my Government has imposed a duty of 25 per cent. upon its value, which I must pay to its custom-house, before I can offer the cloths in my market. Last year, you gave me 50,000 yards for $100,000, and the operation was a fair one in my trade; but, as I must pay, this year, $25,000 in duties upon the same purchase, I cannot give you but $75,000 for the 50,000 yards." The English manufacturer replies, "Very well, sir, we cannot lose your market; and, if your Government has taxed our cloths, as you say, we must assume the tax. We must let you have the same 50,000 yards of cloth for $75,000, this year, which we sold to you last year for $100,000." The merchant takes the cloth, pays the $75,000, brings it to New York, pays his $25,000 of duties at the custom-house there, and offers his cloths in the same market as last year. How can he sell? The cost to him last year was $100,000, paid to the foreign manufacturer. The cost, this year, is $75,000 paid to the manufacturer, and $25,000 paid to our custom-house making

$100,000 in all; and can he not sell at the same prices as last year? Most certainly he can; and, in that case, what protection does the manufacturer of cloths in this country derive from the duty? Certainly none. If the foreign article can be brought here, and sold in our markets as cheap as before the duty, he derives no direct benefit from the tax. It is a diminution of the profits of the foreign manufacturer, or his loss, if you please; but the domestic manufacturer takes nothing by it, if the price of his product is not raised in our markets, or if the foreign competing product is not excluded. And in the supposed case, where the foreign producer pays the duty, beyond question neither of these consequences follow from it, as direct protection. It will not do, then, as a principle, to say that we can impose duties upon the foreign producer to protect our manufacturers, if commerce survives and imports continue; because the case supposed demonstratively shows that, while the foreign producer pays the duty and sends the goods, the cost in our market, and to our consumer, is not enhanced, and that the market itself is as open to the foreigner as it was before the duty. In these cases there is no effective protection to the domestic manufacturer. Prohibition must take place, or the price must be raised in our markets, as effects of the duty, or our manufacturer derives no benefit from it.

I will make another illustration upon the other side of the argument. Take the same supposed case, except to assume that the consumer, in our country, pays the whole duty. Then the New York merchant pays the British manufacturer the $100,000 for his cloths, as he did the previous year. In addition to this, he pays the $25,000 duties at the New York custom-house, and places his cloths upon his shelves for sale at the cost of $125,000, instead of $100,000, as in the last year. The duty has raised the price in our markets to its extent, and the merchant finds ready purchasers at the enhanced price. Is our manufacturer then protected? What is to hinder that same British manufacturer from sending to New York as many cloths as he can sell? and how does the duty injure him? He is compelled to pay, at our custom-house, the $25,000 of duties upon the $100,000 worth of cloths; but as he sells for $125,000, he can do this and still take his $100,000 home with him, which was all he asked before the duty. At this price, then, there is no protection to the domestic manufacturer; but as soon as the price recedes from the $125,000, for the supposed quality of cloths, he is protected, because the foreigner must pay the $25,000 of duties, while he pays nothing. If both sell an equal lot of cloths for $120,000, as the duty remains the same, the foreigner must pay $25,000 of his purchase money to the custom-house for duties, and gets but $95,000 for his cloths; while the domestic manufacturer gets the whole $120,000, no tax having been imposed upon his production. The protection is, therefore, an effective protection to him of 25 per cent., a part of the tax falling upon the foreign producer, and the remainder upon the domestic consumers.

Upon these illustrations, I wish to propound the following inquiries, to be answered by those who have studied this subject more deeply than myself. Do they not show, beyond the power of question, that while the foreigner would consent to pay the whole duty, his goods could be sold in our markets as cheap as before any duty was imposed; and that, although he might fill our treasury, there was no direct protection to the domestic manufacturer? That, upon the other side, if the whole duty fell upon the domestic consumer, and the price of the goods were raised in our markets to the extent of the duty, the foreigner could afford to send his goods here, pay our duty, and supply our market, as well as when there was no duty, thus presenting no effective protection, at this point? And does it not necessarily follow, from these two positions, that the effective protection to our manufacturer is only when the payment of the duty is divided between the foreign producer and the domestic consumer? and that the larger the share, less than the whole, which the market imposes upon the consumer, the better for his interest, because that is the government of his price, and the measure of his direct protection? Is it not true, that he has no other benefit from that portion of the duty paid by the foreign producer, than as it makes our markets less desirable, and less profitable to him, because that goes to depress the price here, and only that portion paid by the consumer is added to it?

Is not this a clear illustration of the protection afforded by a revenue duty? and does it not show that such protection is, and must be, effective, unless so light that the foreigner can afford to pay the whole of it, and thus keep exclusive possession of our markets? These appear to me to be unavoidable conclusions from the reasoning, while the measure I have prescribed for revenue duties seems to be such as would enable the Legislature to keep the competition open and healthful upon both sides, without granting prohibition to one, and visiting exclusion upon the other, or giving monopoly to either.

I am aware that human wisdom, without practical experience, cannot tell what is the extreme revenue point, as to any rate of duty, much less as to the arrangment of an entire tariff; but I believe an approximation can be made from the information already within our reach, which may be corrected, after the operations of trade shall have pointed out its errors, without causing changes seriously detrimental to any interest. My examinations have satisfied me, that a range of duties from 25 to 33 per cent. are as high as most articles of import will bear, consistently with the revenue principle. There may be exceptions, and I think if there are, that iron and sugar are the principal articles. These have for a long time, under our legislation, borne very heavy duties, and continue to be largely imported, and to be very prolific of revenue. Still I think the examinations I have made have conclusively shown that the rates of duty, under the present law, are too prohibitory upon these important articles for revenue duties. The trade in the former has fallen off, upon an average, about 65 per cent., and in the latter 48 per cent., as compared with the year preceding the passage of that law. It may not be necessary to bring them down to the rates I have named to preserve the revenue principle, but I am satisfied that a material reduction is demanded for that purpose.

The rates I have moved are a quarter and a third of the value of the property to be taxed; and is not that taxation enough, as a general rule, for reasonable protection? Will not as large a share of that tax fall upon the consumers, the whole people of the country, as they ought to pay to sustain the manufacturing interest?

Second, upon commerce. The influence of high and prohibitory duties upon this great and essential interest, cannot be otherwise than deeply injurious. They act directly upon trade, and tend to force it from its natural channels, and to diminish its volume and expansion; and, in that way, to the extent of their influence, strike at the life of commerce.

Stability is most essential to healthful commerce, and fluctuations interrupt its channels, increase its hazards, and render it fitful and sickly. Very high duties occasion extreme fluctuations, and prohibitory duties destroy trade and put an end to commerce. The examinations I have made, and the results I have exhibited, of the influence of the present law upon trade—upon the importations—are an exhibition of its influence upon the commercial interest.

The imposition of all duties operates directly upon trade and commerce, and cannot benefit either. Upon them the tax is more directly felt than upon any other interests; because by them the capital must be raised to first meet the payment, and upon them the whole influence is concentrated, whoever may eventually refund to them the duties paid. Still I do not believe that moderate, reasonable, stable duties, such as would be imposed within a wise and just revenue arrangement, would be severely oppressive upon the commercial interest, or would be seriously complained of by it. This interest should bear its share of the common burdens, and, fairly treated, it is as able, and, I believe, as willing to bear it, as any other interest. It has a right, however, to claim exemption from the oppression of duties not required for revenue, and not imposed to collect it; and from prohibitions, which are its destruction. Under any stable, well and wisely arranged revenue system, it can bear the burden of collecting the revenue, which the country shall require from customs, and can preserve health, activity, and vigor; but under a system of prohibitions, and strongly prohibitory duties, injurious both to revenue and trade, it must be sickly, fitful, feeble, and hazardous. Constant changes from extreme to extreme, and constant agitation, are no better for commerce—perhaps much worse. That system of duties which will produce general contentment with all interests, and can therefore be stable, is alone consistent with the prosperity of commerce; and that, I believe, would be found in a fair revenue system.

Third, upon agriculture. The influence of the present tariff law upon the agricultural interest is the most important consideration, because it is the basis of all the other interests, and, in our country, more important than all others. The great mass of our people are engaged in this interest, are dependent upon it for their subsistence and their comforts, and cannot fail to suffer from whatever is injurious to it. Indeed, none of our other great interests can long flourish under any system from which it materially suffers. Its firm prosperity is indispensable to their continued health; and its languishment must soon be followed by their decline, in spite of the power of partial legislation.

The situation of our country most invites, and its true interests most require, the wide extension and firm advancement of this great interest. Our vast unsettled domain is an unproductive waste, no matter how naturally fertile the soil, until agricultural labor reaches and subdues it, and changes that waste into fruitful fields. Hence, the influence of our legislation of this character upon the interests of agriculture becomes doubly important, and has a national, as well as an individual, consequence, paramount to that which attaches to any other of the great interests.

Under this sense of the importance of the examination I am prosecuting, I hope the Senate will bear with me, while I make a detailed and somewhat minute inquiry into the influences of this legislation upon the products of agriculture.

I will take first the article of *wool*. This is an important production of agriculture, over a very large extent of the country, and a principal staple in several of the states. The extent and importance of the interest, as well as the great worth of the wool-growers as a class of our citizens, entitles this article to all the consideration and protecting care which Congress can justly give to any article, or any interest.

How, then, is the value of wool in this country, at the present time, compared with the value of similar qualities of the same article in other wool-growing countries. I do not refer to South America, Smyrna, and like regions, where the sheep is permitted to range uncontrolled and without care, and where the principal value given to the wool is the cost of taking the animal and cutting off the fleece; but to England, Spain, Saxony, and other countries, where wool-growing is made a business of careful cultivation. I cannot answer the question I have asked, as applicable to the present time; but I hold in my hand a volume of testimony, taken before the committee on manufacturers of the House of Representatives, during the session of Congress of 1827–28, from which it appears that wool of the same quality was, then, from 50 to 70 per cent. higher in this country than in England.

[Mr. Wright here referred to the evidence, and read from the testimony of several witnesses to sustain his assertion.]

My examinations have established another fact, which is, that Spain, Saxony, and all the other wool-growing countries of the continent of Europe, export wool to England; showing that they produce the article cheaper than it is produced in England, and can afford to sell in the English markets. These importations it has not been, at any time, the policy of England to prohibit, and, for the benefit of her manufactures, they have usually been permitted entirely free, or at a very light duty.

Wool, then, is higher in our markets than in those of any other country where the article is cultivated, and where the finer and richer qualities are produced. What is now the difference between the prices of fine wools in our markets and in those of England, I do not know; but I do not suppose it is anything like as much as the witnesses referred to stated it to be in 1828. Indeed, I doubted, at that time, whether the witnesses had not made a high estimate of that difference, because it appeared to me that importations would have been greater if the difference in price had remained, for any considerable period, as great as they supposed it to be.

Be that as it may, my object in making these references, and stating these facts, is to inquire whether any senator supposes we can, by our legislation, maintain wool at a valuation in this country from 50 to 70 per cent. above that of all other wool-growing countries? and whether any senator believes we ought to do that, if we can do it? I do not think we should do this, if we could; because, if we give wool that artificial value above the markets of the world, we must give the same increased value to woollen clothes and other manufactures of wool, or otherwise we shall make the destruction of its manufacture in the country certain; and there will be no market, and no price for our wool but the exporting price; and if we must add from 50 to 70 per cent. to the cost of all the manufactures of wool, beyond what they might be purchased for abroad, merely to keep the price of wool in this country up to this high mark, I think the tax will be too heavy for the object; because all must wear woollen goods, while few, in the comparison, will grow wool. I do not, however, think we could accomplish this object, if we should try to do it. There is no portion of the stock of the farmer which can be so easily and so rapidly increased as his flocks of sheep, and with so little outlay of capital; and there is scarcely an improved county in the whole Union where sheep cannot be well and easily grown. If, therefore, we should give to this branch of agricultural industry this great advantage, and these exorbitant profits, how very soon would domestic competition overstock the market, and bring down the price? It is impossible in a country like this, by the power of legislation, or by any other power, to maintain any one branch of human industry in the possession and enjoyment of such an advantage. It is fortunate that it is so; or otherwise, the temptations to unjust and partial legislation would be too fearful, and the oppressions from it might become wholly insupportable.

I am willing to extend to the American wool-grower such fair and reasonable protection as our necessities for revenue will warrant—say 30 per cent.; and is not that reasonable protection to our farmers, who choose the business of wool-growing? Is not $30 in every $100 a reasonable advantage, compared with those engaged in other branches of farming, who cannot be protected at all? Is it not as high a tax for their benefit as the public will be contented to bear? Is it not as strong encouragement as the business will warrant, without inviting so many to it as to overstock our markets and render the protection useless?—for all will see that, when they shall be compelled to seek an export market, our duty will not aid them. I am compelled to say I think this degree of protection would better promote the interests of our wool-growers than a higher, or more prohibitory duty; because it would be stable, the revenue being necessary; and because, admitting a moderate foreign competition at the great disadvantage of $30 in the $100, it would not invite that flood of domestic competition, which perfect prohibition would be almost certain to bring upon them, and the consequent extreme fluctuation which over-competition never fails to produce. I believe our wool-growers will be satisfied with this degree of protection; if the taxes upon the articles they are compelled to purchase and consume are proportionately reduced.

Hemp. This is another agricultural production within the reach of protection, or which has been hitherto so considered. Yet it will be seen that the present duty upon this article, upon the actual importations for the three quarters of 1843, is only equal to an *ad valorem* rate of 32 per cent., and if put, therefore, at 30 per cent., the reduction cannot be material. The present duties upon some of the manufactures of hemp are enormous, while others are low revenue duties. The duties actually paid upon untarred cordage and yarn are 174 and 199 per cent., while those paid upon sail duck are but 22 per cent. These are inequalities for which there can be no reason, connected with a proper protection to the agricultural production.

I am not acquainted with this branch of agriculture, but I have understood that the difficulty does not arise in the growing of hemp; that our soils are as rich and suitable, and produce the crop as easily and abundantly, as those of any other country; but that we either do not possess the skill, or are not willing to use it, because it is injurious to health, properly to rot the hemp for exposed uses. Our hemp-growers practise the dew-rotting, while the water-rotting is said to be indispensable for durability, when put to exposed uses, such as sails, cordage, and the like. I do not suppose any one expects, by any degree of protection, to force the dew-rotted hemp to these uses; and I have never been able to perceive how any duty we may impose is to give us the skill, if we have it not, to water-rot our hemp; or, if we have the skill, and will not use it, because the process is an unhealthy one, how an increase of duty is to change that disposition. I have never understood that the question was one of expense, and, for that reason, requiring protection; and I am happy to learn that some experiments have been recently made to export hemp from this country, with some promise of success. In any way, therefore, in which I have been able to view the interests of agriculture, as connected with this product, I am forced to consider a duty of 30 per cent. a sufficient protection, and I think the hemp-growers will so consider it.

Sugar. This is an agricultural production, which has grown into importance in our country, within a few years, comparatively speaking; and yet it has already become the great staple of one section, and the cultivation and production are rapidly increasing. I am wholly unacquainted with this branch of agriculture, and cannot, therefore, form any opinion as to the extent of protection required for it. The article is one which has been very heavily taxed, under almost all our tariff laws; formerly, much more as a rich source of revenue, than from any object of protection to the domestic production. It has proved to be an article which will bear a higher rate of revenue duty than almost any other considerable article of import in our whole list. The duty imposed under the present law is much less than that under the tariff of 1816, or any intermediate law, other than the gradual reductions under the compromise act; and yet the rates, as have been seen, are from 67 to 101 per cent. under this law. It will be also observed, that the falling off in the trade, in this article, upon a comparison with the six years, has been 55 per cent.; and with the single year 1842, but 48 per cent.; much less, in both cases, than most of the other articles subject to such extreme rates of duty. These facts are referred to, for the purpose of showing that the article will bear a very high revenue duty, and I do not doubt that all the protection required, and certainly all which it would be reasonable to impose upon an article of such universal consumption, could be afforded without a violation of the revenue principle.

Of the principal agricultural staples of this country, the three named are all which have occurred to me as asking protection, or being within its reach. Of all our other great staples, we are exporters, and not importers; and the markets of other countries, the open market of the world, are our markets for these products, and must govern our prices. Protection, therefore, by impost duties imposed by us, is wholly illusory and useless. Any duty imposed by us upon the foreign articles in our markets cannot raise the price of our articles in a foreign market.

Take the article of *flour*. This is an important product of agriculture over a very large portion of the Union; and, of it, the country exports largely. I am aware that a high duty is imposed upon the importation of foreign wheat and flour, by the present law; but does that duty benefit the wheat-grower? Where is his price made? Certainly in our commercial and exporting cities. There the surplus of our wheat must go, and does go, to find its market: and there the market price is established which governs the sales throughout the country. What controls the price in those cities? Supply and demand, which control the price of everything in every market. What demand? The whole demand for flour, no matter whether to be consumed at home or to be exported. All purchasers in the same market pay the same price, without reference to the purpose for which they buy. There is always, as a general rule, a surplus of flour in our commercial markets, beyond the demand for domestic consumption; that surplus must seek a foreign market, and the price it will command for exportation controls the price of the whole mass. Our duty, therefore, is wholly inoperative, and cannot exert the slightest influence upon the price of flour, thus controlled, even in our own markets. Flour, then, cannot be protected, because we export flour, and the open markets of the world are our markets, and must control our prices.

The argument in favor of the prohibitory system upon manufactured articles, is, that by forcing a larger proportion of our laborers into manufacturing employments, we shall withdraw them from agriculture, and thus diminish its productions, while they will become consumers, instead of producers of its products, and thus the agricultural interest will receive a double benefit from the policy. I shall by-and-by, have occasion to inquire how far labor is likely to be benefited by a policy which is designed and calculated to make dear bread. But, passing that consideration for the present, I will examine this argument as applicable to the profits of grain-growing as an agricultural pursuit. In just so far as the manufacturing employments of this country increase the general demand, in the markets of the world, to precisely that extent is the wheat-grower benefited by the policy, in the single article of the sale of his wheat. Beyond that, this effect cannot be experienced so long as our wheat and flour market is an exporting market. If the policy could be carried so far as to force a sufficient portion of our laborers into manufactories, to consume all our flour, and leave no surplus for exportation, then might the wheat of our farmer come within the reach of protection; because, then, a prohibitory duty upon foreign wheat would give him the monopoly of our markets, and enable him to control the price in them. Until that state of things can be produced, our wheat and flour cannot be benefited by an impost duty. So long as we are exporters, and foreign markets are our markets for these articles, the price of the wheat of our farmer cannot be benefited by our duty. The increased home demand would benefit him so far as it should affect the price of his wheat in the export market, but no farther; and beyond that he could derive no benefit, while our country should export wheat.

Does any senator hope to see the time when this country will not export breadstuffs? I do not hope to see that time. I think the masses of the people of this country will find speedy cause to regret such a period, if it shall ever occur. They will be likely to find that a monopoly of bread is anything but a protection to their comforts.

The articles of *beef*, *pork*, *butter* and *cheese*, agricultural productions of the North and West, stand in the same relation to this policy with wheat and flour. They are great staples of these sections of the Union, and they are all articles of export. Their market is the market of the world, and the prices they command are measured by the wants of the world, not merely of our Union. Import duties upon all these articles are dead letters upon the statute book, so far as the interests of our farmers are concerned. They afford no revenue to the public treasury to lighten his taxes, and add nothing to the price of his products. I speak comparatively. There are imports under all these heads, but not of that character which conflict with the farmer's market. Delicacies, luxuries, bearing these general names, are imported in very small quantities, for the uses of those who regard their appetites more than their pockets. Take the article of cheese as an example. The value of the importations, for the three quarters of 1843, was $3,850, the quantity being 30,033 pounds. This showed a foreign cost of more than 12½ cents per pound, and the duty was 9 cents per pound, bringing the article, to the consumer, up to a price probably not less than 25 cents per pound, while the market cheese of this country commanded about 5 cents per pound in our largest commercial markets. So with wheat. Choice seed wheat is occasionally imported, which gives the article a place upon the list of imports, while the quantity brought into the country does not, in the least, affect the market price of the wheat of our farmer. So with the other articles named.

The manufactories are spoken of as furnishing valuable markets to the farmer for these articles of his produce. Where do the manufacturers purchase their supplies? In the great commercial markets, where they sell their manufactured goods. By what price do they purchase? By the same which others paid in the same markets. New York and Boston are the great exporting markets for the flour of this country. Did any one ever think of going to Lowell, the largest manufacturing village in the country, to learn the market price of flour? Certainly not; but the manufacturer of Lowell goes to the Boston or New York market, both to learn that fact, and to purchase the flour for the consumption of his factory; and when there, he purchases for the same price which the merchant pays, who purchases to export to England, France, South America, or any other foreign market. The former gets no more from the manufacturer than from the exporting merchant. So with all other like articles of supply for the manufacturing establishments.

It is undoubtedly true that these establishments open a limited retail trade to the farmers in their immediate vicinage, for fresh provisions and temporary supplies, which are both convenient and lucrative; but this is a benefit too narrowly circumscribed to be taken into the account, when discussing the great and general interests of agriculture throughout this wide country.

Cotton, *rice* and *tobacco*, are great agricultural staples of the southern and southwestern states, which are also compelled to seek foreign markets, and are therefore beyond the reach of protection from import duties. Of these articles, the cotton is by far the most important, as it is much the most important article of export from our country. I believe the estimates are, that about one-fifth of the ordinary annual crop is consumed at home; the remaining four-fifths being, of course, compelled to seek a foreign market. What proportions of the tobacco and rice find a home market, and what proportions are exported, I am unable to say. It is enough that the interests of all these branches of agriculture are in much better and abler hands than mine here; and in those hands I shall cheer fully leave them.

Not to go further in this examination of agricultural productions, here are eleven principal articles, three only of which can be materially and practically benefited by protecting duties; and it is for the wisdom and the justice of Congress to decide how far the great public and private interests of all will be consulted by taxing the eight for the benefit of the three, beyond that degree of taxation which a supply of the public treasury shall demand, and the proper rates of duties for raising revenue shall warrant.

If such the relative advantages and burdens, flowing to the manufacturing, commercial, and agricultural interests, from the prohibitory system of duties, what are the relative claims of these several interests to the favors and bounties of the Government, growing out of the actual profits of capital now invested in them respectively? Upon this point I pretend to no extent or accuracy of information, and my object is to throw out the crude impressions I have imbibed, rather to elicit information from others, than under any expectation of communicating information myself.

In agriculture the great mass of the capital of the country is employed; and what does it yield, in net annual proceeds? The senator from South Carolina [Mr. McDuffie] has said he did not believe the net profits of the planters of his state exceeded, upon the average, 5 per cent. upon the capital invested. I was surprised, at the time, to hear the gentleman make so high an estimate. I have reflected much upon the subject, and taken some pains to make inquiries from others, and do not believe that the net profits of the capital invested, upon a fair appraised value of the property in the market, in any agricultural county in my state, taking an average of years, will exceed 3 per cent., and I should not feel surprised to know that it did not exceed 2 per cent. I know that the moderate but independent farmers of my section of the Union, worth from $3,000 to $8,000, and $10,000, as industrious and frugal as any class of the citizens of this country are, or can be; who can pay off their expenses and lay up from $100 to $200, at the close of the year, not counting the labor of themselves and their families upon the one side, or their living upon the other, consider themselves as doing well. The investments of capital are more secure in this branch of industry, and to that extent should yield less returns. I do not doubt that many will think me wild in the judgment I have pronounced, and perhaps I am; but if gentlemen will institute careful inquiries, I have no doubt they will be surprised at the very moderate profits derived from the capital employed in agriculture, as a general average for the country.

In commerce the case is very different. Here the hazards are extreme, and success usually brings extreme profits. There appears to be an attraction in this pursuit, growing out of the very hazards which surround it. Vast fortunes are, sometimes, suddenly accumulated, and, like the lotteries, men are prone to look at the prizes, not at the blanks which are drawn. Still I very much doubt whether, as a whole, the net profits of the capital invested are not less in this than in either of the other great divisions of business. I have often thought that, were any branch of human industry presented, however lucrative the compensation promised, where the hazards to life and health were seen to be as great as are the hazards which attend the employment of capital in commerce, and where so many wrecks could be seen along its shore, no human being would be found to engage in it. I have heard calculations of the rate per cent. of commercial men who fail in business, and it was fearfully great, though my memory will not permit me to state, with confidence, what the rate was.

How, then, is it in the manufacturing and mechanical branches of industry? Here, more than in the other branches, forecast and calculation can be employed. The agriculturalist must take the chances of the seasons, the merchant the peril of the seas, and both the changes of the markets; while the latter is the only hazard of the manufacturer and mechanic, whose employments do not rest upon artificial and changing legislation. I can speak from an acquaintance somewhat extensive as to the mechanics of the country as a class of citizens; and where industry and prudence are carefully observed, no class of men in our country are more certain to reach comfortable independence. Among the most useful, independent, and respectable citizens, wherever I have enjoyed a personal acquaintance, I have always found the mechanics, as a class, holding a very prominent place. Hence I have been led to believe that the profits of capital and the fruits of industry in their employments are as good as in any others I have known, as a general remark.

With the large manufacturing establishments I have scarcely any acquaintance. I must speak of them, therefore, from report, and I shall do so principally from what has been said of the profits of their capital, in the course of this debate. And what has been said upon this point? Their dividends have been spoken of as ranging from 6, 7, 14, and 20 per cent. up to 30 and 40 per cent. per annum. These latter rates, I am compelled to suppose, must be somewhat exaggerated. I have, however, been informed, from sources upon which I place strong reliance, that some of the establishments engaged both in the cotton and the woollen manufacture, are able to divide to their stockholders 7 per cent. upon their capital stock, half-yearly, and to accumulate a surplus amply sufficient to cover all contingent losses. This is too much for interests sustained by the universal taxation of all other branches of industry. If this is so, it proves conclusively to my mind, that the present prohibitory duties should be modified, and fair revenue duties substituted, that a healthful competition may moderate these profits, by a reduction of the prices of the manufactured articles to the consumers. This is far beyond the profits of capital in other branches of industry, and too much to be sustained by burdens imposed upon them.

It remains for me to consider the influence of the system of prohibitions, and prohibitory duties, upon *labor* as a distinct interest; the labor of those operatives, in all the great departments of industry, which is compensated by stipulated wages, and has no other or further interest in the capital which employs it, or in the profits or losses arising from the employment of that capital.

This division of the subject, and the careful consideration of this head, is rendered more appropriate and important, because the advocates of the system of high and prohibitory duties place its defence and justification mainly—nay, I may say almost exclusively—upon the ground of protection to this labor. To give it more constant and more profitable employment is their great avowed object; and some of the most earnest of those advocates, in this debate, have gone so far as to say that, if this ground could not be sustained, the system itself could not be defended and justified.

This avowed object is a worthy one. No great interest in any country more justly demands or deserves the watchful regard of legislators than this labor, and no member of this body feels more earnestly anxious than I do to shape all our legislation so as to bring the fewest burdens upon, and the greatest benefits to it. Under the influence of this disposition, I shall enter upon the examination of what I think are, and must be, the influences of such a policy upon this description of labor in our country.

One position cannot fail to be admitted. If the high duties raise the price of the necessaries of life to our laborer, the cost of his food, his clothing, and his comforts, to that extent, they are a tax upon him, and lay him under the necessity of having more constant employment, or higher wages, or both, to meet the increased expenses of his living. And this consequence must attach to him in whichever of the great branches of industry he may be employed. The tax he must pay upon these necessaries must be equal, whether he be engaged in manufactures, commerce, or agriculture.

While the high duties remain, and are effective to raise the price and extend the market for manufactured articles, those engaged in the manufacturing branches of industry may be able to employ more labor, and to pay better prices, in consequence of the duties; but it has been already shown that duties, imposed for protection and not for revenue, never have been, and never can be, sustained at a stable point; that, as soon as they shall have the effect to give artificial values to the protected articles, the burden of the tax will be felt by all other interests, the disproportionate profits to the protected interests will be seen, discontents will be engendered, and the duties will be reduced. This will suspend employment at the high rates of wages, and the laborer will be thrown wholly out of employment.

Again: If too prohibitory, commerce will be destroyed, the collection of revenue defeated, and reduction of the duties back to the revenue point will become compulsory. This will have the same effect to render the employment of the laborer inconstant and fitful, as well as to unsettle the rate of his wages. And if these two almost unavoidable consequences do not follow, the increased profits, arising from the artificial values given to the products, will produce domestic competition, break down the monopoly, reduce the business to the level of other pursuits, and thus destroy the effect of the duties upon the wages of labor. In either of these events, the influence upon the wages of the laborer must be temporary, and the consequence of the temporary increase of his compensation must be inconstant employment at any rate of compensation.

In this aspect of the case, it is important to examine the nature of the connection between this labor and the capital which employs it, in the manufacturing branches. And it should be premised, that, in any state of duties, any advance in the rates of wages will only be a consequence of an advance in the products of that labor, and so far from keeping pace with the latter, be the enhancement of the value of the products what it may, the only increase in the compensation to labor will be what is required to command the requisite amount of it from the other great branches of industry. If the goods of the manufacturer should be doubled in value, it by no means follows that he would double the wages of the labor he employs. That would depend upon the rates of wages which his agricultural and commercial neighbors were able to pay, and the rate of wages he would establish would only be such as to take from them the labor he should require. An advance of 5 per cent. would effect this object, and he certainly would not go beyond its accomplishment. This principle is not only true when applied to labor employed in manufacturing, but is equally applicable to the wages of labor in all the pursuits of industry. No capitalist, whatever may be his employment, pays more for labor than will command such as he requires, be the profits of his business what they may. If the wheat of the farmer, or his wool, or his beef, double in value, he does not, in consequence, double the wages of his laborers. If the adventure of the merchant double his capital invested, he does not, in consequence, double the wages of his sailors and cartmen. A permanent advance in products generally draws after it an advance in the wages of labor, but always as a consequence; the labor is the last to advance, and, when the enhancement of the value of products is extreme, labor never keeps pace with them. The ordinary wages of the able-bodied day laborer of the North, in the hay and harvest season, is $1, in money, or one bushel of wheat; but let wheat advance to $2.50 per bushel, as it sometimes does, and the wages of the laborer may be $1.50, never more, and more likely $1.25. The operation of this rule is universal.

Let the usual revulsion come, after one of these periods of high prices, as it always must come, and what is the effect upon labor? Employment, at any rate of wages, almost ceases. The farmer and the merchant curtail their operations within the narrowest possible limits; and the manufacturer closes his factory, and stops altogether. This compels the laborer, at once, to work for any rate of wages he can get, when any employment at all is offered. Such are the fruits of extreme fluctuations upon labor; and it has been seen that fluctuations must be a consequence of high and prohibitory duties, and a consequent artificial standard of value, in any branch of industry.

Again: The manufacturer can make his business the subject of very accurate estimate and calculation; and hence he is able to establish the rates of his laborers' wages so as, with a very great degree of certainty, to protect himself from loss. He is about to make a certain quantity of a certain description of goods, say cotton or woollen cloths. He can tell precisely what the materials will cost him, how long it will take his mills to work them up, what will be the ordinary wear and tear of his machinery, what his allowance for accidents, what the interest upon his capital, and, from the prices current of the day, what the cloths will sell for in the market. He knows, then, what he can afford to pay for the labor, his only risk being a change in the market, before his cloths can be placed there. Will he exceed in his rate of wages what he thus ascertains he can afford to pay? Never. He will sooner close his mills, and let his capital remain idle. Will he pay for his labor all which this calculation shows him he can afford to pay? That does not follow, if that be more than will command from others the labor he wants. Hence, in this branch of industry, the laborer must work for the ordinary rate of wages, be the profits of the manufacturer what they may; while, if prices are low, he must work for what the manufacturer can afford to give without loss to himself, or the factory is closed, and he finds no employment there at all. In other words, the profits upon his capital are the whole object of the proprietor of the manufactory; and he will not work it to his own loss, knowing it to be so. If, therefore, fluctuations come, which he can foresee—if prices fall below a healthful line—the weight is thrown from himself on to the shoulders of the laborer, and he must bear the loss in a reduction of his compensation, or he must be thrown out of employment altogether.

Another consideration, I suppose must materially affect manufacturing labor. I am not personally acquainted with the subject, but I suppose that labor is rendered more dependent than labor in the other branches of industry, because the laborer, by long employment in a manufacturing establishment is, to a great extent, unfitted to perform profitable labor in any other calling. Is this not so as to the great body of manufacturing laborers? and does not, therefore, the sudden closing of the factories, and the entire arrest of their employment, reduce them to peculiar dependence, unknown to any other classes of laborers in our country? Such are my impressions, and if they are well founded, they will show the great power which the manufacturing capitalist must hold over the employment, and, by necessary consequence, over the living, the comforts, and the independence of the manufacturing laborer. Is it wise or politic, in reference to the labor of this country, to endeavor to shape our laws so as to force it into these dependent situations, from the more free, and equally comfortable and respectable employments of agriculture and commerce? I cannot think so.

I have admitted that, while the high duties shall be effective to the manufacturing interest, it can afford to make a better compensation to labor, although the rates of compensation, so artificially improved, as well as the entire labor under the system, must thereby be rendered unstable, fluctuating, fitful, and uncertain; yet how will the same system of duties and prohibitions affect the *commercial* branch of our industry? I have before attempted, and I believe successfully, to show that this whole policy must be a direct burden upon commerce. Upon this interest it is that the tax is directly felt. Here the capital must be raised to pay the duties. Here the hazards of the markets, at the enhanced prices, must be encountered. And can this great branch of industry make better and higher compensation for its labor under such a system? Palpably not; and yet its labor is equally taxed, and equally demands increased compensation. Suppose the duties are prohibitory. To that extent commerce is destroyed, and the call for labor to carry on its operations is also destroyed. Its whole operations, too, under such a system, must be unsteady, uncertain, changeful, and fluctuating; and so must be its demand for labor, and its ability to compensate it; and yet its labor, under all these disadvantages, must bear its full share of the burdens of the system. Its food, and clothing, and comforts, must bear the same taxation with the other branches of labor, and be injured in the rate of its compensation, in the steadiness of its employment, and in the extent of the demand upon which it relies. Need I say more to prove that moderate, reasonable, stable revenue duties are infinitely more advantageous to the labor employed in commerce, than a system of prohibitions even intended to protect labor?

How is it, then, with the labor employed in *agriculture?* The wool-grower, while the protective duties shall have the effect to raise the price of his wool, may be able more fully to compensate the labor he is called upon to employ; but what is his demand for labor? Nothing like that of the man who tills the soil, and makes grain-growing his business. Upon this point I speak with some confidence, as I believe I possess accurate personal information. That portion of the country in which I resided from infancy to manhood was then a grain-growing, and is now a wool-growing district. The consequence has been a vast change in the hired labor employed by the farmers. Their hay-cutting season is now the only one in which the demand for labor is extensive, most of the farmers intending to tend their flocks of sheep, and manage their limited tillage, with small additions to the labor of their own families; and the mass of the labor of their hay-fields is now performed by transient laborers from the neighboring British province of Canada. The rate of wages is high, but the employment very temporary; and in consequence, that class of native laborers which, when I was a boy, depended upon employment from those farmers, is not now found there. They have gone west to the grain-growing sections.

The hemp and sugar-growers of the southwest may require the same, or even more labor, in consequence of their protection; and may also be able to pay better prices, so long as the duties shall have the effect to enhance the value of their products in the market. Of these agricultural employments I cannot speak from personal acquaintance, and I am therefore disposed to indulge the most favorable presumptions in regard to the labor employed in them.

What is the influence upon the labor employed in tillage, in raising the wheat and other grains of the North and West, and in making the beef, pork, butter, and cheese of those sections, and in cultivating the cotton, rice, and tobacco of the South? They will require the same labor in proportion to their productions. Their labor is equally taxed with that in the other branches; and their own clothing and other necessaries and comforts, save the provisions which they produce, bear the same burdens with those consumed by their fellow-citizens in other employments. Will the system of high and prohibitory duties enable them to pay more for their labor? It has been seen that their products must seek the open markets of the world, and that our duties cannot affect their price. If the duties shall be so high as to break up, or materially interrupt the exchanges of commerce, to that extent their markets must be injured and the value of their products depressed. How, then, can they afford to pay higher wages for labor, under such a system, than under one of stable revenue duties, which leaves their markets open, commerce healthful, and themselves and their labor but moderately taxed, and that to supply the national treasury, which they must, in some form, contribute to supply? They cannot. They cannot so well afford to compensate labor for its toil; and yet these employments are the great resource of at least nine-tenths of the labor of this whole country.

Entertaining, most deeply, these impressions in relation to the influences of the prohibitory system of duties upon the labor of this country, I have expended a good deal of time and research to inform myself as to the results of a like policy upon this great and vital interest in countries where the system is much older, and has been much more rigidly enforced, than as yet with us. One natural and necessary consequence of the system has appeared to me to be to increase the power of capital over labor, by forcing it into artificial channels, and thus increasing its dependence; to increase the profits of capital at the expense of labor, and finally to give to the former a monopoly to impoverish and oppress the latter.

As England is the country to which we are most usually referred for lessons of wisdom upon this subject, and the British Government is the one which claims and receives the credit of having most perfectly protected its domestic interests, and especially its labor, I have referred to British history to satisfy my inquiries upon this point. The examination has been a tedious one, and briefly and imperfectly as I intend to exhibit it to the Senate, I shall be compelled to be tedious in the performance of that task.

And first, as to wool. The *export* of wool from Great Britain was prohibited by law from 1660 down to 1825, while the article was permitted to be *imported* free of duty down to the year 1802. Here the agricultural interest was made subservient to the manufacturing, by the strongest provisions of law. The British wool-grower was compelled to sell his wool in the markets of his own country, and all the world were at liberty to compete with him there upon equal terms. In 1802, a very light revenue duty of 2s. 3d. sterling per cwt. was imposed upon imported wool, which was raised in 1813, to 6s. 8d., and in 1819, to 56s., equal to 6d. per pound. This high duty was continued but for a short period; when, to favor the manufacture, the import duty was brought back to 1 farthing per pound upon wool costing 1s. sterling per pound or under, and 1d. per pound upon all other wool, where it now remains.

In 1337 Parliament passed a law, "prohibiting the wear of any cloth made beyond sea, and interdicting the export of English wool."

In 1525 the manufacture of wool was domestic, and pretty equally distributed over the kingdom.

In 1533 a law was passed, reciting "that the city of York afore this time had been upholden principally by making and weaving of coverlets, and the poor thereof daily set on work in spinning, carding, dyeing, weaving, &c.;" that the manufacture, having spread into other parts, was "thereby debased and discredited;" and enacting, as a remedy for this evil, that henceforth "none shall make coverlets in Yorkshire but inhabitants of the city of York."

About the same time an act was passed to restrain the manufacture in Worcestershire to the town of Worcester and four other towns.

Here was protection to the woollen manufacture, carried not merely to the prohibition of all imports of woollen goods, and the wear within the realm of all cloths made beyond sea, but to the prohibition of the manufacture, in certain branches, by any of the inhabitants of the country, except in certain specified towns; in other words, protection by law against domestic as well as foreign competition.

In 1677 a law was passed, declaring upon its face that it was for the encouragement of the woollen manufacture, which required that all persons should be buried in woollen shrouds, and that the coffins should be lined with woollen cloth, if lined with cloth at all. Heavy penalties were imposed for any violation of this act, which went to the clergyman of the parish, whose duty it was made to prosecute for the penalties when incurred; and he was to read the act to his congregation on a specified Sabbath in each year. This law the historian says was enforced, and remained a statute of the realm for more than one hundred and thirty years.

As early as the year 1700, manufactures of wool were exported from Great Britain to the amount of more than £3,000,000 sterling per annum. In 1787 the average exports were about three and a half millions, up to, and until after, at which date all importations were entirely prohibited. In 1819 importations were permitted at a duty of 50 per cent.; which duty was subsequently reduced, and in 1834, was but 15 per cent. upon goods not made up, and 20 per cent. upon those made up, or partly so.

In 1834, the entire manufactures of wool in the kingdom were valued at £21,000,000, a little less than one-third of which were exported.

This brief sketch will show with what minuteness and rigid care this interest has received legislative protection in England, and how readily and perfectly even the agricultural interest is subjected to its advancement; and under that government, where the will of Parliament is the constitution and the only limit of power, they are not compelled to resort to prohibitory duties to reach such an object, but prohibitions in terms, as well of exportations as of importations, are readily and freely resorted to, when thought to be more efficient.

The duty upon bar-iron, in 1787, was £2 16s. 2d. per ton, and upon iron in pigs 27½ per cent.; but iron castings and manufactures of iron were prohibited. At this period, the exports of iron were very small, only some eleven or twelve thousand tons per year. In 1819, the duty upon bar-iron had been raised to £6 10 0, and upon iron in pigs to 17s. 6d, while the importation of iron castings was permitted at a duty of 20 per cent., and wrought iron and the manufactures of iron at 50 per cent. In 1834 the duty upon bar-iron had been reduced to £1 10 0, upon iron in pigs to 10s, upon castings to 10 per cent., and upon wrought-iron and the manufactures to 20 per cent. In this year, the exports of iron were 145,000 tons, and in 1838, 255,317 tons. The substitution of pit for wood coal, about a century ago, gave a wonderful impetus to this manufacture in Great Britain, and reduced the price of iron one half in a comparatively short period.

The manufacture of cottons to any considerable extent in Great

Britain, is comparatively of recent origin. It is supposed to have existed to some extent in the early part of the seventeenth century; but down to a period as late as 1773, cotton was only used for filling upon a linen warp. This manufacture was also at first domestic, and very generally scattered over the country. The weavers purchased their linen warp of the Irish, their cotton wool in their own markets, and from these materials made their cloth in their own houses, and sold it where they could find purchasers. About 1760, the merchants of Manchester commenced to purchase the warp and cotton, and send agents into the country to hire the weavers to manufacture cloth for them. At this time the whole value of the manufacture in the kingdom was but £200,000 per annum. In 1767, Hargrave invented the *spinning-jenny*, and soon after Arkwright invented the *spinning-frame*. About 1785 Compton invented the *mule-jenny*, and Cartwright the *power-loom*. After these improvements the manufacture extended itself with unexampled rapidity, although this has never been an interest so peculiarly favored by British legislation as the woollens interest. At an early period this branch of manufacture was directly discouraged, and almost prohibited by law. In 1721 a law was passed imposing a penalty of £5 upon the weaver, and £20 upon any person who should sell a piece of cotton calico within the realm. This was to protect the woollen and linen manufactures; and fifteen years after this time, this legislation was so modified that calicoes *manufactured in Great Britain* were permitted to be worn, "provided the warp thereof was entirely of linen yarn."

At this early period importations of cotton wool were permitted free of duty; and as early as 1788, the manufacturers were protected by an import duty of from 44 to 50 per cent. In 1819, these duties were raised to 50 and 67½ per cent.; and in 1834 were reduced to 10 and 20 per cent.

Nothing can exhibit more forcibly the advance of the cotton manufacture in Great Britain, or of the production of cotton wool in this country, than a brief reference to our exports of that article to that country. In 1791, the first cotton wool was imported into England from the United States, and the quantity was 189,316 pounds. In 1792, the quantity was less, being only 138,328 pounds. In 1793, Whitney invented the *cotton-gin*, and in 1794 we sent to Great Britain 1,601,760 pounds of cotton; in 1795, 5,276,300 pounds; and in 1837, (forty-two years,) this export had reached the enormous amount of 444,211,537 pounds. Previous to 1831, the import duty into Great Britain did not exceed six per cent. It was then raised to 10s. sterling per cwt., which duty was found too burdensome to the British manufacture, and in 1833 it was reduced to 2s. 11d. per cwt. At about this period, the estimated value per annum of the manufactures of cotton, in the realm, was £34,000,000 sterling, more than a third beyond the value of the manufactures of wool at the same period. Of this amount of manufactures, about one-half are annually exported, and find their market out of the kingdom.

Such is a very brief sketch of these three important branches of manufacture, wool, iron, and cotton, in Great Britain, from their infancy, until they became extensive and important exporting interests; and it deserves remark, that that one of the three which depends entirely upon a foreign material, and which has been the least favored by legislation, had become by far the most important of the three, and much the most extensive and important manufacturing interest in the kingdom. Another remark should also be made, and it is that all these interests have long since advanced beyond the reach of protecting duties, by becoming exporting interests, and being compelled to seek the open markets of the world for a very large share of their productions. The present import duties, being low revenue duties, is conclusive proof upon this point.

This brief history shows a further fact connected with the arguments urged in support of the prohibitory policy of this country. It is that Great Britain has reached that condition which the advocates of that system here seem to suppose is so very desirable, and will be such a source of wealth, happiness, and independence to this country—the condition when the population of the country require all its produce of provisions for their own sustenance. There the agriculturalist has that home market, the exclusive benefits of which hold so conspicuous a place in these arguments.

What has been, and what is now, the influence upon the labor of Great Britain of this home monopoly of food? This is the point I am at present discussing, and it is in reference to the influence upon labor that I now propose to examine the protective and prohibitory system of that Government, and its general legislative policy in respect to the agricultural interest. Here, again, I shall be compelled to be tedious, but to myself the examination is not without deep and exciting interest. I propose to confine myself principally to breadstuffs, and mostly to the article of wheat.

I find that, from the conquest in the eleventh century down to 1436, (nearly four hundred years,) the *exportation* of breadstuffs from England was entirely prohibited, while I find no notice of any restraint upon importation. The declared policy during this period was to secure an abundance of provisions, and low prices. In other words, it was a system of protection to labor at the expense of capital.

In the year last named, a law was passed to permit the exportation of breadstuffs when the home price should have fallen to a certain specified point. For wheat it was about 36 cents per bushel, and other grains in proportion. The policy of this legislation was to relieve agriculture from the depression of its own overstocked markets, but under the restriction, that exportation must cease when the domestic price should rise above the point named.

Laws were also passed to regulate and restrain the domestic trade in breadstuffs. These laws made it highly penal for purchasers to buy up and engross the stocks in grain, and prohibited purchasing in one part of the kingdom to sell in another.

In 1562, exportation was permitted when the domestic price should fall to about 54 cents the bushel of wheat; and in 1571, the permission was extended to the price of about $1 07; but an export duty of about 10¾ cents was imposed, to be paid to the public treasury.

In 1624, the laws imposing restraints upon the internal trade in breadstuffs were materially modified.

In 1670, the point of exportation was extended to the price of about $1 47 per bushel for wheat, the same export duty being imposed. The same law *prohibited* importations when the home price should be at or below the point of exportation, and imposed an import duty of 22 1-5 cents per bushel until the home price should rise to $2 22 cents, when importations could be made free of duty.

This appears to be the first law adapting the policy of direct protection to agriculture by prohibitions and import duties.

In 1673 only three years after, all the laws restraining the internal trade in grain were wholly repealed, evidently in furtherance of the same policy of removing the restrictions upon agriculture and extending its privileges.

In 1689, sixteen years later, the policy on the subject of the exportation of breadstuffs was precisely reversed. The export duty of 10¾ cents per bushel was repealed, and a bounty allowed of about 14 cents per bushel, to be paid from the public treasury, upon the exportation of wheat, when the home price should be at or below $1 33 per bushel. This swept away the last remaining vestige of legislation, designed, or calculated, to make bread plenty or cheap; and adopted fully the policy of legislating, as our system proposes to do, to make it scarce and dear.

From this period until 1773, almost a century, the legislation fluctuated—at some periods exportation being wholly prohibited, and at others the sums paid in bounties upon exportation being very large. In the single year 1750 these bounties paid amounted to $1,062,270. At the early part of this interval, the import duty was increased to about 45¾ cents per bushel upon wheat, when the home price was at or below $1 52 per bushel; and half that duty above that price and below $2 30, when importations were permitted free. In 1699, 1703, 1704, and 1747, additions were made to this duty, the last law fixing it at 63 cents per bushel when the domestic price was at or below $1 25, and continuing very heavy duties until that price chould rise to the former limit of $2 30.

In 1773 a great change was made. Importations were allowed at a merely nominal duty, when the home price should rise to $1 37 per bushel for wheat, and exportation was entirely prohibited when that price should be above $1 22. This law also first allowed importations of wheat in bond. Here was an extensive remission of the former protective policy in favor of the consumers of breadstuffs, and consequently in favor of labor. From this time until 1791 no material change took place in the general policy of the legislation, though several laws were passed increasing the import duty when the price of wheat was at or below the limit before fixed of $1 37 per bushel, the last bringing that duty up to 69 cents per bushel.

In 1791 new demands were made for further protection to the agricultural interest. Deep fears were expressed that the country would be brought to a dependence upon foreign wheat for its bread, unless greater encouragement was given to the domestic wheat grower. The duty was then 69 cents per bushel, but that duty ceased when the home price should rise above $1 37. The consequence of this agitation was the continuance of that duty until the home price should rise above $1 43, and the addition of heavy duties between that price and $1 54 per bushel.

In this legislation is furnished the clearest evidence that the consumption of bread-stuffs in the kingdom was exceeding its fair natural production, and the brief sketch I have given of the advance of the manufacturing interests will show that at this period it was that the manufactures of woollens, iron, and cotton, were making their most rapid extensions, forced along by very high protecting duties or positive prohibitions. The consequence of this farther protection to the grain-growing interests was a forced movement in that direction. Lands much more suited to grazing were taken in and put to tillage under the artificial encouragement and the necessities of the country for bread, and mark the first consequence.

In 1793, at the expiration of but two years, the bounties upon the exportation of wheat from the realm were revived. The domestic markets had become so soon overstocked, and as the land-owners could not sustain the consequent fall in the home price, a bounty must be paid to them, from the public treasury, for exporting their surplus to foreign countries, and selling it there cheaper than they were willing to sell it in the markets of their own country.

In 1797 the Bank of England suspended specie payments, prices of commodities and of bread-stuffs with others rose greatly, and demands for further protection to the grain-growers was the speedy consequence; and in this year, and also in 1803 and 1804, moderate additions were made to the import duty.

A second law, in 1804, fixed the import duty at 86¼ cents per bushel, when the price should be at or below $1 80, and a moderate duty between that price and $1 89. This act continued the bounties on exportation when the home price should fall to $1 35.

In 1805, 1806, 1809, and 1813, laws were passed increasing the import duty; the last fixing it at $1 13 per bushel, when the price in the domestic market should be at or below $1 80.

In 1814, all restrictions upon exportation were taken off, and all bounties upon exportation repealed.

In 1815, after a desperate struggle in the country and in Parliament, a law was passed *prohibiting* importations *for domestic consumption*, when the price of wheat was at or below $2 30 per bushel, and allowing them, *free of duty*, when the price rose above that point.

Here this branch of British legislation reached its climax, and between that time and 1827, several acts were passed permitting importations of bread-stuffs, for specified periods, or in limited quantities, or under special orders from the crown or the board of trade, at very moderate duties; and upon one occasion the lords commissioners of trade actually admitted the importation of a considerable quantity of bread-stuffs, in the face of the law, and subsequently sought and received the sanction of Parliament for their act.

In 1827 a modification of this extreme protection took place. The import duty was fixed at 57 cents per bushel when the price of wheat should be at or below $1 72; and for every fall from that price of 22 cents, 44 cents were added to the duty; and for every rise in the price of 22 cents above the point fixed, ($1 72,) 44 cents were to be taken from the duty, until wheat should come to be about $2 per bushel, when the duty was to be stationary, and merely nominal—only equal to about 2¾ cents per bushel. This act was limited upon its face, and was to expire on the 1st of May, 1828. This was the first direct introduction of the sliding-scale of duties, which still characterizes the British corn laws; and these modifications of the law of 1815 were predicated upon the admission that the protection to this interest had been carried to excess under that law.

In 1828 a general law fully adopting the sliding-scale, so called, gave again permanent regulation to these duties. The point fixed for importations at a merely nominal duty, was a domestic price a trifle above $2 per bushel. For a fall of 1s. sterling below this price, 2s. 8d. were added to the duty per quarter of eight bushels; for a fall of a second shilling per quarter, four shillings more were added to the duty; and so on, irregularly increasing the duty as the home price of wheat should fall, until, at the price of $1 85, the duty should be 57 cents per bushel; and from that point the duty was to increase exactly as the price should fall.

After this period no material change is believed to have taken place until the now existing law, which fixes the duty at 55½ cents per bushel when the price of wheat is $1 41½, and diminishes the duty exactly, or almost exactly, as the price rises, until it reaches $2, when the duty becomes fixed, and merely nominal—1s. per quarter of eight bushels.

Such is a brief and very imperfect sketch of the protection which British legislation has given, first to the *consumers*, and then to the *producers*, of bread-stuffs.

A mere glance at the legislation in reference to a few other articles of provisions will close this review. In 1787, the import duty upon hams and bacon was $10 43 per cwt.; that duty in 1819 was raised to $12 43, and is now just half that amount, $6 21 per cwt. The importation of salted beef and pork was prohibited in 1787 and in 1819, and now the duty is $2 66 per cwt. In 1787, the import duty upon butter was but 55½ cents per cwt., and in 1819, and at the present time, it is $4 44. Upon cheese, the duty in 1787 was 33⅓ cents per cwt., and in 1819, and at the present time, it is $2 31. Such has been the protection extended to these important agricultural productions, which are equally necessary articles of food.

Such has been the British system of protection to domestic interests, as the terms are used in this debate—to great branches of manufucture, and to the great and leading interests of agriculture—and what have been the fruits to the British population, to the British masses, to British labor?—for this last is my present point of inquiry.

Need I refer to the present condition of the laboring masses of Great Britain to answer this question? Are authorities required to establish and illustrate the condition of that portion of the British population? I shall not attempt to adduce them. The very argument upon which the present tariff law is sustained, and its policy justified, by its most intelligent as well as most distinguished advocates here, admits all I wish to infer, as the fruits of the British system. What is that argument? That our manufactures, our agriculture, our every interest, require to be protected against "*the pauper labor of Europe*," and of what country in Europe so much as Great Britain? What other country holds such stern competition with us in almost all our manufacturing interests, and especially in wool, iron, and cotton? Not one, and not all the countries of Europe combined. Protection, then, is demanded most emphatically against the pauper labor of England, of Great Britain. And hence my argument drawn from the practical workings of the British system, cannot be inapplicable or inappropriate.

Again, I will repeat, I am examining the influence of this prohibitory and monopolizing system upon labor, upon the condition and comforts of the laboring classes, and upon the wages of labor.

What, then, is the present condition of the day-laborer in Great Britain? What in England itself? That of poverty, want, and hunger. Poverty in his dwelling, in his clothing, in his food. I remember to have seen, within one or two years, extracts from some public document, I believe some examination before a committee of

Parliament, in which it was stated that the agricultural laborer of England did not consume as much wholesome bread by about one-fourth as the same description of laborers in France, and nearly one half less than the same laborer in this country; that he did not have, on the average, to exceed one full meal of butcher's meat per week; and that the laborers in the manufactories were not as well fed as those employed in agriculture. The same document stated that the laborer in Ireland was scarcely acquainted with the articles of meat and bread, as articles of his own food, the potato being almost his exclusive living.

Such have been the fruits of this system of prohibitions and monopoly of bread to labor, in Great Britain, and such is the condition to which a rigid adherence to it for many centuries has reduced the common laborer of that country. It has produced an impassable separation between labor and capital, and an examination of the official documents upon which the modern British legislation is predicated will show that the great inquiry is, how will any proposed measure affect capital; the rents of land; the revenues of the wealthy classes; the credit of the stocks?—not how it will affect the working man or his comforts. The tendency there has been to benefit capital at the expense of labor, until it has made the capitalist an aristocrat, rolling in wealth, holding the labor of the country under his feet, by his monopoly over all the pursuits of industry, and the Government of the country and the control of its policy, in his hands, by the power of the loans which the profits of his capital arising from this legislation has enabled him to make to it. It has made the Government a proud, splendid, and powerful bankrupt, buried under a mountain of debt which it never hopes to pay; and it has made the working man a starving beggar—a legalized pauper.

Can a like policy and like measures fail to produce like results upon the laboring man of this country? They have produced them to an almost equal extent in France, Spain, Austria, and every other country where the monopolizing policy has controlled the legislation. In Great Britain they have been produced most perfectly, because there the policy has been adopted most extensively and pursued most rigidly; but everywhere the marked effect has been to separate capital and labor, and to place the latter entirely in the power of the former; and an invariable consequence has been to increase the profits of capital, and diminish the wages, the comforts, and the independence of labor. Ireland affords the most striking example of the extent to which the power and oppression of capital over labor can be carried. There even the landlord is a permanent absentee, not simply from his estate, but from the country, and everything which will sell is carried away to extinguish his rents and swell his gains, while that which will not, remains to subsist an almost naked and almost starving tenantry, suffering under the oppressions of a merciless agent of their absentee landlord.

I have letters, informing me that persons are now engaged, in various parts of the country, endeavoring to prejudice the minds of our honest Irish laborers against those who seek to modify the present tariff law, alleging that it is done to benefit British labor, at the expense of the labor of this country. Do they hope to convince these warm-hearted sons of oppression, who have fled from this system at home, that it will be a blessing to confer it upon them here? Are they to be made to believe that the British policy, which has brought the laborer in Great Britain to absolute starvation, is a policy which is to promote their happiness in this country? They will pay, as cheerfully as any portion of our population, such taxes as the support of the Government may require, but their experience at home will not be likely to make them easily believe that taxation will bring them either comforts or independence.

Still, it is said, we require protection against the pauper labor of their country, and of other European countries. This is not the ground assumed at an earlier stage of this policy. Then it was, that our manufacturers required protection against the increased cost of the raw materials for their manufacture in this country over that cost in the manufacturing countries of Europe. I hold in my hand the minutes of testimony taken before the committee on manufactures of the House of Representatives, during the session of Congress of 1827–28, and previous to the passage of the tariff law of 1828. The testimony to which I refer related to the manufacture of wool; and every witness who answered the interrogatory agreed in stating that wool could be manufactured as cheap in this country as in England, the manufacturer here having the wool and other materials at the same price.

[Mr. Wright here read the testimony of several witnesses, among which were the following:—

Col. James Shepherd, of Northampton, Massachusetts, witness, was asked the following question, and gave the following answer:

" *Question.* Of an equal quality of wool, at present prices, in England and the United States, can the English manufacturer make a cheaper fabric than can be made in the United States? If so, how much cheaper?

"*Answer.* The difference in the price of the fabric would be the difference of the price of the wool, in my opinion, as I think we can manufacture it as cheap as they can!"

Mr. W. read the testimony of Abraham Marland of Andover, Massachusetts; William W. Young, of Wilmington, Delaware; James Walcott, Jr., of Southbridge, Massachusetts; and Joshua Clapp, of Boston, Massachusetts, to the same purport.

He then read the testimony of Joshua W. Pierce, of Somersworth, New Hampshire, as follows:—

"*Question.* Without reference to the price of wool, can the fabric be manufactured as cheap in the United States as in England?

"*Answer.* I think it can. All my information brings me to this conclusion; and one reason I would assign is, that we substitute a much larger share of the labor of females than they do in England, in the woollen manufacture."

He also read the testimony of Elenterre Irene Dupont, of New Castle county, Delaware, as follows:—

"*Question.* Without reference to the difference in the price of wool, can the fabric be manufactured as cheap in the United States as in England?

"*Answer.* The woollen manufactory is not fairly established in this country, but I know no reason why we cannot manufacture as well, and as cheap, as they can in England, except the difference in the price of labor, *for which*, in my opinion, *we are fully compensated by other advantages.* Our difficulties are not the cost of manufacturing, but the great fluctuations in our home market, caused by the excessive and irregular foreign importations. The high prices we pay for labor are, in my opinion, *beneficial* to the American manufacturer, as for those wages he gets a much better selection of hands, and those capable of, and willing to, perform a much greater amount of labor in a given time. The American manufacturer, also, uses a larger share of labor-saving machinery than is used in the English manufactories, which very much diminishes the effect of the higher rates of wages upon the actual cost of our goods."]

Here is the sworn testimony of practical manufacturers in 1828.

They did not, then, suppose that they required protection against "the pauper labor" of England. Whether time has changed their interests, in this respect, I am unable to say. I do not suppose it has materially, as I am not aware that the wages of labor have risen in this country, or fallen in England, so as to widen the disparity between the two countries, very essentially, since 1828.

Whether these witnesses were, at the time, laboring under a mistake in judgment upon this point, is another question which I am not able to decide. I will confess that I had some doubts, when the testimony was given; and yet it satisfied me that the disparity, if any, must be much less than seemed to be generally supposed.

Another remark is suggested here, from the answer of the last witness. Our cotton and woollen manufactures must now certainly be fully and firmly established; and I suppose the skill possessed in these branches must be as perfect, as to the qualities and kinds of goods manufactured, as that possessed by manufacturers elsewhere. In 1828, this was one of the principal grounds upon which protection was sought. It was contended that our manufacturers wanted time to establish their business, and acquire the skill necessary to compete with foreign establishments. Has sufficient time to accomplish these objects been allowed, that now the ground is changed upon which continued protection, beyond that which the collection of the revenue will afford, is still demanded? I suppose that must be so, and hence it is necessary to examine this new ground, and more especially as to its influence upon labor.

If we are to adopt the prohibitory system to protect our manufacturing interests against the pauper labor of Europe, when is the ground for that protection to cease? Certainly not until one of two events can be brought about. It must continue either until pauper labor shall cease to exist in Europe, or until the system shall produce pauper labor here, which can compete upon equal terms, with the pauper labor of other manufacturing countries. Who ever expects to see the time when there will not be pauper labor in England, and the other European countries? Certainly no one, while the present institutions, and systems, and policy, of those Governments continue. The first event, therefore, is not to take place, and thus relieve our manufacturers from their demands for protection against the pauper labor of Europe.

How is it as to the second of these events? Will the prohibitory system, fully introduced and rigidly adhered to, reduce the labor of this country to a similar state of pauperism, and therefore of equal competition, with the labor of Europe? It has been seen that such has been one of its fruits, in every country where it has been rigidly enforced. Suppose the system to be carried to the British extent in this country, and that a sufficient portion of our population be induced by it to resort to manufacturing and the mechanic arts to consume all our agricultural productions: can that portion of the population which continues in agricultural pursuits consume all the manufactured products of the portion engaged in that branch? Certainly not the one half of them. As one man employed in agriculture can feed several engaged in other pursuits, so one man employed in manufactures can clothe several engaged in agriculture. What, then, is to become of the surplus of manufactures? Now there is a surplus of agricultural productions, and that surplus is and must be exported; and hence those productions are beyond the reach of protection from our duties. So must the surplus of manufactures, in the assumed case, be exported; and then will manufactures be beyond the reach of our protection, while the agricultural productions, being all consumed at home, will be brought within the reach of protection from our duties.

Such is precisely the present condition of Great Britain, and her agricultural interests prove as ready to demand her legislative protection, and a monopoly of her home markets, as did her manufacturing interests, in their infancy, while the latter have passed beyond the reach of benefit from the policy, by having become her exporting interests.

Suppose this revolution accomplished in our country, and that all our agricultural products are consumed at home, and all our exports are made to consist of our manufactured products: how will then be our manufacturing labor? It will be beyond the reach of protecting duties, because its products would have to be sold in the open markets of the world, and to meet the competition of the world, the pauper labor of Europe and all. No import duties of ours can enhance the value of their products, or give to them the monopoly of a market. They must meet competition, as the great mass of our agricultural productions now do, wherever a market can be found. Then, however, our agriculture, like that of England at the present time, will claim the protection within its reach, the exclusive possession of the markets of its own country. It will command and secure that protection, for it is, and will be, the commanding interest. It will here, as in other countries, draw the capital of the nation to itself, for the security of the investment, when the control of the national policy shall enable that capital, thus invested, to dictate its own profits.

When such a state of things shall have been produced by a prohibitory policy on the part of this Government, what will measure the compensation to labor? and what, especially, to manufacturing labor? The manufacturer can make his calculations as well then as now. He can tell the cost of his materials, the interest upon his capital invested, the wear and tear of his machinery, and the promise of his market, as well under such a system as under the present; and, consequently, he will know as certainly what he can afford to pay for labor, and when his interests wlll be better served by closing his factory than by employing laborers to run it. What will he do? Will he not pay such rates of wages for labor as he can afford to pay, or employ no laborers at all? Most certainly he will. What will be his movable item of cost in deciding the question whether he shall work his mills or suffer them to remain idle? Most certainly the wages of his labor. He cannot control the cost of the materials of his manufacture, or the cost of the provisions and other necessaries of the laborers he is to employ; and he will not abate the profits upon his capital; but he can and will control the wages of his labor.

If, then, pauper labor in Europe meets him in the foreign market, he must and will have pauper labor at home to compete with it, or he will close his mills and employ no labor. And suppose he does that, what is this mass of unemployed manufacturing labor to do? Where is it to resort? Will agriculture take it up? Certainly not; because that will extend its productions beyond a supply for the home market, and destroy its monopoly and high prices, by compelling it to export.

This is precisely the result of the experience of Great Britain, as before shown, and of all other countries which have pursued the monopolizing policy. The result in all has been dear bread and cheap labor; the prosperity of capital and the subjection of the masses; the triumph of the power of money over the moral and physical power of men. It must be so in this country, if ever the time shall arrive that its manufacturing, rather than its agricultural, becomes its exporting interest. Then the laborer will be fettered and bound down to such fixed employment as capital shall find it for its interest to give, and the wages of labor must, as in England now, be controlled by the prices at which the products of manufacture can be sold abroad. I will make a brief reference to testimony taken before a committee of the House of Commons of the British Parliament in 1842, to show the working of the system upon the wages of labor there. The witness was a Mr. Joseph Walker, an extensive manufacturer, at Wolverhampton, England. Speaking of the duties upon the foreign iron used in their manufactories, and the effect of that duty upon the wages they are able to pay for labor, he says, "that difference must come out of the wages of labor here; for we actually export the goods that we make of foreign iron; and when we export them, we must sell them at the price the foreigner does."

"*Question.* You mean to say that that burden compells you to reduce the wages so as to enable you to compete with the foreigner? *Answer.* It has the effect of reducing them the whole amount of the duty."

Again: speaking of duties upon articles of provisions, the witness says: "Undoubtedly all the duties put upon the importation of food of all descriptions—on coffee, sugar, corn, and everything of that sort—are a direct disadvantage to the laboring man of England; because it is evident that the manufacturer must sell his goods at the price at which the foreigner sells his; and, in order to do that, he must reduce his wages to the workmen." Again:

"*Question.* Do the wages of the workmen at Wolverhampton rise and fall with the price of food, and other articles of necessity? *Answer.* No: I think not. I do not think it operates. The wages of labor depend upon the demand for the goods, not upon the price of the provisions. We witness, now, low wages and a high price of provisions; high prices of bread, meat and groceries." Again: "*Question.* Unless the price of your manufactures was lower, how would you be better able to meet the foreign manufacturer than you now are? *Answer.* We are now compelled to fall back upon a reduction of wages to meet the foreign manufacturers, because the cost of the raw material is the same to them and to us; and it is, therefore, the workmen who suffer. If we do not get 10s. for a piece of goods in a foreign market, and we are obliged to take 8s., we must then either cease to send the goods there, or fall back upon the wages to reduce it to 8s."

Here is the sworn testimony of an intelligent manufacturer of goods in England for an export market, and here his exposition of the influence upon the wages of labor, of the condition I have assumed; when the productions of agriculture find consumers at home to their full extent, and when the manufacturing has become the exporting interest.

I have said I do not wish to see the time when this country shall cease to export the bread-stuffs and other articles of food. Here are my reasons. This witness has stated them from a practical experience. I do not wish to see the time when our duties will fall upon the hungry laborer, because he must have food; and this testimony shows that the capitalist will not let them fall upon him. If compelled to pay a duty upon his iron, he will deduct the amount from the wages of his laborer; and the laborer must work for such wages as he can get, or he cannot eat his highly-taxed food. Such are my views of the unavoidable final fruits of the prohibitory system upon labor and the laboring man.

So much has been said, in the course of this debate, about the present prosperity of the country, and the agency of the present tariff law in producing the prosperous change, that I feel compelled to offer a remark or two upon that subject. And, in the first place, it is my duty to inquire to what extent the country can now be said to be in a prosperous state. It is important to settle the fact, before it will become necessary to seek for the cause.

The commercial exhibition, which I have presented for the year 1843, certainly does not furnish much ground for exultation, so far as that great interest is concerned. I am aware that trade is holding out a somewhat better promise for the present year; though nothing I have yet seen indicates very abundant importations for this year. I suspect that gentlemen have rather looked at the duties collected, under the present very high rates, than at the value of the importations; for they will remember, if the imports should rise up to what has been considered in former years a healthful and prosperous state of commerce, with the present very limited free list, the revenue collected must be enormous under the present rates of duty.

How is it with agriculture? Is that interest prosperous? I can speak within my own limited acquaintance, and not beyond it. In the county of my residence, the beef and pork and butter and cheese of the farmer, during the last fall, which was the season for the sale of those productions, found one of the dullest markets which that section of the country has ever known, and at prices at least from 15 to 20 per cent. reduced from the previous very low year. Such is the state of agricultural prosperity there, and I am informed and believe that all the northern and western counties of my state have met the same experience. Bread-stuffs, and especially wheat, I believe did a little better last fall, and found ready markets at moderately fair prices.

The manufacturers, it is said, have been doing a very lucrative business under this law, and I presume that interest may be called prosperous; and I think the prosperity derivable from this legislation, must be limited mainly to that interest.

I do believe that the law has exerted some influence in the restoration of the public credit; and the belief that it would, operated strongly in inducing me to vote for it; but a much more moderate law, and one arranged upon fair revenue principles, while it would have had at least an equal effect in that direction, would have less embarrassed agriculture and commerce, and laid a more safe and healthful foundation for the lasting prosperity of our manufactures.

In speaking of our prosperity, senators seem to forget our condition at the time the law passed. The evils of our bloated credit system had passed over the country, blighting everything like prosperity, and leaving only debt and distrust. Time has measurably restored confidence where it was deserved, and the sponge of the bankrupt law has wiped away the hopeless load of debt. In this condition, the country is as certain to rise into a state of prosperity, as the young and sound constitution, to recover health, after the seeds of the disease which has prostrated it have been eradicated. Here is the great and resistless cause of the moderate degree of prosperity which has yet appeared, and it will be scarcely in the power of bad legislation to prevent its onward progress, though it may, as I believe this law will, if not properly modified, materially retard it.

Finally, I will ask, can a system of taxation be made a system of blessings to a whole people? Is it possible that a country can be taxed into prosperity, and wealth, and happiness? If the tax-collector be benefited, must not the tax-payer feel the burden? If one interest is positively promoted by the arrangement of the tax, must uot some other one be burdened by it? It is a tax, and must be paid, and all therefore cannot receive, and none pay. Would

Congress think of imposing taxes, if revenue were not wanted? Would any one think of imposing high duties if there were no expenses of the Government to provide for? I suppose not; and hence it seems to me that the duties we do impose should be imposed to raise the means to meet those expenses, not to defeat revenue by prohibiting importations.

Let me not be misunderstood. My argument is not between protection and no protection. It is between that degree of protection which is incident to revenue and consistent with it, and prohibition, destroying revenue and conferring monopoly. I am willing to throw the whole mass of the revenue from customs—from sixteen to twenty millions of dollars a year—between the domestic and foreign competing interests, for the protection of the former; but I am not willing to shut out competition, break up our commerce, and destroy our revenue, to favor any interest. I believe such a policy unequal and unjust; that it will unreasonably burden the exporting interests, and must finally fall with crushing weight upon the working man.

AGRICULTURAL ADDRESS.

[Read by JOHN A. DIX, at the Exhibition of the New York State Agricultural Society, held at Saratoga, September 16th, 1847.]

Before proceeding to read the Address, Mr. Dix made the following remarks :—

Mr. President and Gentlemen of the Society:—I have come here, at your request, to perform a melancholy duty—to read to you and to this assembly, the Annual Address prepared for the occasion by Silas Wright. In the order of your proceedings it was to have been delivered by himself. The providence of God has overruled your arrangements. The voice which was to have been heard by the thousands assembled here, is silenced forever. He who was to have stood before you where I now stand, and to have borne a prominent part in your proceedings, has gone down in the fulness of health and strength, to the tomb. The large space which Mr. Wright filled in the public eye, his great talents and the moral elevation of his character, render that bereavement a national calamity. The general gloom which the intelligence of his death carried with it, attests the profound respect in which he was held by his countrymen, and the strong impression which his character and services had wrought in the public mind.

The admonition contained in these hidden dispensations of Providence is the more solemn, when those who are conspicuous for their intellect and their virtue, are called from the field of their labor, while they are yet fresh and vigorous, and when the path they tread seems but an avenue to higher distinction. It is thus that the career of Mr. Wright has been terminated, while his faculties were in full vigor, and while much of the high promise of his life was yet to be fulfilled. His death is the more impressive at this time, and in this place, from the peculiar circumstances by which his name is connected with the proceedings of the day. The intellectual labor in which he had been engaged, at the invitation of the society, was performed. The address he was to have delivered, was completed during the very last hours of his life. Thus, the accomplishment of the task he had undertaken for the society, may be said to have been coincident with the termination of his earthly career.

I am not here, Mr. President and gentlemen, to pronounce a eulogy on the character or public services of Mr. Wright; but to perform the more humble part of reading to you the address, which lies before me—the last labor of his life—and which seems to come as a legacy to the society, to his friends, and to his countrymen. At the same time, I have thought it might not be inappropriate or unsatisfactory to refer briefly to some of the circumstances attending his decease.

It is well known that Mr. Wright for the last twenty years has held, without interruption, various public trusts requiring incessant mental labor, and leading to a habitually sedentary life. In the intervals of his service in the Senate of the United States, from 1833 to 1845, a portion of his time was devoted to the cultivation of his garden and a few acres of land, by his own hands. While governor of the state he purchased an additional quantity of land, and when relieved from the duties of the executive office, he applied himself with great diligence and zeal to the improvement of it. His labor was not merely that of superintendence. He was himself a principal laborer in all his agricultural operations. He hired an able-bodied, hard-working man, and went with him into the field, ploughing, mowing and harvesting, performing himself a full share of labor; and, after the fatigues of the day, retiring to his study and passing his evenings in reading and in correspondence. To these excessive exertions of body and of mind, and to the too rapid transition from a life of comparative bodily inactivity to one of severe manual labor, is doubtless to be traced the sudden attack, which terminated his existence. I need not dwell upon details, which have been so widely circulated, and are now so generally known. Suffice it to say, that on the morning after he had revised the address, which I am about to read, and after having made a few corrections, leaving it word for word as it now is, and probably precisely what it would have been if he had lived to deliver it himself, he was seized with a severe pain in the breast at the village post-office,—walked calmly to his house with a few friends, and in two hours he had as calmly breathed his last.

Such, gentlemen, were the last hours of Silas Wright! The same calmness which distinguished him throughout all the changes of his life, accompanied him at its close. From the first moment of his attack he appeared to understand its fatal character, and he submitted to it without a struggle or a murmur.

In him perished one of the purest models of a citizen and a statesman the country contained. He may be said, indeed, to have been an impersonation of the true character and spirit of her institutions. In the traditions and legends of early ages, before these eras of legitimate history, their periods are markedly the lines and actions of distinguished personages, invested with the ruling characteristics of the communities of which they were intended to be the types. The spirit of the political system is thus illustrated by the individual example. Mr. Wright might have been copied without any coloring of the imagination, as an exemplification of the genius of ours—of what it is, and what it ought to be—of its simplicity, its purity and its strength. Plain and unostentatious in his manners, serene amid all the agitations of life, unambitious of wealth and honors, singularly courteous and kind in his intercourse with others, equally dignified—whether dealing with the most complex questions of public policy in the Senate chamber, or when tilling, with Roman simplicity, his own field—he recalled to mind those classical examples of distinguished patriotism and virtue, which gave lustre to the times in which they existed, and which have come down to us consecrated by the memory of ages.

The close of his life was in harmony with its whole course. It was appropriate that the last labors of his hands should have been performed with the implements of husbandry, and that the last effort of his mind should have been given to the cause of agriculture, a pursuit to which the great mass of his countrymen are devoted, and on which the purity of the body politic, and the durability of our social system, pre-eminently depend.

With these remarks, which I could not forbear to make, and for which I trust the occasion will furnish my apology, I proceed to read the address.

Mr. President, and Gentlemen of the State Agricultural Society:—

Had it been my purpose to entertain you with a eulogium upon the great interest confided to your care, the Agriculture of the State, I should find myself forestalled by the exhibition which surrounds us, and which has pronounced that eulogy to the eye, much more forcibly, impressively, eloquently, than I could command language to pronounce it to the ear of this assembly.

Had I mistakenly proposed to address to you a discourse upon agricultural production, this exhibition would have driven me from my purpose, by the conviction that I am a backward and scarcely initiated scholar, standing in the presence of masters, with the least instructed and experienced of whom, it would be my duty to change places.

The agriculture of our state, far as it yet is from maturity and perfection, has already become an art, a science, a profession, in which he who would instruct must be first himself instructed far beyond the advancement of him who now addresses you.

The pervading character of this great and vital interest, however; its intimate connection with the wants, comforts, and interests of every man in every employment and calling in life; and its controlling relations to the commerce, manufactures, substantial independence, and general health and prosperity of our whole people, present abundant subjects for contemplation upon occasions like this, without attempting to explore the depths or to define the principles of a science so profound, and, to the unitiated, so difficult, as is that of agriculture.

Agricultural production is the substratum of the whole superstructure; the great element which spreads the sail and impels the car of commerce, and moves the hands and turns the machinery of manufacture. The earth is the common mother of all, in whatever employment engaged and the fruits gathered from its bosom, are alike the indispensable nutriment and support of all. The productions of its surface and the treasures of its mines, are the material upon which the labor of the agriculturist, the merchant, and the manufacturer, are alike bestowed, and are the prize for which all alike toil.

The active stimulus which urges all forward, excites industry, awakens ingenuity, and brings out invention, is the prospect or hope of a market for the productions of their labor. The far mer produces to sell; the merchant purchases to sell; and the manufacturer fabricates to sell. Self-consumption of their respective goods, although an indispensable necessity of life, is a mere incident in the mind impelled to acquisition. To gain that which is not produced or required, by the sale of that which is possessed, is the great struggle of laboring man.

Agricultural production is the first in order, the strongest in necessity, and the highest in usefulness, in this whole system of acquisition. The other branches stand upon it, are sustained by it, and without it, could not exist. Still it has been almost uniformly, as the whole history of our state and country will show, the most neglected. Apprenticeship, education, a specific course of systematic instruction, has been, time out of mind, considered an indispensable pre-requisite to a creditable or successful engagement in commercial or mechanical pursuits; while to know how to wield the axe, to hold the plough, and to swing the scythe, has been deemed sufficient to entitle the possessor of that knowledge to the first place and the highest wages in agricultural employment.

A simple principle of production and of trade, always practically applied to manufactures and commerce, that the best and cheapest article will command the market, and prove the most profitable to the producer and the seller, because most beneficial to the buyer and consumer, is but beginning to receive its application to agriculture. The merchant, who, from a more extensive acquaintance with his occupation, a more attentive observation of the markets, better adapted means, and a more careful application of sound judgment, untiring energy and prudent industry, can buy the best and sell the cheapest, has always been seen to be the earliest and surest to accomplish the great object of his class, an independence for himself. So the mechanic, who, from a more thorough instruction in the principles and handicraft of his trade, or a more intense application of mind and judgment with labor, can improve the articles he fabricates, or the machinery and modes of their manufacture, and can thus produce the best and sell the cheapest, has always been seen to reach the same advantage over his competitors, with equal readiness and certainty; and that these results should follow these means and efforts, has been considered natural and unavoidable.

Still the agriculturist has been content to follow in the beaten track, to pursue the course his fathers have ever pursued, and to depend on the earth, the seasons, good fortune and Providence, for a crop, indulging the hope that high prices may compensate for diminished quantity or inferior quality. It has scarcely occurred to him, that the study of the principles of his profession, had anything to do with his success as a farmer, or that what he had demanded from his soils should be considered in connection with what he is to do for them, and what he is about to ask them to perform. He has almost overlooked the vital fact, that his lands, like his patient teams, require to be fed to enable them to perform well ; and especially has he neglected to consider, that there is a like connection between the quantity and quality of the food they are to receive, and the service to be required from them. Ready, almost always, to the extent of their ability, to make advances for the purchase of more lands, how few of our farmers, in the comparison, are willing to make the necessary outlays for the profitable improvement of the land they have?

These, and kindred subjects are beginning to occupy the minds of our farmers, and the debt they owe to this society for its efforts to awaken their attention to these important facts, and to supply useful and practical information in regard to them, is gradually receiving a just appreciation, as the assemblage which surrounds us, and the exhibitions upon this ground, most gratifyingly prove.

Many of our agriculturists are now vigorously commencing the study of their soils, the adaptation of their manures to the soil and the crop, the nature of the plants they cultivate, the food they require, and the best methods of administering that food to produce health and vigor and fruit; and they are becoming convinced that to understand how to plough and sow and reap, is not the whole education of a farmer; but that it is quite as important to know what land is prepared for the plough, and what seed it will bring to a harvest worthy of the labors of the sickle. Experience is steadily proving that, by a due attention to these considerations, a better article, doubled in quantity, may be produced from the same acre of ground, with a small proportionate increase of labor and expense, and that the farmer who pursues this improved system of agriculture, can, like the merchant and mechanic referred to, enter the market with a better production, at a cheaper price, than his less enterprising competitor.

The change in the agriculture of our state and country, opens to the mind reflections of the most cheering character. If carried out to its legitimate results, it promises a competition among our farmers, not to obtain the highest prices for inferior productions, but to produce the most, the best, and the cheapest of the necessaries of human life. It promises agricultural prosperity, with cheap and good bread, furnished in abundance to all who will eat within the rule prescribed to fallen man, in the sacred volume of the Divine law.

Steady resolution and persevering energy, are requisite to carry forward these improvements to that degree of perfection dictated alike by interest and by duty; and the stimulus of a steady and remunerating market will rouse that resolution, and nerve that energy. Without this encouragement in prospect, few will persevere in making improvements which require close and constant mental application, as well as severe physical labor. Agriculture will never be healthfully or profitably prosecuted by him whose controlling object is his own consumption. The hope of gain is the motive power to human industry, and is as necessary to the farmer as to the merchant or manufacturer. All who labor are equally stimulated by the prospect of a market which is to remunerate them for their toil, and without this hope, neither mental activity, nor physical energy, will characterize their exertions. True it is that the farmers of our country, as a class, calculate less closely the profits of their labor and capital, than men engaged in most other pursuits, and are content with lower rates of gain. The most of them own their farms, their stock and farming implements, unincumbered by debt. Their business gives but an annual return. They live frugally, labor patiently and faithfully, and at the close of the year, its expenses are paid from its proceeds, the balance remaining being accounted the profits of the year. Although a moderate sum. it produces contentment, without a computation of the rate per cent. upon the capital invested, or the wages it will pay to the proprietor and the members of his family. The result is an advance in the great object of human labor, and, if not rapid, it is safe and certain. It is a surplus beyond the expenses of living, to be added to the estate, and may be repeated in each revolving year.

If, however, this surplus is left upon the hands of the farmer, in his own products, for which there is no market, his energies are paralyzed, his spirits sink, and he scarcely feels that the year has added to his gains. He sees little encouragement in toiling on, to cultivate beyond his wants, productions which will not sell; and the chances are, that his farm is neglected, his husbandry becomes bad, and his gains in fact cease.

To continue a progressive state of improvement in agriculture, then, and to give energy and prosperity to this great and vital branch of human industry, a healthful and stable market becomes indispensable, and no object should more carefully occupy the attention of the farmers of the United States.

Deeply impressed with the conviction of this truth, benevolent minds have cherished the idea that a domestic market, to be influenced only by our own national policy, would be so far preferable, in stability and certainty, to the open market of the commercial world, as to have persuaded themselves that a sufficient market for our agricultural products is thus attainable. It is not designed to discuss the soundness of this theory, where it can be reduced to practice; but only to inquire whether the state of this country, the condition of its society, and the tendency and inclination of its population, as to their industrial pursuits, are such, at the present time, or can be expected to be such, for generations yet to come, as to render it possible to consume within the country, the surplus of the productions of our agriculture. The theory of an exclusively domestic market, for this great domestic interest, is certainly a very beautiful one, as a theory, and can scarcely fail to strike the mind favorably upon a first impression. Still examination has produced differences of opinion between statesmen of equal intelligence and patriotism, as to its influences upon the happiness and prosperity of a country and its population. Any examination of this question would lead to a discussion, properly considered, political, if not partisan; and all such discussions it is my settled purpose to avoid, as inappropriate to the place and the occasion.

I simply propose to inquire as to a fact, which must control the application of theories and principles of political economy touching this point, to our country and its agricultural population, without raising any question as to the wisdom of the one, or the soundness of the other. Is the consumption of this country equal to its agricultural production, or can it become so within any calculable period of years? How is the fact? May I not inquire without giving offence, or transcending the limits I have prescribed for myself in the discussion? Can a fair examination, scrupulously confined to this point, take a political bearing, or disturb a political feeling? It is certainly not my design to wound the feelings of any member of the society, or of any citizen of the country; and I have convinced myself that I may make this inquiry, and express the conclusions of my own mind as to the result, without doing either. If I shall prove to be in error, it will be an error as to the fact inquired after, and not as to the soundness of the principle in political economy dependent upon the fact for its application, because as to the soundness of the principle, I attempt no discussion and offer no opinion. It will be an error as to the applicability of a theory to our country, and not as to the wisdom or policy of the theory itself, because of the soundness or unsoundness of the theory; when it can be practically applied, I studiously refrain from any expression, as inappropriate here. With the indulgence of the society, I will inquire as to the fact.

Our country is very wide and very new. It embraces every variety of climate and soil most favorable to agricultural pursuits. It produces already almost every agricultural staple, and the most important are the ordinary productions of extensive sections of the country, and are now sent to the markets in great abundance.

Yet our agriculture is in its infancy almost everywhere, and at its maturity nowhere. It is believed to be entirely safe to assume that there is not one single agricultural county in the whole Union, filled up in an agricultural sense—not one such county which has not yet land to be brought into cultivation, and much more land, the cultivation of which is to be materially improved, before it can be considered as having reached the measure of its capacity for production. If this be true of the best cultivated agricultural county in the Union, how vast is the proportion of those counties which have entire townships, and of the states, which have not merely counties, but entire districts, yet wholly unpeopled, and unreclaimed from the wilderness state?

When to this broad area of the agricultural field of our country, we add our immense territories, organized and unorganized, who can compute the agricultural capacities of the United States, or fix a limit to the period when our surplus agricultural productions will increase with increasing years and population? Compare the census of 1830 and 1840 with the map of the Union, and witness the increase of population in the new states, which are almost exclusively agricultural, and who can doubt the strong and resistless inclination of our people to this pursuit?

Connect with these considerations of extent of country, diversity of soils, varieties of climate, and partial and imperfect cultivation, the present agricultural prospects of this country. Witness the rapid advances of the last dozen years in the character of our cultivation, the quality and quantity of our productions from a given breadth of land, and the improvements in all the implements by which the labor of the farmer is assisted and applied. Mark the vast change in the current of educated mind of the country, in respect to this pursuit; the awakened attention to its high respectability as a profession, to its safety from hazards, to its healthfulness to mind and body, and to its productiveness. Listen to the calls for information, for education, upon agricultural subjects, and to the demands that this education shall constitute a department in the great and all pervading system of our common school education, a subject at this moment receiving the especial attention, and being pressed forward by the renewed energies of this society. Behold the numbers of professors, honored with the highest testimonials of learning conferred in our country, devoting their lives to geological and chemical researches, calculated to evolve the laws of nature connected with agricultural productions. Go into our colleges and institutions of learning, and count the young men toiling industriously for their diplomas, to qualify themselves to become practical and successful farmers; already convinced that equally with the clerical, the legal, and the medical professions, that of agriculture requires a thorough and systematic education, and its successful practice the exercise of an active mind devoted to diligent study.

Apply these bright and brightening prospects to the almost boundless agricultural field of our country, with its varied and salubrious climate, its fresh and unbroken soils, its cheap lands and fee simple titles, and who can hope, if he would, to turn the inclinations of our people from this fair field of labor and of pleasure? Here the toil which secures a certain independence is sweetened by the constant and constantly varying exhibitions of nature in her most lovely forms, and cheered by the most benignant manifestations of the wonderful power and goodness of Nature's God. Cultivated by the resolute hands and enlightened minds of freemen, owners of the soil, properly educated, as farmers, under a wise and just adminis-

16*

tration of a system of liberal public instruction, such as should and will be, and aided by the researches of geology and chemistry, who can calculate the extent of the harvests to be gathered from this vast field of wisely directed human industry?

The present surplus of bread-stuffs of this country, could not have been presented in a more distinct and interesting aspect than during the present year. A famine in Europe, as wide-spread as it has been devastating and terrible, has made its demands upon American supplies, not simply to the extent of the ability of the suffering to purchase food, but in the superadded appeals to American sympathy in favor of the destitute and starving. Every call upon our markets has been fully met, and the heart of Europe has been filled with warm and grateful responses to the benevolence of our country, and of our countrymen, and yet the avenues of commerce are filled with the productions of American agriculture. Surely the consumption of this country is not now equal to its agricultural production.

If such is our surplus in the present limited extent and imperfect condition of our agriculture, can we hope that an exclusive domestic market is possible to furnish a demand for its mature abundance? In this view of this great and growing interest can we see a limit to the period, when the United States will present, in the commercial markets of the world, large surpluses of all the varieties of bread-stuffs, of beef, pork, butter, cheese, tobacco, and rice, beyond the consumption of our own country? And who, with the experience of the last few years before him, can doubt that the time is now at hand, when the two great staples of wool and hemp will be added to the list of our exportations?

These considerations, and others of a kindred character, which time will not permit me to detail, seem to me, with unfeigned deference, to prove that the agriculture of the United States, for an indefinite period yet to come, must continue to yield annual supplies of our principal staples, far beyond any possible demand of the domestic market, and must therefore remain, as it now is and has ever been, an exporting interest. As such, it must have a direct concern in the foreign trade and commerce of the country, and in all the regulations of our own and of foreign Governments which affect either, equal to its interest in a stable and adequate market.

If this conclusion be sound, then our farmers must surrender the idea of a domestic market to furnish the demand, and measure the value of their productions, and must prepare themselves to meet the competition of the commercial world in the markets of the commercial world, in the sale of the fruits of their labor. The marts of commerce must be their market, and the demand and supply which meet in those marts must govern their prices. The demand for home consumption, as an element in that market, must directly and deeply interest them, and should be carefully cultivated and encouraged; while all the other elements acting with it, and constituting together the demand of the market, should be studied with great care, and, so far as may be in their power, and consistent with other and paramount duties, should be cherished with equal care.

Does any one believe, that for generations yet to come, the agricultural operations of the United States are to be circumscribed within narrower comparative limits than the present; or that the agricultural productions of the country are to bear a less ratio to our population and consumption than they now do? I cannot suppose that any citizen, who has given his attention to the considerations which have been suggested, finds himself able to adopt either of these opinions. On the contrary, I think a fair examination must satisfy every mind that our agricultural surplus, for an indefinite future period, must increase much more rapidly than our population and the demand for domestic consumption. This I believe would be true without the efforts of associations, such as this, to improve our agriculture. The condition of the country, and the inclination and preference of our population for agricultural pursuits, would render this result unavoidable; and if this be so, when the impetus given to agricultural productions by the improvements of the day; the individual and associated efforts constantly making to push forward these improvements with an accelerated movement; the mass of educated mind turned to scientific researches in aid of agricultural labor; the dawning of a systematic and universal agricultural education; and the immense bodies of cheap, and fresh, and fertile lands, which invite the application of an improved agriculture, are added to the account, who can measure the extent or duration of our agricultural surplus, or doubt the soundness of the conclusion, that the export trade must exercise a great influence upon the market for the agricultural productions of the country for a long series of years to come?

Such is the conclusion to which my mind is forced, from an examination of this subject, in its domestic aspect simply; but there is another now presented of vast magnitude and engrossing interest, and demanding alike from the citizen and the statesman of this republic, the most careful consideration. All will at once understand me as referring to the changes and promises of change in the policy of the principal commercial nations of the world, touching their trade in the productions of agriculture. By a single step which was nothing less than commercial revolution, Great Britain practically made the change as to her trade; and subsequent events have clothed with the appearance of almost superhuman sagacity, the wisdom which thus prepared that country to meet the visitation of famine, which has so soon followed, without the additional evil of trampling down the systems of law to minister to the all-controlling necessities of hunger. Changes similar in character, and measurably equal in extent, though in many cases temporary in duration, have been adopted by several other European Governments, under circumstances which render it very doubtful how soon, if ever, a return will be made to the former policy of a close trade in the necessaries of human life.

New markets of vast extent and incalculable value, have thus been opened for our agricultural surplus, the durability and steadiness of which it is impossible yet to measure with certainty. It is in our power to say, however, that a great body of provocations to countervailing restrictive commercial regulations, is now removed, in some instances permanently, and in others temporarily in form; and it would seem to be the part of wisdom, for the agriculture of this country, by furnishing these markets to the extent of the demand, with the best articles, at the fairest prices, to show to those countries, and their respective Governments, that reciprocal commercial regulations, if they offer no other and higher attractions, present to their people a safeguard against starvation.

Such is the connection, now, between our agriculture and the export trade and foreign market, and these relations are to be extended and strengthened, rather than circumscribed and weakened, by our agricultural advances. The consumption of the country is far short of its production, and cannot become equal to it within any calculable period. On the contrary, the excess of production is to increase with the increase of population and settlement and the improvements in agriculture and agricultural education. These appear to me to be facts, arising from the condition of our country, and the tastes and inclinations of our people, fixed beyond the power of change, and to which theories and principles of political economy must be conformed, to be made practically applicable to us.

The American farmer, then, while carefully studying, as he should not fail to do, the necessities, the wants, and the tastes of all classes of consumers of his productions in this country, must not limit his researches for a market within those narrow bounds. He must extend his observations along the avenues of commerce, as far as the commerce of his country extends, or can be extended, and instruct himself as to the necessities and wants and tastes of the consumers of agricultural productions in other countries. He must observe attentively the course of trade, and the causes calculated to exert a favorable or adverse influence upon it; watch closely the commercial policy of other countries, and guard vigilantly that of his own; accommodate his productions, as far as may be, to the probable demands upon the market, and understand how to prepare them for the particular market for which they are designed. Next to the production of the best article at the cheapest price, its presentation in market in the best order and most inviting condition, is important to secure to the farmer a ready and remunerating market.

So long as our agricultural shall continue to be an exporting interest, these considerations, as second only to the science of production itself, will demand the careful attention and study of our farmers, and in any well-digested system of agricultural education, its connection with manufactures and the mechanic arts, with commerce, with the commercial policy of our own and other countries, and with the domestic and foreign markets, should hold a prominent place. A thorough and continued education in these collateral, but highly necessary branches of knowledge to the farmer, will prove extensively useful to the American citizen, beyond their application to the production and sale of the fruits of his labor. They will qualify him the more safely and intelligently to discharge the duties of a freeman; and, if called by his fellow-citizens to do so, the more beneficially to serve his state and country in legislative and other public trusts.

I hope I may offer another opinion in this connection, without giving offence, or trespassing upon the proprieties of the place and occasion. It is, that this education in the just and true connection between the agricultural, the commercial, and the manufacturing interests of our country, equally and impartially disseminated among the classes of citizens attached to each of these great branches of labor, would effectually put an end to the jealousies too frequently excited; demonstrating to every mind, so educated, that, so far from either being in any degree the natural antagonist of the other, they are all parts of one great and naturally harmonious system of human industry, of which a fair encouragement to any part is a benefit to all; and that all invidious and partial encouragement to any part, at the expense of any other part, will prove to be an injury to all. The education proposed will do all that can be done to mark the true line between natural and healthful encouragement to either interest, and an undue attempt to advance any one, at the expense of the united system, merely producing an unnatural and artificial relation and action, which cannot fail to work disease and injury.

The labors of this society, and of kindred associations, have done much to inform the minds of our farmers in these collateral branches of knowledge useful to them, and much remains to be done. The science of production claims the first place, and is a wide field, as yet so imperfectly cultivated as to afford little time for collateral labors. To secure a stable and healthful market, and to learn how to retain and improve it, also opens an extensive field for the mental labors and energies of the farmer. Between these objects the relation is intimate and the dependence mutual. The production makes the market, and the market sustains the production. The prospect of a market stimulates to activity in the field of production, and the fruits of that activity urge the mind to make the prospect real. Success in both contributes to the health and vigor and prosperity of agriculture, and of that prosperity commerce and manufactures cannot fail largely to partake.

All are willing to promote the cause of agriculture in our state and country. Most are ready to lend an active co-operation, and all are cheerful to see accomplished any valuable improvement in this great branch of productive industry. The difficulty hitherto has been in adopting any general plan to effect this desirable object. Hence, most usually, when the public mind has been awakened to the subject, arbitrary, and in many cases visionary, experiments have been introduced, based upon no philosophical investigation of cause and effect, but upon some accidental trial, by a single individual, of some novel mode of culture, which, under the circumstances attending the experiment, has met with success. This single experiment, without an inquiry into, or a knowledge of the cause which, in the given case, has secured the successful results, is at once recommended as an infallible rule of husbandry. The publication and dissemination of detached experiments of this character, for a long period constituted the most material additions to the stock of literary information connected with agriculture, supplied to our farmers; while many of the experiments were too intricate and complicated to be reduced to practice with any certainty of accuracy, and others were so expensive that the most perfect success would not warrant the outlay. Unsuccessful attempts to follow the directions given for making these experiments, brought what came to be denominated "book-farming," into great disrepute with the industrious, frugal, and successful farmers of the country, and excited a jealousy of, and a prejudice against this description of information upon agricultural subjects, which it has cost years of patient and unceasing effort in any measure to allay, and which are not yet removed.

In the meantime geological research, heretofore principally confined to investigations into the mineral kingdom proper, has been extended to its legitimate office, and has brought within its examinations the formation of the various soils, and their minute constituent parts. Chemistry has commenced where geology closed, and by a careful analysis of these constituents of the various soils, of the principal agricultural products, and of the usual manures, is laboring to establish, upon philosophical principles, the true relations between the soil and the manure to be applied, and between both and the crop to be planted and produced. It is seeking out, with rapid success, the appropriate food of the various vegetables cultivated by the farmer, the soils and manures in which the food for each is found, and the way in which it may be most successfully administered. So with the food of the domestic animals, and the most economical manner of feeding it.

These investigations are the reverse of the former system of arbitrary experiments. There a result was made to justify the arbitrary means adopted to produce it. Here causes are ascertained, and, being so ascertained, are relied upon to produce their natural effect, which effect is the result sought.

The importance of this great subject is effectually arousing the attention of the literary and scientific men of the country, and the success already experienced is drawing to these researches minds qualified for the labor, and energies equal to its rapid advancement. The progress made is bringing together the unsettled mind of the country, and producing the very general impression that the time has arrived when the foundations of a systematic, practical agricultural education should be laid, and the superstructure commenced.

It is universally conceded that agriculture has shared but lightly in the fostering care and Government patronage which have been liberally extended to commerce and manufactures, nor is it believed that additional public expenditure is necessary to enable the state to do all that can be reasonably required of it, to accomplish this great object. Our educational funds are rich, and the colleges, academies and common schools of the state share liberally in the distributions from them, while a Normal School for the education of teachers, instituted at the seat of Government, is also mainly supported from these funds. These institutions present the organization, through which, perhaps better than through any independent channel, this instruction can be universally disseminated among the agricultural population of the state. The annual additions to the school district libraries may be made with reference to this branch of education, and thus place within the reach of all the discoveries as they progress, and the rules of husbandry deduced from them, as they shall be settled and given to the public from the pens of the competent professors engaged in pursuing the researches.

This society, and like associations, may, through appropriate committees, their corresponding secretaries, public-spirited commercial men, and otherwise, collect and imbody in their transactions, facts and information respecting the markets, foreign and domestic; the present and probable supply of agricultural products; the mode and manner of presenting the principal productions in the various markets in the most acceptable form; the state and prospects of trade at home and abroad, and the changes present and prospective in the commercial policy of our own and other countries, with the probable influences upon the agricultural market. The commercial and agricultural press will doubtless come powerfully to the aid of the associations, in all efforts of this character, and having these great objects in view.

In this way the foundation may be gradually laid, and the materials collected for the commencement of those agricultural studies, which time and application, with the constant evidence of their utility in practice, would ripen into a system, to be ingrafted upon the course of regular studies pursued in the colleges, academies, and common schools, and made a branch of the studies of the male classes in the Normal School, placed under the superintendence of an instructor selected for that purpose, and qualified to prepare his classes for teaching the studies in the common schools of the state.

Thus a generation of farmers would soon come forward, well educated in the great and essential principles of agricultural production; in the true relations existing between agriculture, commerce and manufactures, and in the adaptation and preparation of their products for the agricultural markets. Such farmers, with the continued aid of the schools in which they were taught, would become the best manual-labor instructors for their successors.

The passage of time reminds me that I am extending these remarks beyond the proprieties of the occasion, and the patience of the audience. A single reflection shall close them.

However confidently the opinion may be entertained, that other circumstances and relations might present a prospect for the agriculture of our state and country, more stable, independent, and flattering, certain it is, that the future here opened is full of cheering promise. We see in it the strongest possible security for our beloved country, through an indefinite period, against the scourge of famine. Our varied soil and climate and agriculture double this security, as the disease and failure of any one crop will not, as a necessary consequence, reduce any class of our population to an exposure to death from hunger. We see also, in addition to feeding ourselves, that our surplus is almost, if not altogether, sufficient, if faithfully and prudently applied, even now to drive famine from the length and breadth of Europe. And that it is in our power, by faithful mental and physical application, soon to make it equal to the expulsion of hunger from the commercial world. We see that, dependent upon the commercial markets, our agriculture may bring upon our country a high degree of prosperity, and enable us, when extraordinary occasions shall call for its exercise, to practise a national benevolence as grateful to the hearts of the humane as to the wants of the destitute. And we see that, by the wider diffusion and more secure establishment of a successful agriculture among our citizens, as a permanent employment, we are laying broader and deeper the foundations of our free institutions, the pride and glory of our country, and prized by its freemen as their richest earthly blessing; the history of all civil government, confirmed by the experience of this republic furnishing demonstrative proof, that a well-educated, industrious, and independent yeomanry, are the safest repository of freedom and free institutions.

LIFE

OF

JOHN CALDWELL CALHOUN,

12mo. 457 pp.

WITH A FINE PORTRAIT.

PRICE $1 25, IN SHEEP OR EMBOSSED MUSLIN.

It is dedicated to the people of South Carolina; is written with marked ability, and with a high appreciation of the political principles and character of Mr. Calhoun.—*Charleston Mercury.*

A most valuable accession to the biographical literature of the country—*New York Daily Globe.*

Mr. Jenkins has performed an acceptable service in preparing such a work as is well calculated to satisfy the present interest in the life and character of the great Carolinian.—*New York Journal of Commerce.*

The book is written in a style that will be admired by the reader, and is another evidence that the author's mind has been highly cultivated; and is producing fruits that will speak well, in all future time, for his qualifications as an author.—*Auburn Daily Advertiser.*

It is a volume that can be read with pleasure and profit by all who wish to be well-informed concerning events that have recently occurred. It is neatly printed. and is embellished with a portrait of the man whose life it records. We commend it as a candid and reliable biography, well worthy of being read by all who seek information on which to base their judgment of the man and the administration to which it relates.—*Niagara Democrat.*

The author is a deservedly popular one, having given to the country several excellent and unprejudiced biographies of different distinguished statesmen, including Gen. Jackson, Silas Wright, and John C. Calhoun—all of which have had an extensive sale; and we are certain that the work before us will meet with the same favor.—*Cold Water (Mich.) Sentinel.*

JENKINS'

UNITED STATES EXPLORING EXPEDITIONS.

Voyage of the U. S. Exploring Squadron under the command of Captain Wilkes, together with explorations and discoveries by D'Urville, Ross, and other navigators and travellers; and an account of the Expedition to the Dead Sea under Lieutenant Lynch. By John S. Jenkins. Published by James M. Alden, Auburn, N. Y.

This valuable work has already passed through three large editions. It is beautifully illustrated, and forms a handsome octavo volume of 517 pages. Price, in cloth, $2,25: in sheep, $2,50.

The following are some of the numerous flattering encomiums which the work has received from the public press:—

The voyages of D'Urville, Ross and others, the results of which are here detailed, have been productive of great good, in the extension of geographical and scientific knowledge; and it is every way desirable to possess fuller information concerning them. The necessary expensiveness of the original works will, no doubt, confine them, for the most part, to public libraries, or to the shelves of the wealthy; but, in this volume, we are happy to say, all that is of general interest, and adapted to popular reading, may be found. Mr. Jenkins has manifestly bestowed much labor on his book, and is an adept in the very difficult art of condensation. He has not merely abridged his materials, nor is his work a mere selection from other authors, but bears every mark of being a faithful digest from authentic sources. He is master of a terse style, by which he is enabled to avoid all diffuseness and unnecessary embellishment, and makes his statements with directness and precision.

In the present day, when most men must depend on summaries, like the present, for a great part of their knowledge on a large class of subjects, it is a matter of satisfaction to light upon a book, which communicates so much, in a cheap and compendious form. We have examined it with some care, and are persuaded that the author has executed his task with discretion and fidelity. Our interest in reading it has increased to the end, and we shut the volume with a sense of gratification in having easily acquired much valuable information, and with regret that we have reached the close.—*Old Colony Memorial.*

We took it up, therefore, expecting to find it a mere compilation, or, perhaps, an abridgment from the U. S. Exploring Expeditions of Wilkes and Lynch, with some added references to D'Urville and Ross. Had it been no more than this, it would have been a valuable thing for ordinary readers, since there are few who will buy the weighty volumes of Wilkes, and fewer still who will read them through. Most people, in this age, have too much to do to read quartos. They are obliged to wait till some one shall kindly condense them, and give us the *multum in parvo.*

The author of this volume is just the person for such a work. He understands the public taste, and adapts his labors to the million. In this case, however, he has in the first part travelled far beyond the record of Capt. Wilkes, whose narrative has been merely the thread on which he has strung the facts procured from many other sources. For instance, he has gleaned up everything of interest with regard to the South Sea Islands, from the days of Capt. Cook downward, and interwoven it with the visit of the Exploring Expedition to those Seas. We have, therefore, collected before us, at a view, all that ordinary readers wish. So it is with respect to the South American cities at which the Expedition stopped.

In the second part, Lynch's Expedition to the Dead Sea has been used in the same way, while everything else of interest with regard to that portion of the world, has been gathered from other sources. We have, therefore, in a narrow compass, all the really valuable information to be obtained on this subject.—*Albany State Register.*

To the thousands of people in this land who are unable to purchase the several works herein consulted and abbreviated, the labors of Mr. Jenkins will be very acceptable. He has done his work well—has made one good book out of a dozen others.—*Western Literary Messenger.*

This volume is an octavo of over 500 pages, printed in beautiful style, and embellished with the finest engravings on wood. It is verily a world in a nutshell—fifty dollars' worth of books in one volume. All that is of real interest and value in the large and expensive works of the United States Exploring Expedition, and Lynch's Expedition to the Dead Sea, together with the results of twenty other books of voyages, travels and history, pertaining to the Pacific, South America, California and New Holland, are here compressed into one volume. We have read some passages with much gratification; and promise ourselves great enjoyment in a more careful perusal. Although every page, every paragraph, teems with information, yet the author has found space for many entertaining anecdotes and pictures of scenery and customs. It is a book which may be read with great interest and profit at every fireside.—*Auburn Daily Advertiser.*

A book like this would possess more worth in the estimation of a reflecting mind, than five hundred of the ordinary light publications of the day.—*Havana Republican.*

The comprehensive octavo of Mr. Jenkins will not take the place of its original sources, in the libraries of men of wealth, and of public institutions; yet its sale will by no means be confined to people of very limited means. The mass of book-buyers will prefer it, not only because they will avoid seven-eighths of an expense otherwise incurred, but also thus save an equal proportion of time. The book is not a mere abridgment, nor a selection from the larger works of Wilkes, Lynch, etc.; nor are its gleanings alone from their fields. We are given to understand that every line of the work is from the pen of Mr. Jenkins; and, in his preface, he tells us that a large proportion of his facts is derived from other works than any of the above-mentioned. Some twenty books of travel and history are cited as authorities, besides a "number of others referred to in the notes."

The volume is truly much in little—a summary and closely detailed review of all late explorations in and around the Pacific. In five hundred pages we have the results of many thousand. Some idea of its compression of volumes into a small space may be gained from the fact, that Lieut. Lynch's Expedition to the Dead Sea is thrown into fifty-five pages, in which the "important results and actual information" are given. At this day, when a golden key is not the only one that unlocks the treasures of learning; when all information must be laid before "the people" in an accessible shape; and when, in the bustle of the age, men can only read as they run; we cannot but regard Mr. Jenkins's book, so cheap and compendious, as a precious windfall to the multitude. And we may remark here, that some of our country friends—especially the "poor scholars" who live at a distance from public libraries—would be greatly favored by cheap editions of such works as Ticknor's Spanish Literature, Prescott's works, etc. It would not interfere with the sales of the fine edition, and would rather be an additional source of profit to the authors and copyright-holders.

So far as we have examined it, the volume before us is executed very understandingly. The style is close and perspicuous, and the screws are applied to diffuse remark without the sacrifice of picturesque elegance of narration.—*Literary World.*

This is a handsome octavo volume of 517 pages, containing, as its title intimates, a compilation of scenes, incidents, adventures, etc., in, and descriptions of, various countries visited by celebrated navigators and travellers. It is divided into two parts. Part one comprises accounts of expeditions to the Pacific and the South Seas: Part two embraces a narrative of the voyage of Lieutenant Lynch to the Dead Sea, together with scenes and incidents in the Holy Land, from the writings of various travellers.

The work contains copious and interesting descriptions of the most important places and localities visited by the several travellers, from whose writings the book has been prepared. The information it contains is arranged in an attractive form, well suited to popular reading, and the work, as a whole, is admirably adapted to impart valuable knowledge.—*Boston Daily Journal.*

Now these Exploring Expeditions gave a vast amount of new information, and Mr. Jenkins has sought to present it in an attractive and condensed form. For an accurate knowledge of the places and localities described—of the Pacific and the Jordan—it will be found servicoable. Indeed, Mr. J. has not strictly followed his authors. He has gone outside of them, and obtained information gathered since their works were published—an anachronism for which the reader will not scold him.

To show the extent of Mr. Jenkins' labor, we may mention that the important results and actual information obtained by Lieut. Lynch, in his Dead Sea Expedition, are compressed in some forty-five pages. Yet nothing material is omitted! This is real service rendered. For Lieut. Lynch was verbose to a fault—right in his spirit; bold as an adventurer; truthful; but no writer.

We do not see why such books could not be introduced into our schools, so that while scholars are taught to read, they may be taught, also, living information. What lad is not interested in the Jordan and the Dead Sea? What scholar not anxious to know more about the Pacific and its wonders?—These are living topics. The one is hallowed by every association of the Past, and the other made alive by every interest of the Present. If boys in our schools—the more advanced, certainly—could have put in their hands books more to interest and instruct—could not the intelligent teacher do more towards making them good readers and well-informed men?—"*The Daily True Democrat,*" *Cleveland.*

The account of the United States Exploring Expedition, as detailed by Lieut. Wilkes, though highly interesting, is much too prolix for common readers.—Five octavo volumes require more patience and perseverance than ordinarily fall to the lot of individuals. There are also many young people who have not time to read, nor money to purchase extensive works, but who could profit much by a cheap, judicious synoptical class of publications. This is precisely the course adopted in schools —first rudiments, and then more expansive views in ample volumes. Mr. Jenkins has not barely abridged the works referred to in the title page; he has written, or rather compiled, a new work, making use of the authors referred to, and introducing considerable valuable matter from other sources. The reader may purchase here, for two dollars, all that is of consequence in volumes costing elsewhere from five to ten times that sum.—*Northern Christian Advocate.*

We are indebted to the publisher for a copy of the above work, which gives, in an attractive and condensed form, an account of the expeditions to the Pacific and the South Seas, together with a variety of interesting information in relation to the localities described in its pages. * * * It is a volume of over 500 pages, handsomely executed, and will no doubt meet a quick demand.—*Rochester Democrat.*

One of the most valuable and attractive books of the present year. * * * No library can be complete without it.—*American Citizen.*

www.ingramcontent.com/pod-product-compliance
Lightning Source LLC
LaVergne TN
LVHW020125110826
845151LV00001B/274

* 9 7 8 1 4 2 5 5 4 1 5 7 6 *